# Salish Systems

## Kinship Networks of the Northwest

Jay Miller, PhD, ed

© 2019

Contents




# Introduction

Gathered together herein are highpoints in the study of Salish kinship systems representing this distinctively localized Northwest language family of 23 members (see p. vi) distinguished between 16 in four Coast branches (Central = Comox, Pentlatch, Sechelt, Squamish, Halkomelem <= Chilliwak, Musqueam, Cowichan>, Nooksack, Straits <= Saanich, Sooke, Songhees, Samish, Lummi, Semiahmoo>, Lushootseed Puget, Twana; Tsamosan Olympic = Quinault, Cowlitz, Lower & Upper Chehalis <Satsop, kx, čš>; Oregon Tillamook <Siletz>; Nuxalk Bella Coola) and 7 Interior Plateau members (Lillooet, Thompson, Shuswap, Okanagan, Kalispel-Spokan-Flathead, Coeur d'Alene, Moses Columbian).

Leslie Spier (1925: 74), while based in Seattle, first treated Salish in its own right, Iva Osanai (1941) brought it into the UChicago sphere of kinship studies, and Bill Elmendorf (1961) looked in greater detail at its split into lineal Coastal and bifurcate collateral Interior Salish forms. While George Murdock derived Salishan from Hawaiian cousin type (1949: 350), he later called it, because it combines bilaterality with residence options (1965: 31), the fundamental kinship system of North America.  Salish kinship is classificatory, descriptive, bilateral, and concerned with generation, affinity, collaterality, bifurcation, polarity, relative age, speaker's gender, and decadence.

Lewis Henry Morgan set the early agenda for American kinship studies, aided by input from George Gibbs (see p. 39) and other remote sources, by insisting that unilineal systems of clans, gens, phratries, moieties, and engendered ancestors were original to North America but later 'degenerated' into other reported corporate, cognatic, bilateral forms.  As a result, kinships not based on matrilines of mothers to daughters or patrilines of fathers to sons baffled early scholars, even as they traced their very own bilateral kin within modern nation states.  In place of unilineal patterns, therefore, kindreds emerged as the new model, with a stem kindred having a continuous primary claim to a name, place, or item that makes it seem unilineal.

Scholars republished here grappled with key terms (below), such as *sept* for a corporate unit descended from a common ancestor who marry outside exogamously of it; or a *deme*, a corporate group which is endogamous, like a religious congregation, where Catholics marry other Catholics, Muslems other Muslems, Buddhists other Buddhists, etc. Because our diversified Salishan language stock is specific to the Northwest, with a strong cohort of cooperating scholars, their studies of contrasts and comparisons have produced satisfying results for both kinship's on-going use and behaviors, as well as glimpses into past features of these daughter languages leading to reconstructions of proto-Salish.

Oveall these systems are place based since names are attached to land and its resources, both physical and spiritual. The same name can be held by other members of the family as long as they live far apart to avoid confusions. Names in oral tradition usually go back through four generations to eight great grandparents, though leading families will maintain much longer dynastic claims going back to the beginings and recreations of the world, often over four or five ages, each distinguished by a named culture hero.

Origins of Salish have been traced to Boundary Bay near the mouths of the Fraser River, and thus neither interior as proposed by Franz Boas nor fully coastal, but more estuarian with abundant and varied resources. Early in Proto Salish formation, Kutenay moved east upriver and on into the Plains. Nuxalk developed in the interior, then moved to the coast, adopting marine terminology from neighboring Wakashan. Tillamook early moved down the Salish Funnel along the glacial outflow that became the Chehalis River, later traveled and occupied by Tsamosans. Moving up the Fraser into the interior were ancestors who split into Thompson, Lilooet, and Shuswap, with other Interior Salish following later onto the Columbia River and overland into Montana. All harvested, hunted, and fished until a few centuries ago when the arrival of the horse encouraged greater mobility, huge bison hunts into Montana, and more effective and concentrated leadership under dynastic families for both Salish and Sahaptians.

Overall, these systems were more complex than found in available literature, as shown by the community at Minter headed by a noble woman and famous for its elite training academy.

## Editing

Wherever possible, native spellings have been updated, with all *native terms* in *italics* whenever possible; punctuation, often cumbersome, has been retained, and abbreviations for all kin terms have been unified to the single letter system {F = father, M = mother, below} instead of the double letter one {fa = father, mo = mother} or triple ones {chi = child, sib = sibling, nib = nibling}. Every Spokane is now Spokan, for the tribe not the city. Bella Coola is Nuxalk whenever possible. Complex punctuation has been simplified, with some added spacing to help clarity. Native words are in italics if possible without confusion. Bibliographies are attached at the end of their texts.

Whenever possible spellings in modern International Phonetic Alphabet have been supplied using GenSal fonts. A sustained example is the Lushootseed kin terms provided to Arthur Ballard and updated by Zalmai Zahir, PhD. Among Salish, Klallam uniquely and consistently emphasizes relative age, as noted by scholars herein, as shown in past spellings by Erna Gunther (*Klallam Ethnography*, UWPA 1 (5): 171-314  1927: 258-9) on the left and Timothy Montler's (Saanich, North Straits Salish Classified Word List, Canadian Ethnology Service, Mercury Series, Paper #119 1991: 1-171) present ones on the right:

> The specific terms for the older and younger of two relatives of the same degree, as
> the older and younger brother, are used only when it is necessary to make clear to which
> reference is made. In every case the term for the younger is considered a slighting

Contents

word, a "small" word, as my {speaker} ... put it.

suxstō'nuq          older sibling          šəyəɫ elder, laƛ̓ eldest
satcui'ɬ            younger sibling        sə'ey'čən
                    youngest               he'ič own, sə'čal'ɬ other

sena'txwin          older brother's wife, husband's older brother
senata'xwin         younger brother's wife, husband's younger brother

yū'tɬ               oldest child
tcetī'tsin          intermediate child
ō'ō'tc              youngest child
stī'qwin            older sibling's child
tEqwinoi'ɬ          younger sibling's child

k!ɬwēhō'uñ          parents-in-law of one's child after child's death, meaning 'crying together'
                                                      qʷəɬx̱ʷa'əñ'

                    ancestor, tradition, speeches          čəleñən
                    person who has lost all relatives      ləsčənañət


Terms

Agnatic = traced thru males
Levirate = remarriage to ♂Sb of deceased H.
Nepotic = collateral, side lines, such as neice & nephew
Reciprocal = shared with each other, such as the same term for both GP & GC.
Sororate = remarriage to ♂Sb of decease W.
Uterine = traced thru females

Units

Deme = endogamous corporate grouping of bilateral kinship
Guild = special, private membership often called a secret society composed of elite members and
     given to dramatic intimidating public displays.
Ramage = Kin lines ranked by age senority
Sept = exogamous corporate grouping of bilateral kinship

Diagrams

# Kinship Systems

### Matri- lateral / lineal  ♀ O  traced through FEMALES

⊥
=●⁻ O⁻ △⁻ △=
⊥
=●⁻ △⁻  ⁻△=⁻ ●=
⊥              ⊥
=●⁻ △⁻ ●=⁻
⊥        ⊥
=●⁻ △⁻ ●=
⊥        ⊥

### Patri- lateral / lineal  ♂ △  traced through MALES

▲
⊥
=▲⁻ O⁻ O⁻ ▲=
⊥
=▲⁻ O⁻ O⁻  ⁻▲=
⊥              ⊥
=▲⁻ O⁻ ▲=
⊥        ⊥
=▲⁻ O⁻ O⁻ △⁻ ▲=
⊥                ⊥

### Bi-lateral  ♀+♂  traced through BOTH sides

●=⁻⁻ ▲=
⊥        ⊥
=●⁻ ▲ ▲⁻ ●=
⊥ ⊥ ⊥ ⊥
=●⁻ ▲ ▲ ●=⁻△⁻ ⁻
⊥⊥ ⊥ ⊥ ⊥
=●⁻ ●= ▲ ⁻
⊥ ⊥ ⊥
=●⁻ ▲⁻ ●=
⊥ ⊥ ⊥

key

| ♀ O | females  - darkened to trace descent lines | = marriage |
| ♂ △ | males  - darkened to trace descent lines | ⊥ descent, children, offspring |
|  | either gender | ⁻ ⁻⁻ siblings, brothers & sisters |

v

Diagrams


G  grand  M mother  F father  Z sister  B brother  D daughter  S son
A aunt  U uncle  Nc neice  Nw nephew  Nb nibbling  Sb sibling
o older  y younger  H husband  W wife  Cz cousin


GM          GF
 M     P     F
 Z    *ego*   B
 D    C     S


W     H           Sb
A     U           / = in-law
Nc    Nw    Nb    Cz


Salish Tribes Codes

| | | | |
|---|---|---|---|
| C'A = Coeur d'Alene | I | S = Semiahmoo | C |
| Ch = Chehalis Up↑ & Lw↓ | C | Sc = Sechelt | C |
| Cm = Columbian | I | Sg = Songhees | C |
| Cw = Chilliwack | I | Sh = Shuswap | I |
| Cx = Comox | C | Sm = Samish | C |
| Cz = Cowlitz | C | Sn = Saanich | C |
| | | So = Sooke | C |
| Fl = Flathead | | Sp = Spokan | I |
| | I | Sq = Suquamish | C |
| Kp = Kalispel | I | Th = Thompson | I |
| | | Tl = Tillamook | C |
| Ll = Lillooet | I | Tw = Twana | C |
| Lm = Lummi | C | | |
| Mq = Musquem | C | Branches | |
| Nk = Nooksack | C | H = Halkomelem | |
| Nx = Nuxalk | C | L = Lushootseed | C |
| | | S = Straits | C |
| P = Pentlatch | C | Ts = Tsamosan | C |
| Ok = Okanogan | I | | |
| Qn = Quinault | C | C = coast   I = interior Salish | |

# The House of Salish
## Noble Pedigrees, Privileges, and Names
### Along the Skagit River betwixt Logjam and Rock

Jay Miller

Recent criticism wrongly denies any relevance to "house" (as House of Windsor, House of David) as a key factor of Salish kinship and society, such as would be comparable to the all-important houses of the matrilineal cultures of the North Pacific Coast such as Tlingit, Haida, and Tsimshian.

A telling example occurs in one book, where the editors wrongly note [Levi-Strauss] "has also disagreed with Jay Miller's application of the notion of the "house" to the Salish". Yet Levi-Strauss himself lauds in the very first chapter of the same book: "Reading a recent book by Jay Miller on the culture we refer to as Lushootseed, I found it gratifying that in order to characterize certain traits of the social organization, the author referred several times to aristocratic European houses" (Mauze, Harkin, and Kan 2004: xx, 3).

The counterargument pursued here is that while not integrated in Salish society to the degree of the north coast, claiming a house was an element of the coastal prestige system, especially among important families who could assert dynastic status. The Lushootseed language confirms its importance by the use of the suffix $-al'tx^w$ to indicate such a perpetual house ($si'a\dagger altx^w$ House of Seattle), sometimes linked with the root $g^wec$- / $g^w\partial\dot{c}$- "be born (for), originate" (Bates, Hess, and Hilbert 1994: 109). As such, this house is metaphoric and eternal, rather than merely physical built of cedar planks. Indeed, the named house-holders may seasonally occupy a variety of built homes at strategic resource locations, easing the harvesting, preparation, and storage of that resource by members of the household and their guests.

Scholarly understanding of the features of this Salish House suffers from a lack of published data, much of it existing only in fieldnotes and, of course, alive within Salish communities. This article relies on the dense materials assembled in the early 1950s by Sally Snyder among the Swinomish and other Skagit River communities, and until recently under restricted access within the Melville Jacobs Collection at the University of Washington main library. The Saanich fieldnotes of Diamond Jenness (1935) also discuss the importance of the House for Canadian Salish.

The most vivid published account of the direct link between a great name and its house, here physical as well as metaphoric, involves John Fornsby's encounter with his great grandfather, $k^w\partial skad\partial b$, while picking blackberries with other boys. "There were lots of berries. We crawled around and got to the middle back of the house. The body of my [great] grandfather $k^w\partial skad\partial b$ was right there. We got scared. We went home. We never picked berries. I laughed [with relief] when we got back into the canoe" (Fornsby to Collins 1949: 295-96).

This $k^w\partial skad\partial b$ was a famous Skagit leader based on Whidbey Island around modern Coupeville on Penn Cove, still famous for its local oysters. Sneatlum Point is its southern end, and the landfall of founding ancestors (below). In time a namesake of founder $\underline{x}k'\partial k'ad\partial b$ /$\underline{x}\dot{k}\partial\dot{k}ad\partial b$/ married, among others, a Samish wife named $tsi\ ?ag^wa\dagger$ and one of their middle sons first received the name-title of $k^w\partial skad\partial b$. This historic holder of that name had commissioned half a dozen Lower Skagit carpenters to build him a potlatch house,[1] with a painted post holding up either end of the gable, at what briefly became Skagit City (Fornsby to Collins 1949: 295-96), the ancient site of a prime salmon fishery (below).

Later, the body of this *kʷəskadəb* was reburied behind his potlatch house, which eventually was washed away in a flood. By then *kʷəskadəb* had again been reburied, with proper ceremony, at the Swinomish cemetery. The flood settled one of his house posts – 3 feet wide, 4 feet thick, and 8 feet long – in the back of the bay at La Conner. Johnny Fornsby hired men from Lummi to help him move and set up this housepost at a potlatch when the dead were gathered up from a gravehouse on Deadman's Island and moved to the Swinomish community cemetery.

An earlier *kʷəskadəb* was father of the equally famous Sneatlam [*sniƛəb*], and uncle to Goliah, the spokesman drafted as signer for the northern Lushootseed tribes at the 1855 Treaty of Point Elliot – Mukilteo. One of his daughters married among the Chehalis, to the south.

Sneatlam became renowned throughout the Northwest as an early Catholic prayer leader and an important broker in the regional fur trade based at Fort Nisqually. At least one of his wives was a Makah from Neah Bay. Yet one of his brothers flaunted the rules of nobility by being involved with a slave girl, who thereby became known as 'mistake' (*dᶻaƛəb*).

After his death on 16 December 1852, a carved wooden effigy of Sneatlam stood on a high bank on the eastern side of Whidbey Island, "dressed in his usual costume, and wearing the articles of which he was fond" (Gibbs 1877: 203). To this day, his family has remained important in intertribal and international trading, now brokering as far away as China, especially for fireworks sold at tribal stands before July 4ᵗʰ.

A granddaughter of a *kʷəskadəb* by the name of *ba'da'yɬ* (in Lushootseed, *ma'na'yɬ* in Straits) was captured by raiding Klallams from Dungeness, who quickly married her instead, later returning with her for a formal marriage ceremony, receiving ten slaves, a seagoing canoe, and many blankets from her grandfather in exchange for twenty slaves, a canoe, and other goods from these Klallams. At the wedding, the bride was wrapped in "a big mountain goat hair blanket" and the groom appeared with an enormous "rawhide mask over his face, painted like a face, that he shows when they are landing. That is *sxʷay'ačusən*, the kind he showed, two or three feet on a side, a square of rawhide with long hair and a face" (Elmendorf 1993: 108-100 dates these events to 1780-1810).

(21.2) [Frank Allen narrates] What I'm going to tell is three or four generation ago. Before *č'u'ct* and *təna'taltq*, before their time [told to FA by his great-uncle *wa'xʷəlacuD*].

The Dungeness Klallam get ready to go to Skagit, the people from *c'α'qʷ'* and from *sttiɬəm*, all one tribe, make ready. They're going to Skagit now for war. Going for women and slaves now. They go and get to Skagit, to the mouth of Skagit River, at night, and they land away from the village and haul their canoes into the woods and hide.

Next morning they see two little girls playing on the beach. The Klallam catch them

---

[1] Potlatch is a charged term in the Northwest Coast literature, derived from the local trade jargon (Chinuk Wawa) word simply meaning "to give". Among Lushootseed, the equivalent word is *sgʷigʷi*, merely meaning "to invite" but there are also three other words that can be applied (Miller 1999: 147 #5).

and ask them, "Who are your people?" One of the girls says, "My grandfather's name is *kʷałqədəb*." That is the chief of the Skagit people. They ask the other girl, "Who are your people?" And she names her father and grandfather, but they're just common people.

(21.3) So the Klallam talk to one another now. "Now, what are we going to do?" And one man, *sxʷıla'cəm*, says, "I'm going to take this girl home, this grandchild of *kʷałqədəb*, and keep her for my wife." Now they say to the common girl, "You go now and tell *kʷałqədəb* that we are Klallam and we're going to take his grandchild. Tell him we're not taking her for a slave, but so-and-so is going to take her for his wife. They tell the common girl that they will come again next year to buy the other girl from her grandfather. So they sent that girl home.

The Klallam push their canoes off. They are going home now, and that girl, the grandchild of *kʷałqədəb* cries. They tell her, "Don't cry. You are not going to be a slave. That man is going to be your husband."

As they are going home with the Skagit girl, the Klallam ask her what is her name. The girl says, "My name is *ma'na'ył*." Well, they land home with the girl [later returning to Swinomish for a lavish marriage ceremony, when] ...

All the Skagit and Klallam exchange clothes now. Pull off each other's shirts, have a good time now. "We're going to be relations now!"

(21.6) *kʷałqədəb* says, "Stay with me for two or three days, you people! We're going to get mussels." So they send lots of young men to get mussels, the big rich mussels that are at Skagit. And they fill whole canoes with them and bring them back and cook them now, on hot rocks they cook them with leaves over them. And everybody eats and eats. Oh, those good mussels!

Next thing, *kʷałqədəb* says, "Now you get camas." And they dig camas, the women dig those roots on Skagit Island, and they steam them in an oven, underground, for two or three days. And so they keep eating for two or three days. And so it is done.

(21.7) They get through and now *sxʷıla'cəm* says, "Now, *kʷałqədəb*, you come to my country now. We're brothers and sisters now, and all you people come!" So the Skagit take lots of camas and mussels and all kinds of food and go with the Klallam.

And when they get to *c'a'qʷ'* they land and everybody goes to sxʷıla'cəm's house. They have a good time there, they dance and sing and have lots of food. And they exchange clothes with one another, men and women, and have a good time.

Now sxʷıla'cəm gets up and begins to sing: "*heyɔ• tisiyɔ• hɔ / ta•či tisiyv• hɔ•* [Klallam] (ha! my chief [power] / my power has come now)." [in spoken Klallam: *ha tacsiya'm', ta'či tiya' siyam'.*]

After he sings his *tamanawis* he goes and takes hold of a slave and takes him to *kʷałqədəb*. He takes a woman slave and he calls his wife *ma'na'ył*, "Come on!" His wife comes. He tells his wife, "You give this woman slave to your grandmother, *kʷałqədəb*'s wife." And now he gathers blankets and goods of all kinds and gives them to *kʷałqədəb*'s people, a little all around till everybody has some.

And now we're through with *ma'na'ył*. That is where we are from; my family is from that line on my mother's side. So we are related to the Skagit people from that time.


Extending their range of dynastic marriages, both Sneatlam, as *Neetlum*, and *kʷəskadəb*, as *Wheskienum*, appear in the journal of Fort Langley for June, July, and August of 1830

(Maclachlan 1998: 150, 156-6).  This time, Sneatlum's son was marrying the daughter of a Cowichan leader, a chief variously known as *Shashia*, Joshua, Josia, or Old Joe.  By luck, portraits of he and his son *Cul-chil-hum* were painted by Paul Kane in 1847.  A brief biography, alas, mentions only two sons, leaving uncertain the fate of this daughter married among Skagits when he died blind and heirless in 1870 (Maclachlan 1998: 228-230).

While negotiations had been decided in the spring of 1830, the formal exchange took place in late summer after the Vancouver Islanders had moved across to their Fraser fishery.  "This afternoon [June 17, Thursday] the two Scadchats Chiefs – *Neetlum & Wheskienum* accompanied by a half dozen of others & Sinaughten the Sinnahomes Came here – They have about 20 Skins Lar[ge] & Small…"

On June 29, Tuesday, Nanaimos and Cowichans arrived at the mouth of the Fraser, only to be attacked by Lekwiltok about July 4th, before the Nanaimo settled into their summer village on Friday the 16th.  On July 10th, the Cowichan Shashia demanded 2 guns and 10 blankets for a dozen skins, but he left empty handed "for we have hardly So much property in the Fort."  His concern was, of course, not the fur trade but his upcoming wedding responsibilities.

Neetlum himself visited the fort on August 7th, Tuesday; the Cowichan Shashia on the 8th, then on the 9th "In the evening two very large & three Small Canoes full of Scadchads made their appearance at our wharf – Their Chief (*Needlum*) was already in the Fort – he immediately embarked with them & pushed over to Joe's [Cowichan] camp – All the great men of the river are now assembled there – Our night watch is doubled & every thing in readiness in Case of the worst."

On Friday, August 10th came the culminating exchange in "A great Ceremony – going on the other Side solemnising a marriage that took place last Spring between a Boy of Needlum's and a little Girl of Joe's – Canoes – Guns – Blankets – Slaves etc. etc. are exchanged on the occasion.

On Saturday, the Skagit came across to propose trading, "for which they would have nothing but Blkts [blankets]" but were soon rebuffed.  "They returned to the Cawitchin Camp in the evening & Spoiled Children they are."  On Sunday afternoon, August 12th, the Skagits left for home.

Clearly, through pedigree and alliances, $k^{w}$əskadəb and his family held and hold high rank, meeting the criteria by having a wealth spirit power (below) and by inviting (to at least four potlatches) (Sally Snyder Box 108 Folder 2: page 17  Joe Joe).  Accordingly they kept affirming it with generosity, as indicated by the specially built potlatch house where he was entombed.

This location just above Skagit City served to remind everyone of a major source of his bounty, namely the dense fishery at the lower end of a logjam, two miles long, that blocked the Skagit River from above Mount Vernon to Hamilton.  Spawning salmon clumped there before managing to weave their way upriver.  They were so abundant that harpoons and gaffhooks could be used along with nets.

Until the jam was dynamited apart and away in 1878, peoples along the Skagit had extensive contacts with their neighbors because voyagers either had to drag a canoe through the brush around the jam, or, more readily, portage over into the lower Samish or the Stillaguamish rivers to reach salt water (Collins 1974: 39).

This fishery, potlatch house, and generous leader, therefore, account for the logjam in my title.  They also, as it happens, account for the rock since, according to notes from Alice Campbell:

House

Long ago there were people who turned into rocks [because of the Flood].  This *kʷəskadəb* was the name of one [of them] way up on the Skagit.  It is the name of one of Andrew Joe's relatives.  They came up to ask the people there for a name (certain people used to go to certain places to obtain a name).  If they had known, they could have asked the *sbalix* here [around Concrete, Baker River and Lake] for a name (Snyder 108 5 58 AC).


Even before the Flood, with the founding of human society, the holders of these name-titles were not limited to one place because these ancestors married widely and dynastically.


Ancestors

These few ancestors were the primary founders for this region, the first strictly human generation of the Skagit world.  Their names indeed were and remain mighty.

While most native people lived common, uneventful lives, those with what June Collins (1966) called "renowned names" – which acted more like titles – formed a set of famous chiefly leaders who owned several big cedar-plank houses in various richly endowed locales.  That he (or they) could coordinate the building of more than one large home further spoke to his (their) leadership abilities.  Indeed, in Lushootseed, such a person or family is called *hikʷ siʾab*, in the sense of a grandee who is "big, great, high, most, many, very" (Bates, Hess, and Hilbert 1994: 109) in terms of authority, respect, ability, and, above all, presence.

According to Lower Skagit, *kʾəkʾədəb* /k̓ək̓ədəb/, the first (Lower) Skagit man, was send down to *čubaʾałšəd* /čubaʾałšəd/ (note bene:  Sneatlum Point) by the Creator to found three ancestral families who each first lived in one of the three compartments within one huge plank longhouse set inside a stockade, with those highest in rank in the middle and the eventual colonizers of the Skagit River in the one furthest back (Sally Snyder, Box 108 folder 10: page 33 AJ).

Once this first family was established, they found themselves lured into adopting a new member with vast consequences.  Taking the shape of a young man, the Underwater Wealth Spirit (*tiułəbaxad* /tiułəbaxad/), who was usually both ugly and pitiful to humans, mentally compelled the family of *kʾəkʾədəb* to adopt him after he made himself look presentable as a baby.  A daughter took him to raise, then became pregnant by him.  Since he appeared handsome and hard working, to avoid scandal, they were quickly married, before their son was born.  The husband fixed it so his family could live underwater and took them back home.  But this son was never happy there, and the family came back when he was old enough to quest for a spirit power.

He quested for a year.  Times became hard and famine loomed when the son went to Sneatlam Point and to the bottomless lake across from Greenbanks.  There he got power from the sea and a pair of powerful cedar shields.  On his return, he told his cousin, who was also "pure" from fasting, to have his own parent's home cleaned up and renewed in four days in time for his return.  Everyone worked hard and all was ready when he came into the house with the shields and sang the middle part of his song, which immediately filled the beach with food.  From then on, aided by all these spirit powers, the Skagits grew mighty (Sally Snyder Box 109 folder 2: page 12 -13  AJ, cf Wealth married daughter of *kʾəkʾədəb* #I  Sally Snyder Box 109 folder 2: page 39-40  AJ).

Eventually, trade up and down the Skagit River was managed by *kʾəkʾədəb* at Coupeville for everyone on Penn Cove and by a *daxalxʷəd* – a *sbalixʷ* near Concrete on Lake Shannon at present Baker River – for those above (Sally Snyder, Box 109 folder 1: page 42  AD).

One of these later x̲k'ək'ədəb /x̣k̓ək̓adəb/ married both a Swinomish wife and the Samish wife named *tsi ʔagʷał*, having four boys and three girls.  The next oldest son was the first *kʷəskadəb*, who had two daughters by one wife, and a son by another – who became a 1855 treaty signer and father of a chief, while another son who had a daughter and a son, who also signed the treaty.  His second wife left no descendants (cf Sally Snyder, Box 108 folder 10: page 71  AJ, Box 109 folder 2: page 2  AJ).

One *kʷəskadəb* also had a famous warrior son *t'ax̲tał* /t̓axtał/ who was an endurance runner and athlete.  He would test himself by spitting on a rock and running around Sneatlam Point and back before it dried.  He could outrun deer, elk, cranes, and eagles, killing them with his bare hands (Sally Snyder, Box 108 folder 2: page 97  AJ).  Later young warriors trained by running from Sneatlum Point to Coupeville and on to Fort Casey, a strategic lookout (Snyder Box 108, Folder 2: page 10) now marked by a US defense bunker.

The half-Swinomish namesake son x̲k'ək'ədəb, in turn, had 5-6 wives, with many descendants.  The children of an Oak Harbor women included Goliah, designated a head chief in the 1855 treaty.  From a half-brother descended the woman who married Johnny Fornsby, who as a boy to saw the body of his great grandfather lying in state. (Sally Snyder  Box 109 folder 2: page 31  AJ; sons of x̲k'ək'ədəb #III, Sally Snyder, Box 108 folder 10: page 43  AJ; Box 109, folder 2: page 3  AJ).

Overall, the name of *k'ək'adəb* seems to first occur shortly after the very beginning, going even "deeper, really, from the Flood.  That's why it was hard to tell the history, because the Indian only had one name [over generations]" (Sally Snyder Box 109 folder 2: page 57  AJ).

Other founders were sent by the creator to specific locations, either at the founding of the world or to repopulate it after the Flood.  For the Swadabsh proper on Swinomish slough, the important founder lived a third generation after the Flood, the son of Robe Boy known as *lə̲xalbid.*

## *lə̲xalbid*

Gender equality permeates Salish culture, as shown by the pedigree of the name of the mother of *kʷəskadəb*.  The family of the woman named *tsiʔ əgʷał* came into their own after the Flood (Sampson 1938: 14-16, Matson 1968: 29-38), and thereby came to "own" the story about a man who sensed the Flood was coming, and so tied four seagoing canoes to the top of a mountain with four long ropes that stretched out as the waters rose higher.  When the waters receded, the mooring ropes broke off the high top of the mountain broke and three canoes drifted away.  From the fourth, a man, his wife, son, and daughter landed safely.  They quickly built cattail mat houses for use as a dwelling and storage.

Slowly, life returned.  Little fish came into Swinomish slough and the girl went to play with them, until, one day, a great fish took her away.  Saddened, her brother and his dog wandered away.  He began to shoot small animals, prepare their pelts, and eventually sewed them into a blanket robe.  When he finally came home, his parents were gone to Coupeville and the mat houses burned down as a sign of mourning because they thought both their children were dead.

In great despair, the boy wept until a voice told him to gather up and match all the animal bones he could find, lay them out, and wave his robe over them four times.  Immediately, all these bones became people, but they were chilled.  The voice said to gather charcoal from the burned houses, wave the robe over them, and thus fire was recreated.

Next he waded into the slough, where herring [smelt] swarmed as soon as the hem of his robe touched the top of the water.  These fed the people.  A mountain goat appeared to give everyone wool blankets as clothing to keep them warmer.  These reformed people had no sense, however, so the boy made brains for them from the very soil of that place (Andrew Span Joe, Snyder ms: Tale 68).

Eventually, his own human relations returned and these impromptu beings wandered away.  Ever after known as Robe Boy (*xuyałič'a* /xuyałiča/, "made from a robe"), he married a human woman and had two sons, *tux<sup>w</sup>iqədəb* /tux<sup>w</sup>iqədəb/ (first daylight) and *ləxalbid* (daybreak), who, withstanding snide criticism like their father, seemed to refuse to quest and had a hard time in the community until they revealed successful quests and founded several houses and villages near resource locations and fisheries, celebrated with appropriate rituals.

*ləxalbid* had at least four houses around Fidalgo Island, located in modern terms on the east side near the Swinomish tribal police station, further east at the fort on Sullivan Slough, on the southwest near Martha's Bay and Pull and Be Damned Road, on the northwest at Snee-oosh (*sdiʔus*) Point.

Among the Lushootseed, importantly, socio-cultural institutions were arranged as concentric circles, from the most restricted of food economics to the most expansive of religious expressions in what I have called an "anchored radiance," with everything situated with the drainage of a major river draining into Puget Sound (Miller 1999).

## Drainages

In terms of the overall Puget Basin, Marian Smith, after fieldwork with Puyallup and Nisqually, outlined a comprehensive spatial model with expanding components for each watershed, the maximum extent of allegiance and loyalty for most Lushootseeds.  These units were  (a) hearth mates eating together,  (b) within a cedar plank household,  (c) among houses of all neighboring residents,  (d) of birthright locals – those born there in contrast to inlaws, visitors, and foreigners, including  (e) all seasonal houses, settlements, towns, and resorts,  (f) inter-community networks,  (g) tributary drainages, of  (h) the entire drainage of a watershed or basin.  Integration was enhanced by distinctive styles and hereditary names given to canoe, which transport across time and terrains on mountain, forest, prairie, river, or sea.

Membership within each unit was based on well informed understandings, both subtle and discerning, of local customs such that insiders, in contrast to outsiders, fully appreciated the complexities of "the feud, the snub, the verbal innuendo" and accordingly "were appropriate guests for a ceremonial feast" (Roberts 1975: 79).  To be involved in Lushootseed culture required formal training in and experience with the complexities of oratory, rank, and proper public expressions.  Those of great prestige could also claim diffuse membership in a named House.

Every drainage had customs that set it apart, made obvious by dialect subtleties and by different styles of making fire or using nets, for example, as well as in venerating certain spirit powers and abilities.  The most complex example, for the entire length of the Skagit River, involved net use.

Throughout the Northwest, nets – placed underwater, on land, in the air, or hand held in canoes – were used to capture fish, fowl, and other foods.  Three major types of fish nets were once used along the Skagit, each instituted by the decree of a Changer~Transformer preparing the world for human arrival.  Out in the saltwater, the reef net (*sx<sup>w</sup>alo*, literally meaning 'willow' became make of cords of its twisted bark), developed by Straits Salish speakers, was deployed. In the lower river, the weir net (*qəlʔits*) was developed, and used by Swinomish and others. Upriver, the trawl net (*šəbəd*) was featured, made of a special mountain grass.  The success of the net, however, relied on special *dicta* (formula, spells, power words) closely guarded by the leaders of a family and household because they guaranteed an abundant food supply.

## Lushootseed  Ethno-Chronology

Based on this background and comparisons,[2] then, a Lushootseed chronology must start with the creator high god (*xaʔxa*) who empowers (often mentally) other immortal spirits (*sqəlalitut*) who dwell in the sky, on and in the earth, and under the water.  Foremost among these spirits were four brothers who traveled up the Skagit River, placing pairs of men and women at various locations to create future generations (Collins 1974: 158-59, Snyder Tale 73, Amoss 1978: 66-70, Miller 1999: 60-62).  These brothers, oldest to youngest, were Shield (*sg<sup>w</sup>ədiləč*), Knife, Fire, and Baby, each with sustaining powers and abilities appropriate to their names.  Shield protected and foretold.  Knife taught the proper ways to butcher and prepare game.  Fire showed how to cook it.  Baby told these couples on how to fix family talents, skills, and abilities on their children, as well as limiting access to *dicta*.

The others went away upriver, and Knife may have stopped at the ancient Hozomeen Quarry, but Shield became a rock in the upper Skagit near Portage where he can be heard singing about 3AM by those who had fasted and prepared to learn his song so as to be able to hunt and fish successfully.

This era ended with the time of Starchild and Diaper boy, begat by Stars married to human women.  After they had rescued their mother from slavery and married industrious wives, they gathered up everything useful on the earth and burned it in a great conflagration, then scattered these ashes everywhere so the essence of these materials, resources, and abilities could be more easily found by future generations.

Their children became the chiefly families throughout Puget Sound, each leader learning and guarding the special *dicta* to benefit his family and community.  Powerful dicta were specifically given in compensation for the renewal of the world at the time when mortals and immortals were moving away from the bodily contact of marriage toward the immateriality of adoption (as described for Wealthman and the Sneatlum family).

The land repopulated and thrived until people failed to respect the proper rules, regulations, and avoidances needed for proper living, so a Flood set things right again.  The few survivors included Robe Boy, his son *ləxalbid*, and their many descendants at Swadabsh, as other ancestors refounded communities in other locales.  Though unstated, the host of dead from the Flood must have provided the incentive for the Ghost system still important today since the deluge obviously left behind more refuse and remains than did Fire.

The occasionally references to those few who "drifted away" during the Flood also suggests that one of these Flood casualties was one of the *k<sup>w</sup>əskadəb* who ended up a petrified rock far up the Skagit.  Thus, resolving the conflicting attributes and locations of this name, the

---

[2]  The best descriptions of Salishan worlds represent the Nuxalk (Bella Coola) (McIlwraith 1948), Katzie (Jenness 1955), and Twana (Elmendorf 1960).

Lower Skagit who went upriver to ask for this name were actually showing respect for the people among whom this *kʷəskadəb* ended up lodging.  That is why they did not ask more important tribes around Concrete and elsewhere for a name.  Presumably, *kʷəskadəb* revealed his location to a descendant in a dream that was then followed up by this delegation.

Most recently, the Creator has again asserted his priority by empowering John and Mary Slocum to establish the 1882 Indian Shaker Church, legally incorporated in Washington State in 1910, and still thriving.  As Martin Sampson, Swinomish leader, noted, the advantage of Shakers was "worshipping God direct, they increased their healing over much greater distances."  Unlike shamans, whose spirits remained localized, Shaker spirits could expand into the world as far as needed since they were affiliated with a universal God.  Moreover, though a shaman's spirits deserted him or her at death, the Shaker Spirit led a member "home".

Simultaneously, immortal spirits remain active among initiates of modern *Syowin*, the so-called Smokehouse Religion that allows modern members to "inherit" family spirit powers in the context of this organization.

In modern Lushootseed beliefs about immortals or guardian spirits, such a power attaches itself to a person at birth, but only reveals its presence at puberty through at least two aspects, a being and a song, along with a personifying of the vision itself.  Some or all of these aspects "travel" during the year and only join together during the winter when the person becomes "sick to sing" with the return of his or her spirit partner.  For a woman, her spirit power was regarded as a personal friend, while for a man it was an impersonal force that infused his entire body when it returned (Amoss 1978: 51).

The song, at least, came from the east in the fall, moved slowly south and westward during the winter, and, in late April or so, headed east again.  As a group, spirits came to the Nooksak on Mt Baker before they reached Vancouver Island, where they lingered until spring.

In contrast to these lay or career powers, shamanic curing powers were available at all times.  According to Joyce Wike (1941), while the song traveled, the spirit itself stayed close to the human partner.  Fierce black paint spirits traveled more widely than did those of calm red paint, who stayed nearby and could be used to cure or help others.

During the day, spirits also move around, hovering in the air (rather than treading on the ground), lower in the early morning then higher in the afternoon.  They are constantly aware of human actions and leave if their partner becomes ritually impure or disrespectful.  Then the spirit was said to "lift off" until it could be coaxed back by a shaman.  Spirits liked daylight but, lacking form or substance, were truly ethereal.  Marian Smith (1940a: ) reported that spirits had the most nebulous of existences, with their appetites and pleasures supplied vicariously through their links with humans, especially relatives who were kind enough to remember them and send food and treats through an open fire.


## Comparisons


The role of the *House* (al'al, -altxʷ) among Coast Salish has been much debated by academics, with some denying it entirely.  Physically, this cedar-plank building served as "food processing and storage, workshop, recreation center, temple, theatre, and fortress" (Suttles 91: 214, Kennedy 2000: 76).  Among the matrilineal northern tribes, the house is the pervasive unit, and its influence was felt in the south, where some communities strove to assert claims to a similar but unique house as an aspiration rather than a routine feature.  Thus, standout examples include the Whale House (saɫuɫtxʷ) comprised of five high ranking Comox communities near

Cape Mudge (Kennedy 2000: 52, based on Barnett 1955: 25), and Painted House of the Snoqualmies east of Seattle.

Salish houses, repeatedly, have been called "similar in many ways to a 'House' in the sense of European nobility [holding] property, tangible and intangible, names of heaven-born First Ancestors, confidential knowledge (*sniw'*), ritual property (*ts'uxwten*), legends, songs, dances, secret words (dicta), medicinal remedies, and ceremonial prerogatives (Barnett 1955: 141, 191; Jenness 1935: 52; Thom 2005: 85). All of these are place-based, as inalienable patrimony, such that "senses of place focus attention on the connections and interrelations between myth, legend, ancestor, spirit, song, identity, language, property, territory, boundary and title" (Thom 2005: 409).

In his unpublished notes, Jenness (1935), closely attending to his elder interviews, carefully distinguishes between corporate ownership and the commons.

> The real political unit was therefore not the village, but the big house occupied by a number of kinsfolk – an enlarged or genealogical 'family' to which the Saanich applied the term *hunit's'lakum*, and we in speaking of the similar European nobility use the term House. Each Saanich House, as we many call it then, possessed its own long shed-roofed dwelling,[1] its own camas beds on Galiano and neighboring islands, its own set of ancestral names or titles, and its own stock of legends, songs, and medicinal remedies (Jenness 1935: 29).

The accompanying footnote expands on such privileged property:

> #1. Almost any departure from established custom might become the privilege of a House, heritable by later generations, and by them alone, provided the public had ratified it; and the public ratified it when during some potlatch it heard the statement of claim without demur and accepted the gift that followed the statement. All such privileges or rights, however, hinged upon proof of lineal descent, and the most obvious indication of such descent was the possession of an ancestral title (Jenness 1935: 29 #1).

At Duncan, Cowichan Houses owned nearby weir sites along the river, but

> "On the other hand, the sea near the villages, the hunting grounds and berry patches round about, were common property; any villager, whatever his station in life, might fish and hunt wherever he wished within the village territory" (Jenness 1935: 29).

Elite families owned property that included several houses occupied throughout a year at seasonal resource sites, famous art works, and claims to epics, songs, displays, and rituals. Senior members, both men and women, of elite families doubled as religious and political leaders, depending on the season. Summer was devoted to economy, and winter to religion (cf. Kennedy 2000: 7, 160, 326). The lowest class was largely immobile and marked by a strict provincialism (Kennedy 2000: 125, from Smith 1940: 410).

An apt comparison to Nuchahnulth or Nootkan distinctions between kinship and noble descent indicates "The situation among the people of the West Coast is not unlike that of medieval Europe (a comparison suggested to me [a Welsh national] by a Toquaht chief) where the descent principle was fully utilized only by the elite of society and where the common people neglected to trace their genealogies the further they were removed from aristocratic rank…. In addition, both principles need not be of equal importance for all members of the group (Kenyon 1980: 85-86). Emphasizing ramages of first-borns, Nuchahnulth differed from Salish bilaterality, yet high families in both made claims to hereditary Houses.

## Bibliography


Amoss, Pamela
 1990 The Indian Shaker Church. *Handbook of North American Indians, Northwest Coast.* Wayne Suttles, ed. Volume 7: 633-639.
Barnett, Homer
 1955 *The Coast Salish of British Columbia.* Studies in Anthropology 4. Eugene: Eugene: University of Oregon Press.
Bates, Dawn, Thom Hess, and Vi Hilbert
 1994 *Lushootseed Dictionary.* Seattle: University of Washington Press.
Collins, June
 1949 John Fornsby: The Personal Document of a Coast Salish Indian. Smith 1949: 287-341.
 1950a Growth of Class Distinctions and Political Authority Among the Skagit Indians During the Contact Period. *American Anthropologist* 52 (3): 331-342.
 1950b The Indian Shaker Church. *Southwestern Journal of Anthropology* 6: 399-411.
 1952a An Interpretation of Skagit Intragroup Conflict during Acculturation. *American Anthropologist* 54: 347-355.
 1952b The Mythological Basis for Attitudes toward Animals among Salish-Speaking Indians. *Journal of American Folklore* 65 (258): 353-359.
 1966 Naming, Continuity, and Social Inheritance among the Coast Salish of Western Washington. Papers of the Michigan Academy of Science, Arts, and Letters 51: 425-36.
 1974 *Valley of the Spirits, The Upper Skagit Indians of Western Washington.* Seattle: University of Washington Press.
Duff, Wilson
 1952 The Upper Stalo Indians of the Fraser River of British Columbia. Victoria: British Columbia Provincial Museum, Anthropology in British Columbia. Memoir #1.
Elmendorf, William
 1960 *The Structure of Twana Culture* ~ With Comparative Notes on the Structure of Yurok by Alfred Kroeber. Pullman: Washington State Research Studies, Monographic Supplement 2.
Gibbs, George
 1877 *Tribes of Western Washington and Northwestern Oregon.* Washington: Department of the Interior, United States Geographical and Geological Survey of the Rocky Mountain Region, Part II: 157-241.
 1970 *Dictionary of the Niskwalli (Nisqually) Indian Language* – Western Washington. Extract from 1877 Contributions to North American Ethnology 1: 285-361. Seattle: The Shorey Book Store Facsimile Reproduction.
Haeberlin, Hermann, and Erna Gunther
 1930 *The Indians of Puget Sound.* University of Washington Publications in Anthropology 4 (1): 1-84.
Jenness, Diamond
 1935 Saanich fieldnotes. copy. Victoria, BC: RBCM.

1955 *The Faith of a Coast Salish Indian.*  Victoria:   British Columbia Provincial Museum, Anthropology in British Columbia, Memoir #3.

Kennedy, Dorothy

1993 Looking For The Tribe In The Wrong Places:  An Examination of the Central Coast Salish Social Network.  University Of Victoria:  MA Thesis.

2000 Threads To The Past:  The Construction and Transformation of Kinship in the Coast Salish Social Network.  Oxford University, Exeter College:  Anthropology D. Phil.

Kenyon, Susan

1980 *The Kyuquot Way*:  A Study of a West Coast (Nootkan) Community.  National Museums of Canada, Mercury Series, Canadian Ethnology Service, Paper 61.

Levi-Strauss, Claude

1982 *The Way of the Masks.*  Sylvia Modelski, trans.  Seattle: University of Washington Press.

McIlwraith, Thomas

1948 *The Bella Coola Indians.*  Toronto: University of Toronto Press.  2 Volumes.

Mauze, Marie, Michael Harkin, and Sergei Kan

2004 *Coming to Shore ~ Northwest Coast Ethnology, Traditions, and Visions.*  Lincoln: University of Nebraska Press.

Miller, Jay

1999 *Lushootseed Culture and the Shamanic Odyssey*:  *An Anchored Radiance.*  Lincoln: University of Nebraska Press.

Smith, Marian

1940a *The Puyallup-Nisqually.*  Columbia University Contributions to Anthropology 32.

1940b  The Puyallup of Washington.  *Acculturation in Seven American Indian Tribes*, Chapter 1: 3-36. Ralph Linton, ed.  NY:  D Appleton-Century Co.

1941  The Coast Salish of Puget Sound.  *American Anthropologist* 43: 197-211.

Snyder, Sally

1952-54  Typed Fieldnotes.  Melville Jacobs Collection.  Seattle:  University of Washington, Special Collections.

ms.   Folktales of the Skagit.  Copies at Lushootseed Research and University of Washington Archives.

1964  Skagit Society and Its Existential Basis: An Ethnofolkloristic Reconstruction.  University of Washington:  Ph.D. Dissertation.

1975 "Quest for the Sacred in Northern Puget Sound:  An Interpretation of Potlatch." *Ethnology* 14 (2): 149-161.

Suttles, Wayne

1987 *Coast Salish Essays.*  Vancouver, BC: Talonbooks.

1991 The Shed-Roof House.  *A Time of Gathering ~ Native Heritage of Washington State*: 212-222.  Robin Wright, ed.  Seattle:  University of Washington Press.

Thom, Brian

2005 Coast Salish Senses of Place:  Dwelling, Meaning, Power, Property and Territory in the Coast Salish World.  Montreal:  McGill Anthropology PhD.

Wike, Joyce

1941 Modern Spirit Dancing of Northern Puget Sound.  M.A. Thesis:  U of Washington.

1952 The Role of the Dead in Northwest Coast Culture.  <u>Indian Tribes of Aboriginal America</u>. Sol Tax, ed.  Proceedings of the International Congress of Americanists 29th: 97-103.

Spier

UNIVERSITY OF WASHINGTON PUBLICATIONS
IN
ANTHROPOLOGY

Vol. 1, No. 2, pp. 69-88. Maps 1-9                    August, 1925

# THE DISTRIBUTION OF KINSHIP SYSTEMS
# IN
# NORTH AMERICA.

By LESLIE SPIER.

UNIVERSITY OF WASHINGTON PRESS
SEATTLE

Tribes by # Number

Tolowa (1b) ∞ a d f g i

Hupa (1c)

Whilkut (1e)

Lassik (1h)

Wailaki (1j)

Kato (1k)

Yurok (2a) ∞

Wiyot (3)

Yuki (4a)

Huchnom (4b)

Coast Yuki (4c)

Wappo (4d)

Lutuami (5)

Shasta (6a) ∞ b c d

Achomawi (6e)

Atsugewl (6f)

Northern Yana (7a) ∞ c

Central Yana (7b)

Yahi (7d)

Karok (8)

Northern Pomo (10a) ∞ e

Central Pomo (10b)

Eastern Pomo (10c)

Southeastern Pomo (10d)

Southern Pomo (l0f)

Southwestern Pomo (10g)

Washo (11)

Northern Diegueño (15a) ∞ e

Southern Diegueño (15b)

Kamia (l5c)

Yuma (15d)

Mohave (15f)

Northern Wintun (l6a)

Central Wintun (16b)

Southeastern Wintun (16c)

Southwestern Wintun (16d)

Northeastern Maidu (17a)

Northwestern Maidu (17b)

Southern Maidu (17c)

Coast Miwok (18a)

Lake Miwok (18b)

Plains Miwok (18c)

Northern Miwok (18d)

Central Miwok (18e)

Southern Miwok (18f)

Tachi (20a)

Yauelmani (20b)

Chukchansi (20c).

Gashowu (20d)

Yaudanchi (20e)

Paleuyami (20f)

Northern Pauite (21a) ∞ d e i j l m n o r s

Eastern Mono (21b)

Western Mono (21c)

Kawaiisu (21f)

Tubatulabal (21g)

Kitanemuk (21h)

Serrano (21k)

Luiseño (21p)

Cupeño (21q)

Desert Cahuilla (21t)

Alaskan Eskimo (22)

Eskimo of Cumberland Inlet, Baffin Land,

Kadiak Eskimo (23)

Tinneh (24)

Loucheux (25)

Tukuthe (26)

Hare (27)

Copper Eskimo (28)

Eskimo of Northumberland Island (29)

Cumberland Inlet (30)

Greenland Eskimo (31)
Yellow Knife (32)
Slavey (33)
Tlingit (34)
Haida (35)
Nass (36)
Tsimshian (37)
Carrier (38)
Bellabella (39b) [Nuxalk]

Bella Coola (40) [Nuxalk]
Kwakiutl (41) [Kwakwawawakw]
Nootka (42) [Nuchalnuth]
Comox (43)
Siciatl (44)
Chehalis (45)
Squamish (46)
Cowichan (47)
Thompson (48)
Lillooet (49)

Kwantlen (50)
Songish (51)
Makah (52)
Quileute (53)
Klallam (54)
Snuqualmi (56)
Duwamish (57)
Nisqualli (58)
Shuswap (59)

Kutenai (60)
Okanagan (61)
Colville (62)
Spokan (63)
Kalispel (64)
Coeur d'Alene (65a)
Flathead (65b)
Wenatchee (66)
Yakama (67)
Klikitat (68)
Wishram (69)

Wasco (70)
Chinook (71)
Alsea (72)

Takelma (73)
Sarsi (75)
Blood (76)
Piegan (77)
Gros Ventre (78) [Atsina]
Plains Cree (79)

Assiniboin (80)
Bungi (81)
Wood Cree (82)
Swampy Cree (83)
Paviotso (84)
Uintah Ute (85)
Tabegwaches (86)
Moapa (87)
Shivwits (88)
Kaibab (89)

Havasupai (90)
Southern Ute (91)
Navaho (92)
Hopi (93)
Hano (94)
Zuni (95)
Acoma (96)
Laguna (97)
Cochiti (98)
Jemez (99)

Tewa (San Ildefonso, Santa Clara, San Juan,
    Nambe) (100)
Tesuque (101)
Santo Domingo (102)
San Felipe (103)
Sandia (104)
Isleta (105)
Cocopa (106)
Papago (107) [Tohono O'odham]
Northern Tepehuane (108)
Crow (109) [Absorika]

Wind River Shoshoni (110)
Arikara (111)
Hidatsa (112)
Mandan (113)
Uncpapa (114) [Hunkpapa]

Blackfoot Dakota (115)
Oglalla (116)
Brule (117)
Yanktonai (118)
Yankton (119)

Cheyenne (120)
Arapaho (121)
Grand Pawnee (122)
Republican Pawnee (123)
Skidi Pawnee (124)
Ponca (125)
Omaha (126)
Santee (127)
Sisseton (128)
Menomini (129)

Winnebago (130)
Sauk-Fox (131)
Iowa (132)
Oto (133)
Kansas (134)
Kiowa (135)
Wichita (136)
Osage (137)
Missouri (138)
Quapaw (139)

Caddo (140)
Ojibway of Lake Superior (141)
Lake Michigan (142)
Lake Huron (143)
Ottawa (143)
Kaskaskia (145)
Peoria (146)
Wea (147)
Kickapoo (148)

Piankashaw (149)

Timagami (150)
Wyandot (151)
Seneca (152)
Cayuga (153)
Onondaga (154)
Oneida (155)
Mohawk (156)
Two Mountain Iroquois (157)
Montagnais (158)
Abenaki (159)

Malecite (160)
Micmac (161)
Penobscot (162)
Natick (163)
Mohegan (164)
Munsi (165)
Delaware (166)
Miami (167)
Shawnee (168)
Tuscarora (169)

Cherokee (170)
Tutelo (171)
Chickasaw (172)
Choctaw (173)
Creek (174)
Yuchi (175)
Biloxi (176)
Timucua (177)
Kansas Potawatomi (178)
Ts'ets'aut (179)
Willapa  (180) [Swaal]

∞ = gaps in # numbers
[ ] now preferred names

# The Distribution of Kinship Systems in North America

This paper presents a classification of kinship systems in North America and their distribution.  Historical, sociological, or psychological interpretations can hardly be undertaken without such a basis.

The material has been available for some years.  Lewis H. Morgan published sufficient to cover the region east of the Rockies in his *Systems of Consanguinity and Affinity of the Human Family* some fifty years ago.  But his unfortunate manner of presentation rather prejudiced reworking the data.  Many systems from elsewhere on the continent have been accumulated since, largely due, I believe to the impetus given their investigation by Robert H. Lowie.  Data for part of the Pacific area were brought together by A.L. Kroeber in *California Kinship Systems* and later subjected to more intensive analysts by Edward W. Gifford in *Californian Kinship* Terminologies.  With the exception of Lowie's *Sociological and Historical Interpretation of Kinship Terminologies*, no synthesis of continental scope has been attempted.

This study was begun in 1915 in an attempt to harmonize the Blackfoot data and to compare their systems with those of neighboring tribes.[3]  Through the generosity of William T. Davis of New York and an anonymous friend I was then given the opportunity to classify the material from eastern North America.  It has been possible to complete the task under a Fellowship in the Biological Sciences of the National Research Council in 1923-24.

The data are largely drawn from Morgan's tables.  The Californian data are from Gifford's work, taken directly from his maps in most instances.  I am especially indebted to R.H. Lowie for a large series of systems in manuscript, which he has placed unreservedly at my disposal, and to those who aided him in forming it.  Thanks are due Alanson B. Skinner for unpublished Potawatomi and Bungi manuscripts, Pliny E. Goddard for Sarsi, Eugene A. Golomshtok for Atsugewi, and Erna Gunther for Makah, Wasco, and Salish material from Washington.  Other sources are cited in the bibliography.  I have made no attempt at harmonizing conflicting data.  This requires linguistic specialization and further information.  In most cases the several alternatives are entered on the maps, but I have been quite free in arbitrarily selecting the most harmonious data.

This is strictly an empirical classification.  Beginning with the east, it was obvious that essentially the same systems were in use among tribes occupying large continuous areas.  I have therefore taken a group of similar systems, determined the most frequent mode of classifying each relative, and described that as the norm.  This is more difficult for the western tribes where the systems are more complex and where such features as verbal reciprocity are more frequently common to many groups which are in other respects unlike.  A number of systems, such as the Navaho and Alsea, were classified with [72] difficulty.  So far as the data goes – and it is as likely as not to be incorrect – they belong as much in one class as another.  It seems preferable to suggest their affiliations by classifying them somewhat arbitrarily to establishing a large number of categories.  No two systems are identical; a class is merely a group of systems more alike than they are individually like any other class.

To avoid misunderstanding, I wish it to be clear that I am not now asserting any historical

---

[3]  Spier, Blackfoot Relationship Terms.

connection between the systems of one class.  The Wiyot of northern California, for example, have a system which is closer to that of the Eskimo than to that of any of their neighbors.  That

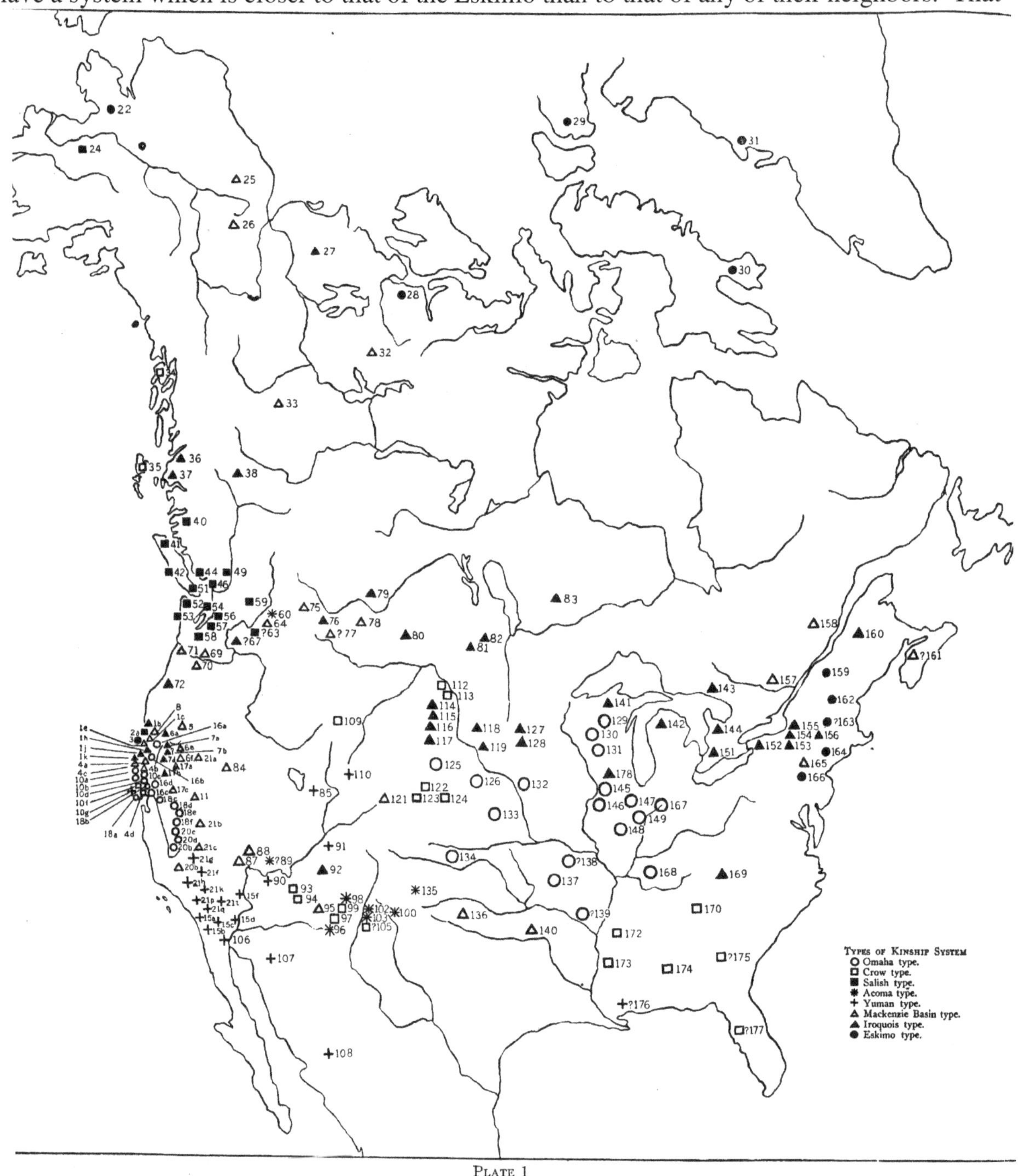


Plate 1

is, they call all cousins of the speaker's generation by the same term, which is not sibling, as the Eskimo do.  Their neighbors, Whilkut, Hupa, and Karok, share a system which classes these cousins with the siblings, although in other respects it resembles that of the Wiyot.  Since I have separated Eskimo from Loucheux and Hare on this basis, I have no choice but to separate Wiyot from Hupa and to class it with Eskimo.  But this does not mean that the Wiyot system is historically related to that of the Eskimo.  The case is different where the several Eskimo groups are concerned.  Here there is not only general similarity of systems, but as the terms are

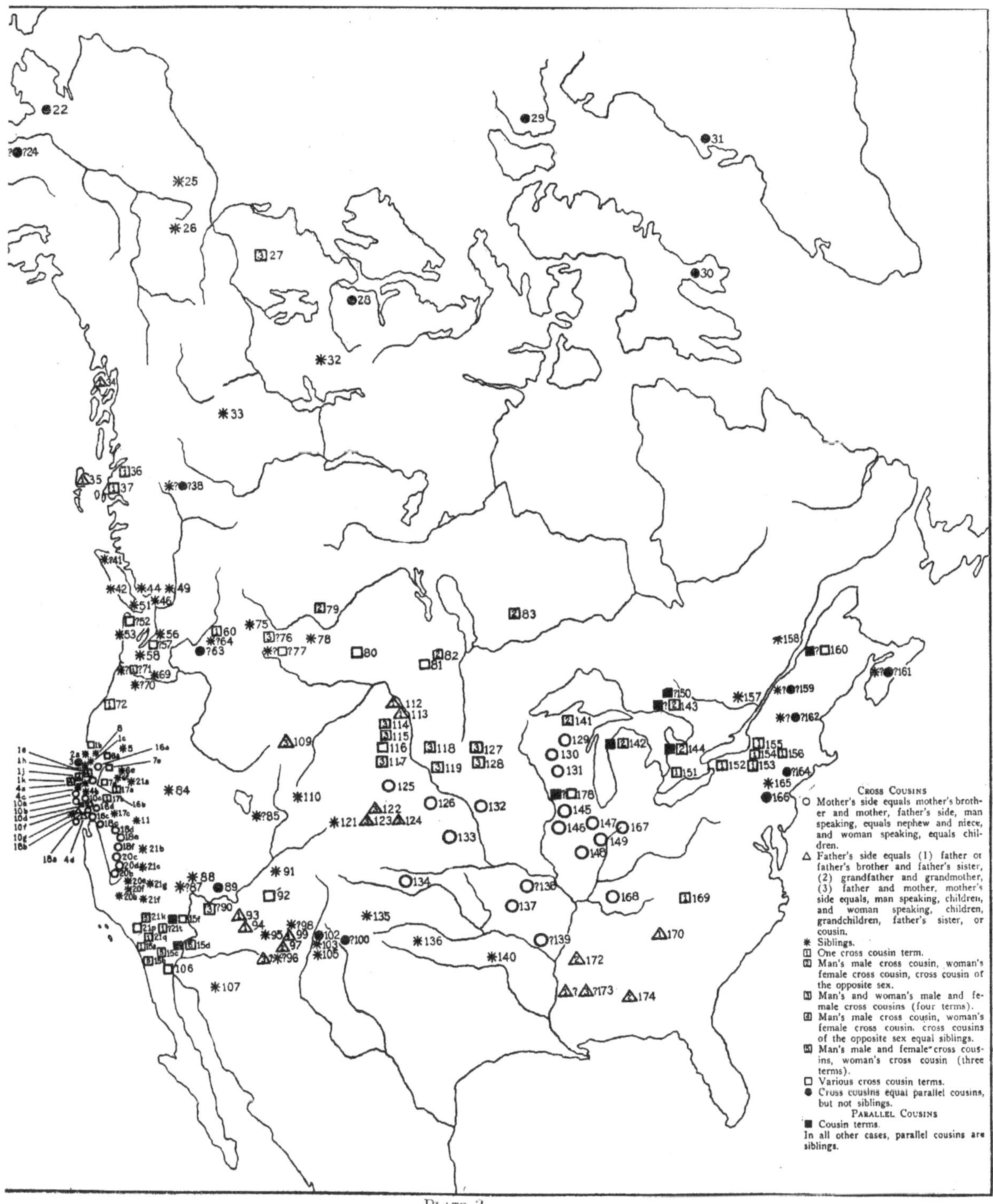



PLATE 2

The Yuman system is generically that of the Mackenzie tribes and the Iroquois, but differs in its development of age distinctions. These are consistently drawn among the parents' siblings, parallel and cross cousins, and nephews and nieces. The classification is based on the relative ages of the connecting relations.

Cross cousin terminology also offers a clue for the discrimination of the Omaha and Crow types. The first class together the mother's brother and his descendants through males: their daughters are always called mothers. The paternal cross cousins are then conceptual equivalents.   Similarly systems of the Crow type class the father's sister with her female descendants through females and their sons with the father.  Again, equivalent forms are used for the maternal cross cousins.  That is, both systems ignore differences of generation in one or the other type of unilateral descent.

The most convenient basis for discrimination, at least in the east, is according to the method of classifying cross cousins.  As a rule the systems are in other respects quite similar: the paternal and maternal siblings are separated, a corresponding distinction is drawn between sororal and fraternal nephews and nieces, and parallel cousins are classed with siblings.  The Mackenzie Basin tribes, the Iroquois, and the Eskimo differ however in their terminology for cross cousins.  They are also called siblings by the Mackenzie tribes: the Iroquois use special cousin terms for them, while the Eskimo class all cousins, parallel and cross, together and apart from siblings.

Plate 3

phonetically analogous, the genetic connection is unavoidable.  Each of such cases will have to be argued on its merits: this study does not attempt it.

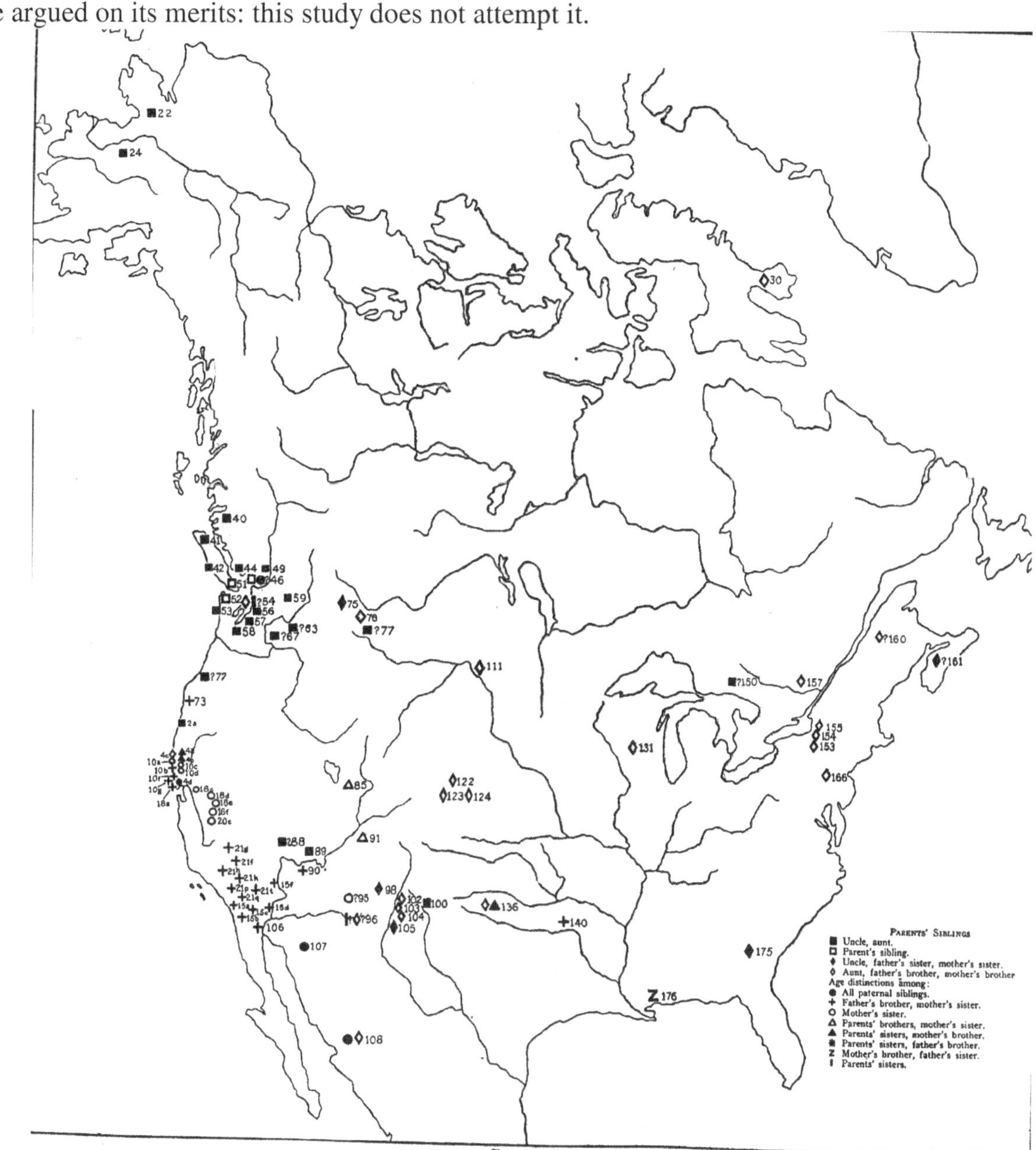


PLATE 4

In all of the preceding, paternal and maternal affiliation is taken into account, at least in the parent and child generations. But among the Salish this is not the case: relatives through males and females are merged, the basis [73] being essentially generation alone. This results in a system which operates with a minimum of terms.

I am not sure that there is justification for placing the Acoma and some of their neighbors in a separate category. Parents' sisters are merged, and this is sometimes true of their brothers. This may represent a transformation in the direction of Spanish and English terminology among these Rio Grande peoples. For the rest, they have a considerable development of verbal reciprocity and a unique way of classifying grandparents and grandchildren.

The most convenient basis for discrimination, at least in the east, is according to the method of classifying cross cousins. As a rule the systems are m other respects quite similar: the paternal and maternal siblings are separated, a corresponding distinction is drawn between

21

sororal and fraternal nephews and nieces, and parallel cousins are classed with siblings. The Mackenzie Basin tribes, the Iroquois, and the Eskimo differ however in their terminology for cross cousins. They are also called siblings by the Mackenzie tribes: the Iroquois use special cousin terms for them, while the Eskimo class all cousins, parallel and cross, together and apart from siblings.

The differences between these classes are not of the same order. The Mackenzie type, the Iroquois, and the Eskimo are much alike: the Yuman type only less like them with its additional age distinctions. The first two might be merged in a single class. Omaha and Crow types are alike in their unilinear groupings, but in other respects they resemble the four just named, that is in the separation of avuncular and nepotic relatives as they are on the male or female side. The Salish type is the most distinct in that it merges these relatives. As this is an empirical classification, the distinctions between the classes are not given as fundamental but descriptive.

## I. Omaha Type

In this system the mother's brother is an "uncle" and his male descendants through males are "uncles." The daughters of these "uncles" are "mothers," whose children are "brothers" and "sisters." The father's sister is an "aunt," her children being "sister's son and daughter" if the speaker is a male, and "son" and "daughter" if female. Their children are "grandchildren."

Ponca (125), Omaha (126), Iowa (132), Oto (133), Kansas (134), Osage (137), Quapaw? (139), Missouri? (138), Winnebago (130), Menomini (129). Sauk-Fox (131), Peoria (146), Kaskaskia (145), Piankashaw (149), Miami (167), Wea (147), Kickapoo (148), Shawnee (168).[4]

In the California systems of this type the "uncle's" daughters are "mother's sisters" (as among the first seven tribes listed below), or "mother's younger sisters."

Northern Wintun (l6a), Central Wintun (16b), Southeastern Wintun (16c), Southwestern Wintun (16d), Coast Miwok (18a), Tachi (20a), Gashowu (20d), Northern Pomo (10a), Central Pomo (10b), Eastern Pomo (10c), Southeastern Pomo (10d), Lake Miwok (18b), Plains Miwok (18c), Northern Miwok (18d), Central Miwok (18e), Southern Miwok (18f), Chukchansi (20c).

## II. Crow Type

In this system the father's sister is an "aunt" and her female descendants through females are "aunts." The sons of these "aunts" are "fathers," whose children are "brothers" (or "fathers") and "sisters." The mother's brother is an "uncle," whose children are "son" and "daughter" (less commonly for a [74] female speaker) and their children "grandchildren." The children of a man's brother and a woman's sister are "son" and "daughter": the children of their other siblings are usually called by nepotic terms.

Crow (109), Hidatsa (112), Mandan (113), Grand Pawnee (122), Republican Pawnee (123), Skidi Pawnee (124), Chickasaw (172), Choctaw (173), Creek (174), Cherokee (170), Mountain Cherokee, Hopi (93), Hano (94), Jemez (99), Laguna (97), Southern Pomo (l0f), Wappo (4d), Tlingit (34), Haida (35); possibly Isleta (105), Timucua (177), and less probably Yuchi (175).

---

[4] Numbers in parentheses refer to maps at the end of the paper {now inserted within text}.

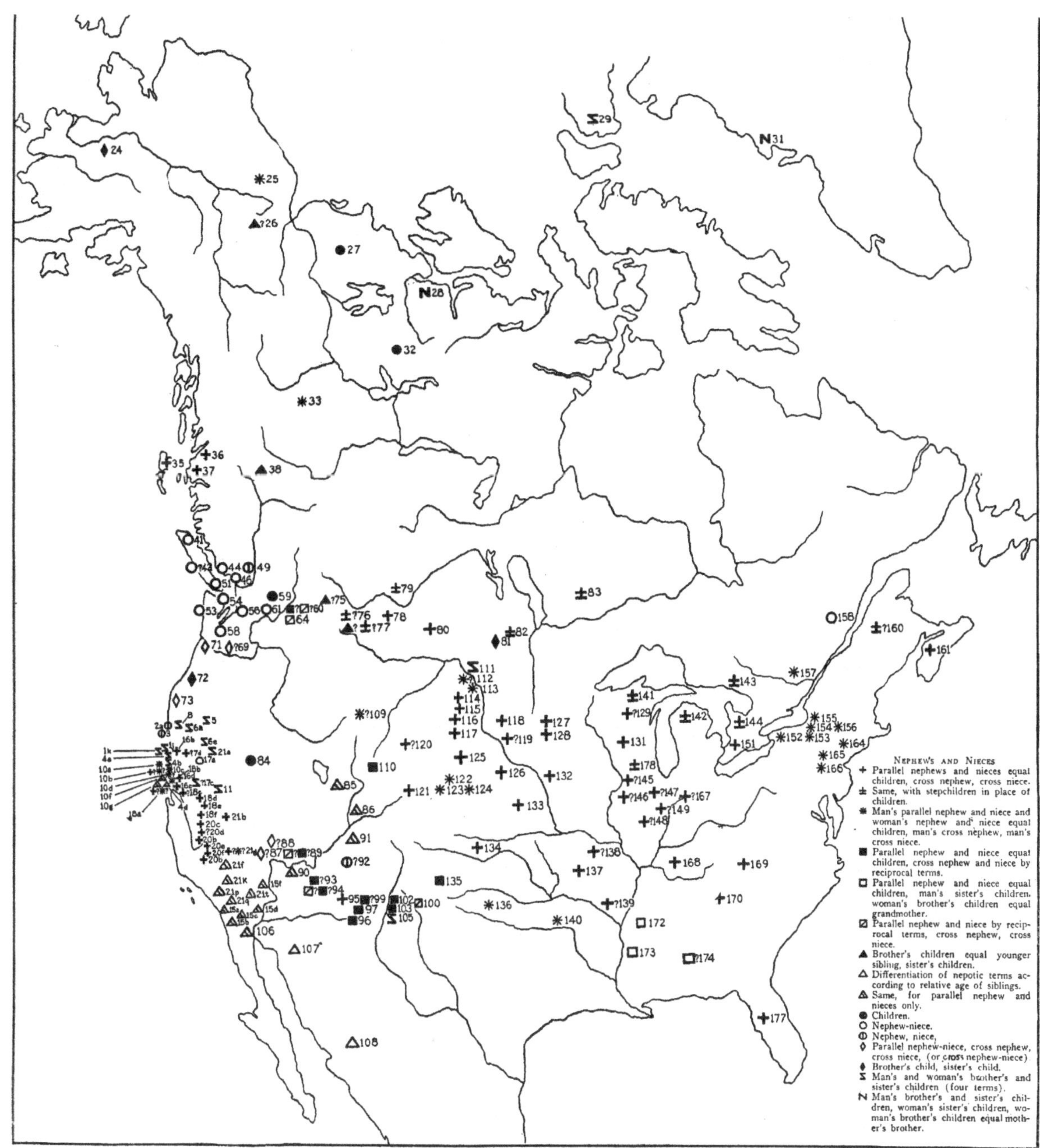





## III. Salish Type

This is characterized by the merging of father's and mother's siblings: that is, there is only one term for "aunt" and one for "uncle." Conversely there is but one term for nephew or niece. There are terms for "grandparent," "child," and "grandchild." Brothers and sisters are usually distinguished as "older sibling" and "younger sibling." Sibling terms are applied to both parallel and cross cousins.

Siciatl (44), Squamish (46), Songish (51), Bella Coola (40), Lillooet (49), Shuswap (59), Snuqualmi (56), Duwamish (57), Nisqualli (58), Klallam (54), Quileute (53), Makah (52), Nootka (42), Kwakiutl (41), Tinneh (24), Yurok (2a): possibly Spokan (163). Possibly Alsea

23

(72), Yakama (67), Kaibab (89), and Tewa (100) should be included here although I have classed them primarily elsewhere.

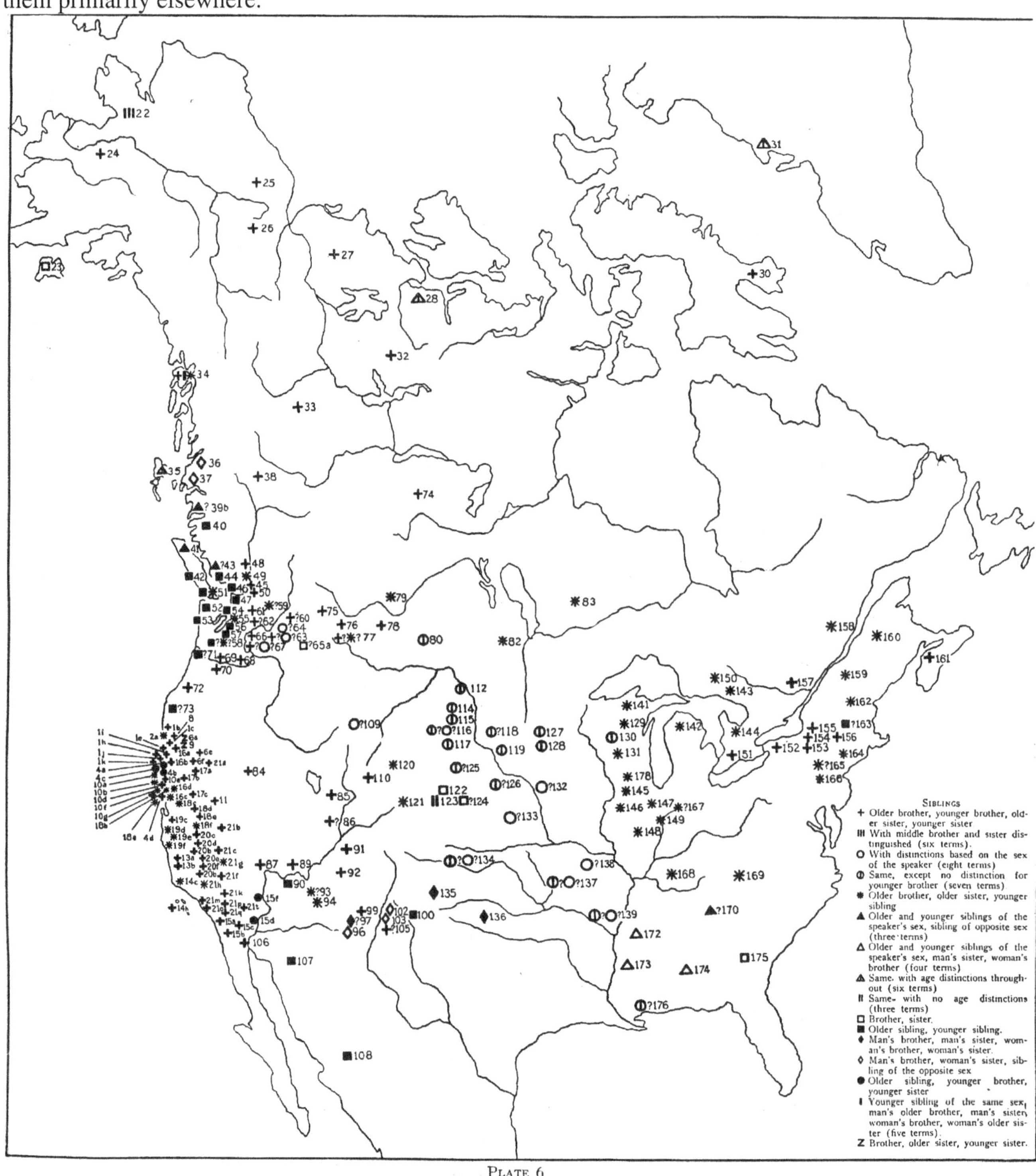


PLATE 6

Two terms, "grandfather" and "grandmother," are used by the Nisqualli, Snuqualmi, Shuswap, Lillooet, Bella Coola, and Yurok.

24

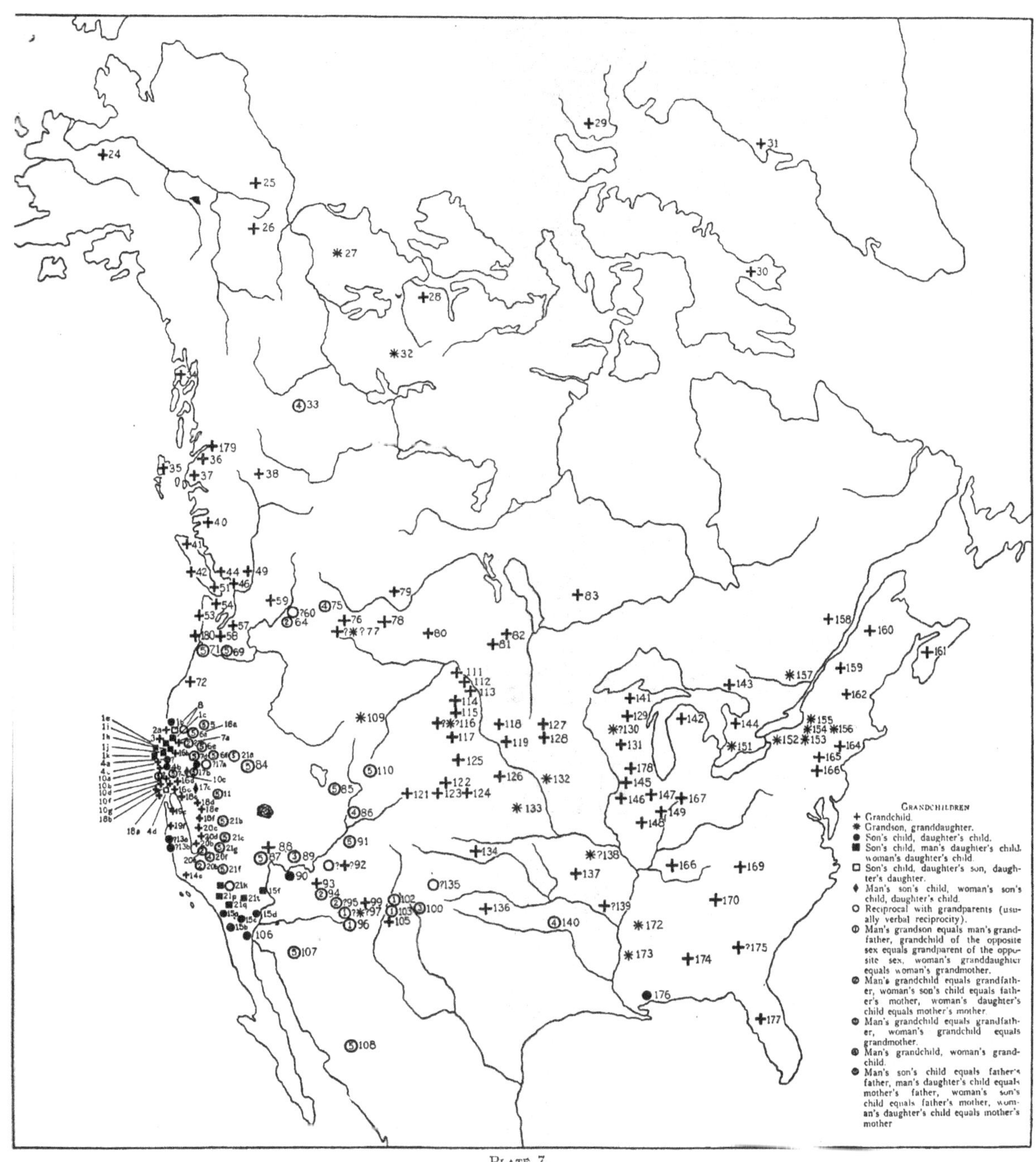



PLATE 7

## IV. Acoma Type

This differs from the preceding largely in the use of three grandparental terms, and the verbal reciprocity between grandparents and grandchildren and between avuncular and nepotic relatives. The grandparental terms are man's grandfather, woman's grandmother, and grandparent of the opposite sex. The corresponding grandchild terms are man's grandson, woman's granddaughter, and grandchild of the opposite sex. Parents' sisters are called "aunt." Mother's brother is usually a separate term: father's brother is "father" or "mother's brother," or he is called by a special term. Reciprocally a man's sister's child is "mother's brother," his brother's children are "son and daughter," "uncle," or "father's brother"; a woman's sibling's

25

children are "aunts."  Commonly three sibling terms are used, man's brother, woman's sister, and sibling of the opposite sex.  Parallel and cross cousins are alike called siblings or by the same special terms:

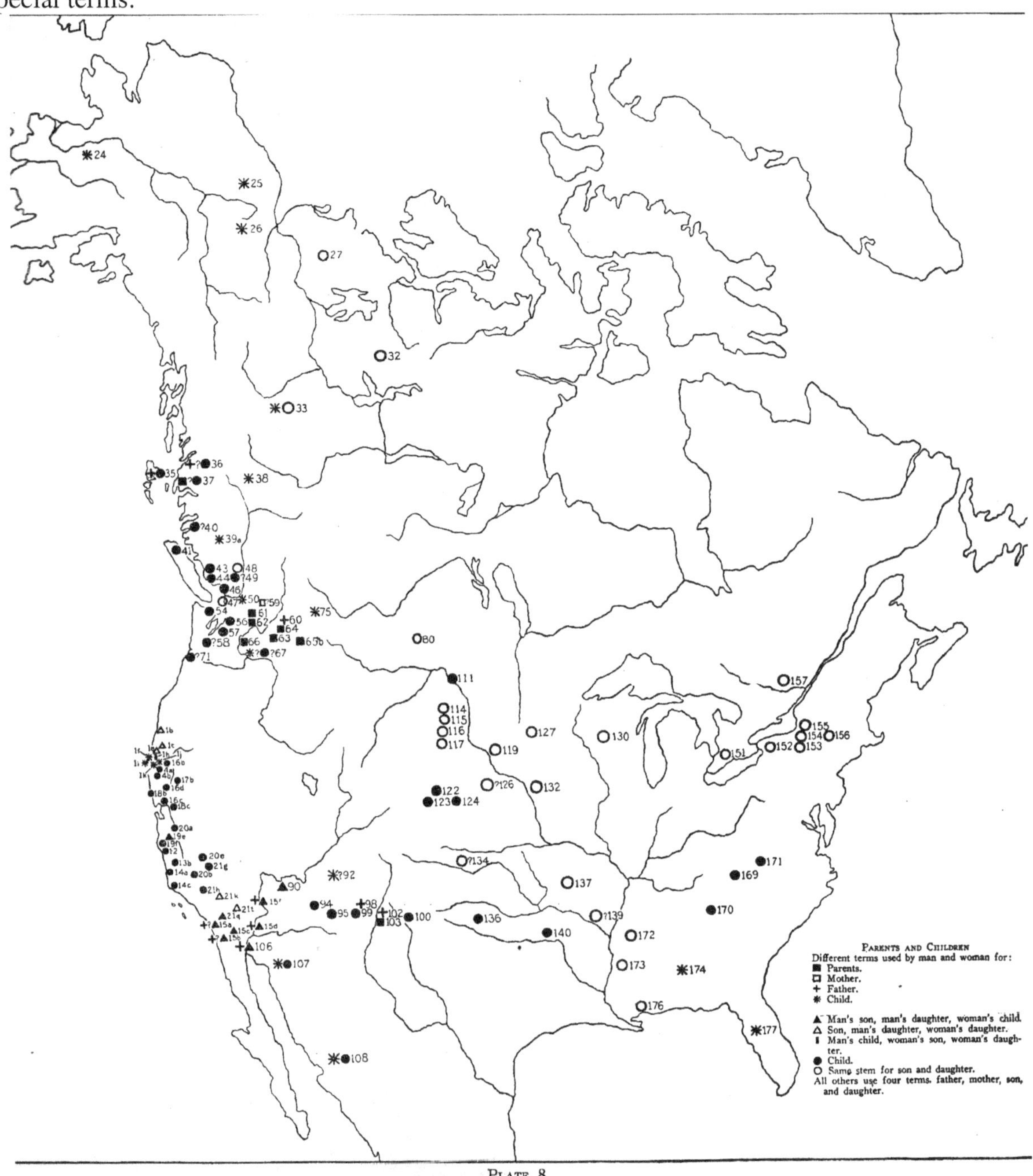

PLATE 8

Kaibab (89), Acoma (96), Cochiti (98), San Felipe (103), Santo Domingo [75] (102), Tewa (San Ildefonso, Santa Clara, San Juan, Nambe) (100), Kiowa (135), Kutenai (60).

Kaibab, Tewa, and Kiowa use terms for grandfather and grandmother: the same terms are used reciprocally for a man's grandchild and a woman's grandchild, except by the Kiowa.  The Kutenai have a term for a woman's grandmother, all other grandparents coming under one caption, reciprocally these terms are used respectively for a woman's granddaughter and for all other grandchildren.

26

Father's brother and mother's brother are included in the same term by Kaibab, Tewa and Cochiti (the last call a woman's uncle "brother").  Reciprocally a man's brother's children are "uncles," again excepting Cochiti.

An aunt is called "mother" by Acoma, San Felipe and Santo Domingo:  conversely the Acoma, for whom alone there are data, call a woman's siblings' children "son and daughter."

Separate terms for man's father and woman's father are in use among Kutenai, Cochiti, Santo Domingo, and San Felipe: the last has also separate terms for mother.
Special terms are used alike for parallel and cross cousins by Kutenai, Kaibab, Tewa, and Santo Domingo.  The Tewa call a female cousin "father's sister," which suggests the Crow type of system.

Among some of these groups the father's sister is "grandmother":  Chickasaw, Creek, Yuchi, and possibly Choctaw, Timucua, and Laguna.  The oldest of the father's sisters is "grandmother" for the Hopi.  The Pawnee groups call the father's sister "mother."

## V.  YUMAN TYPE

The distinguishing feature here is the unusual development of age distinctions.  Father's older brothers and mother's older sisters are distinguished from their younger siblings.  Parallel cousins are older or younger siblings, not according to their ages relative to that of the speaker, but according to those of their parents.  Similarly the children of a man's brother and a woman's sister are distinguished according to the relative ages of their parents.  There are four terms for sibling; older brother, older sister, younger brother, and younger sister.  Parallel cousins are siblings: cross cousins are called by special terms, or less frequently styled siblings.  Children of a man are son and daughter: a woman's children are more frequently called by one term.  Four grandparental terms are used; father's father, father's mother, mother's father, mother's mother, and conversely four grandchild terms, man's son's, child, man's daughter's child, woman's son's child, and woman's daughter's child.

Cocopa (106), Yuma (15d), Mohave (15f), Havasupai (90), Kamia (l5c), Southern Diegueño (15b), Northern Diegueño (15a), Desert Cahuilla (21t), Cupeño (21q), Luiseño (21p), Serrano (21k), Kitanemuk (21h), Kawaiisu (21f), Tubatulabel (21g), Southwestern Pomo (10g), Wind River Shoshoni (110), Uintah Ute (85), Southern Ute (91), Papago (107), Northern Tepehuane (108): possibly Biloxi (176).  Wappo (4d), Southern Pomo (10f), and even Northern Wintun (16a) might be included here, but I have preferred to class the first two with the Crow and the third with the Omaha because of their classification of the father's sister's female descendants and mother's brother's male descendants respectively. [76]

Other age distinctions are made.  Older and younger mother's brother are recognized by the Uintah Ute, Southern Ute, Papago, Northern Tepehuane, and Biloxi, with comparable distinctions made among a man's sororal nephews and nieces depending on the age of his sisters.  The Papago, Northern Tepehuane, and Biloxi also discriminate between father's older and younger sister, and again a woman distinguishes her older and younger brother's children.  The Papago make distinctions among cross cousins as well as parallel cousins according to the age of the parents.  Nepotic terms are verbally reciprocal for Uintah and Southern Ute, almost wholly so for Northern Tepehuane, and in part for Wind River, Havasupai, Papago, Serrano, and Luiseño.

Two terms, older and younger sibling, are used by Havasupai, Papago, and Northern Tepehuane.  Yuma and Mohave use older sibling, younger brother, and younger sister: Tubatulabel and Kitanemuk use older brother, older sister, and younger sibling.

Cross cousins are siblings for Tubatulabal, Kawaiisu, Uintah and Southern Ute, Wind River, Papago, and in part for Mohave.

A woman's children are called 'son' and 'daughter' by Uintah and Southern Ute, Wind River, Kawaiisu, Luiseño, and by Serrano and Desert Cahuilla who distinguish man's and woman's daughters. Tubatulabal and Kitanemuk call a man's children 'child': Papago and Northern Tepehuane do the same but the term is different from that employed by a woman. Man's father and woman's father are separate terms among Mohave, Yuma and Cocopa; while Northern and Southern Diegueño have two terms which may be applied to either relative.

Grandparental terms are father's parent, mother's father, and mother's mother for Serrano, Luiseño, Cupeño, and Desert Cahuilla, and conversely grandchildren are son's child, man's daughter's child, and woman's daughter's child. These terms are all verbally reciprocal. So are those of the Kawaiisu, Tubatulabal, Wind River, Uintah and Southern Ute, and in part Papago and Northern Tepehuane, all of whom have the regular four grandparent-grandchild terms. Grandchildren are classed as son's child and daughter's child by all the Yumans, except the Mohave, and the Biloxi.

## VI. MACKENZIE BASIN TYPE

The characteristic feature here is that all cousins, parallel and cross, are siblings. Four terms are ordinarily employed for these, older brother, older sister, younger brother, and younger sister. Parents are father and mother: children are son and daughter. Parents' siblings are usually father's brother, father's sister, mother's sister, and mother's brother. Nepotic relatives are commonly called by special terms. Grandparents are grandfather and, grandmother: grandchildren are called by one term, Loucheux (25), Tukuthe (26), Yellow Knife (32), Slavey (33), Sarsi (75), Wasco (70), Gros Ventre [Atsina] (78), Arapaho (121), Caddo (140), Shivwits [77] (88), Montagnais (158), Two Mountain Iroquois (157), Munsi (165), and probably Piegan (77) and Micmac (161).

The majority of the Californian and other western tribes that have this system have four terms for grandparents, father's father, father's mother, mother's mother, and mother's father. These are used reciprocally, with but few exceptions, for a man's son's child, a woman's son's child, a woman's daughter's child, and a man's daughter's child respectively.

Hupa (1c), Whilkut (1e), Yuki (4a), Huchnom (4b), Coast Yuki (4c), Lutuami (5), Achomawi (6e), Atsugewl (6f), Washo (11), Southern Maidu (17c), Northern Paiute (21a), Eastern Mono (21b), Western Mono (21c), Moapa (87), Paviotso (84), Wishram (69), Chinook (71).

Other western tribes with this system in its essentials are Paleuyami (20f), Yaudanchi (20e), Yauelmani (20b), Karok (8), Zuni (95), Kalispel (64), and Wichita (136).

There is some possibility that Moapa, Chinook, Piegan, and Micmac make use of special cousin terms.

Father's brother is called father by Zuñi, Eastern and Western Mono, Loucheux, Gros Arapaho, Two Mountain Iroquois, and older or younger father by Wichita and Caddo. Mother's sister is mother for the same groups (except the Eastern Mono) and also for the Sarsi. Again Caddo and Wichita, call this relative mother but distinguish older and younger individuals. Other age distinctions among the parents' siblings are made by the Zuni in their alternative terms for mother's sister and by the Yuki and Huchnom for the same relative, for mother's brother, and for father's sister.

Two modes of classifying nepotic relatives stand out.  A man's brother's children and a woman's sister's children are called son and daughter, child, or step-son and-daughter by Munsi, Micmac, Two Mountain Iroquois, Gros Ventre, Arapaho, Piegan (?), Caddo, Wichita, Zuni, Pauelmani, Yaudanchi, Yellow Knife, Slavey, and Loucheux.  Four terms, man's brother's child, man's sister's child, woman's brother's child, and woman's sister's child, are used by most of the Californians, viz., Yuki, Huchnom, Lutuami, Achomawi, Karok, Washo, Southern Maidu, Northern Paiute, Eastern Mono, and Western Mono.

Relative age of the connecting parent enters into the classification of cousins by the Coast Yuki and possibly of nepotic relatives by the Piegan and Tukuthe.  These features suggest the Yuman system.

## VII. IROQUOIS TYPE

Except that there are special terms for cross cousins, this system is like the last.  Parallel cousins are siblings, or in the cases where cousin terms are used these are not the same as the cross cousin terms.  Four terms are most common for siblings, older brother, older sister, younger brother, and younger sister.  There are separate terms for father, mother, son, and daughter.  Parents' siblings are usually father's brother, father's sister, mother's brother, and mother's sister.  A man's brother's children and a woman's sister's children are usually "children," with the other nepotic relatives called by two terms, nephew [78] and niece.  Grandfather and grandmother are used for grandparents, with one term for grandchild.

Seneca (152), Cayuga (153), Onondaga (154), Oneida (155), Mohawk (156), Wyandot (151), Tuscarora (169), Malecite (160), Ottawa (143), Swampy Cree (83), Wood Cree (82), Plains Cree (79), Ojibway of Lake Superior (141), Lake Michigan (142), Lake Huron (143), and Kansas, Potawatomi (178), Bungi (81), Santee (127), Sisseton (128), Yanktonai (118), Yankton (119), Oglalla (116), Brule (117), Uncpapa (114), Blackfoot Dakota (115), Assiniboin (80), Blood (76), Alsea (72), Yakama (67), Carrier (38), Tsimshian (37), Nass (36), Hare (27), Tolowa (1b), Lassik (1h), Wailaki (1j), Kato (1k), Shasta (6a), Northern Yana (7a), Yahi (7d), Northeastern Maidu (17a), Northwestern Maidu (17b), Navaho (92): possibly Natick (163) and Central Yana (7b).

Cousin terms are in use by the Carrier for the mother's sister's children, by the Navaho for the father's brother's children, and by the Ottawa and the Ojibway groups (except Lake Superior) for a man's parallel cousins and in part for a woman's parallel cousins.

The Oglalla have eight sibling terms, the sex of the speaker entering into the normal categories of older and younger brother and sister.  All the other Siouan tribes have a similar usage, but with a common term for a man's and woman's younger brother, seven terms in all, except the Yanktonai who do not distinguish age among a woman's sisters.  Nass and Tsimshian have three terms, man's brother, woman's sister, and sibling of the opposite sex.  Shasta, Yahi, Malecite, and Bungi have individual ways of classifying these relatives.

One term for child is used by Nass, Tsimshian, Yakama (?), Northwestern Maidu, and Tuscarora.

The father's brother is called father and the mother's sister mother by a large number of these tribes: Yahi, Nass, Tsimshian (?), Navaho (?), Hare, Assiniboin, all of the Dakota groups, and all of the Iroquoian groups, except that mother's sister is recorded as father for the Mohawk, leather's sister is called mother by the Cayuga, Onondaga, Oneida, and Mohawk.  The Blood likewise use a single term for aunt.  Kato, Wailaki, Lassik, and Tolowa call father's sister older sister.

All of a woman's nephews and nieces are called children by Malecite (?), Seneca, Cayuga, Onondaga, Oneida, and Mohawk. The Hare call all nephews and nieces children. Special nepotic terms are used throughout by the Alsea, all the Californians (except the Yahi), but only in part by the Lassik, and possibly by the Navaho. The Carrier call a brother's children younger brother and younger sister.

Four grandparental terms, father's father, father's mother, mother's father, and mother's mother, are used by all the Californian tribes. These terms are used reciprocally for grandchildren by Shasta, Northwestern Maidu of the plains, and Yahi. Tolowa and Northeastern Maidu distinguish only son's child and daughter's child; Northwestern Maidu of the mountains a man's son's child, a woman's son's child, and daughter's child. For both Maidu groups the [79] usage is in part verbally reciprocal. Lassik, Wailaki, and Kato class them as son's child, man's daughter's child, and woman's daughter's child. The Navaho have terms for father's parent, mother's father, and mother's mother: they may use the first reciprocally for son's child. The Alsea have but a single term for grandparent. The Oglalla may have separate terms for father's mother and mother's mother. All of the Iroquois proper, Wyandot, Hare, and possibly Oglalla, distinguish grandsons from granddaughters.

## VIII. ESKIMO TYPE

This system differs from the preceding in that cross cousins and parallel cousins are called by the same cousin terms. There are four terms for parents' siblings. Nepotic terms are usually man's brother's child, man's sister's child, woman's sister's child, with woman's brother's children termed variously. Two terms for grandparents are used, "grandfather" and "grandmother," with one term for grandchild.

Alaskan Eskimo (22), Copper Eskimo (28), Eskimo of Northumberland Island[5] (29) and Cumberland Inlet (30), Greenland Eskimo (31), possibly Wiyot (3), Delaware (166), and less probably Mohegan (164), Abenaki (159), Penobscot (162), and Natick (163).

Siblings are usually differentiated according to relative age. The Alaskan Eskimo resemble the Chukchi and Koryak in their tripartite division, older, younger, and youngest brother and sister.[6]

Copper and Greenland Eskimo women alike call their brother's child by the term for mother's brother. [80]

## COMPARISON WITH EARLIER CLASSIFICATIONS

Resemblances between these systems have been pointed out in earlier papers, but for the most part, attention was drawn only to peculiar modes of classifying certain, relatives.

Morgan's Systems contains many references to just those resemblances between the systems east of the Rockies which form the basis of classification in the present paper. He recognizes in the cross cousin nomenclature an important means of discriminating among them. He remarks on the identity of the Iroquois, Dakota, Assiniboin, Ojibwa, Ottawa, Potawatomi,

---

[5]  So I interpret Morgan's Northumberland Inlet.
[6]  Lowie, *Historical and Sociological Interpretations of Kinship Terminologies*, 294.

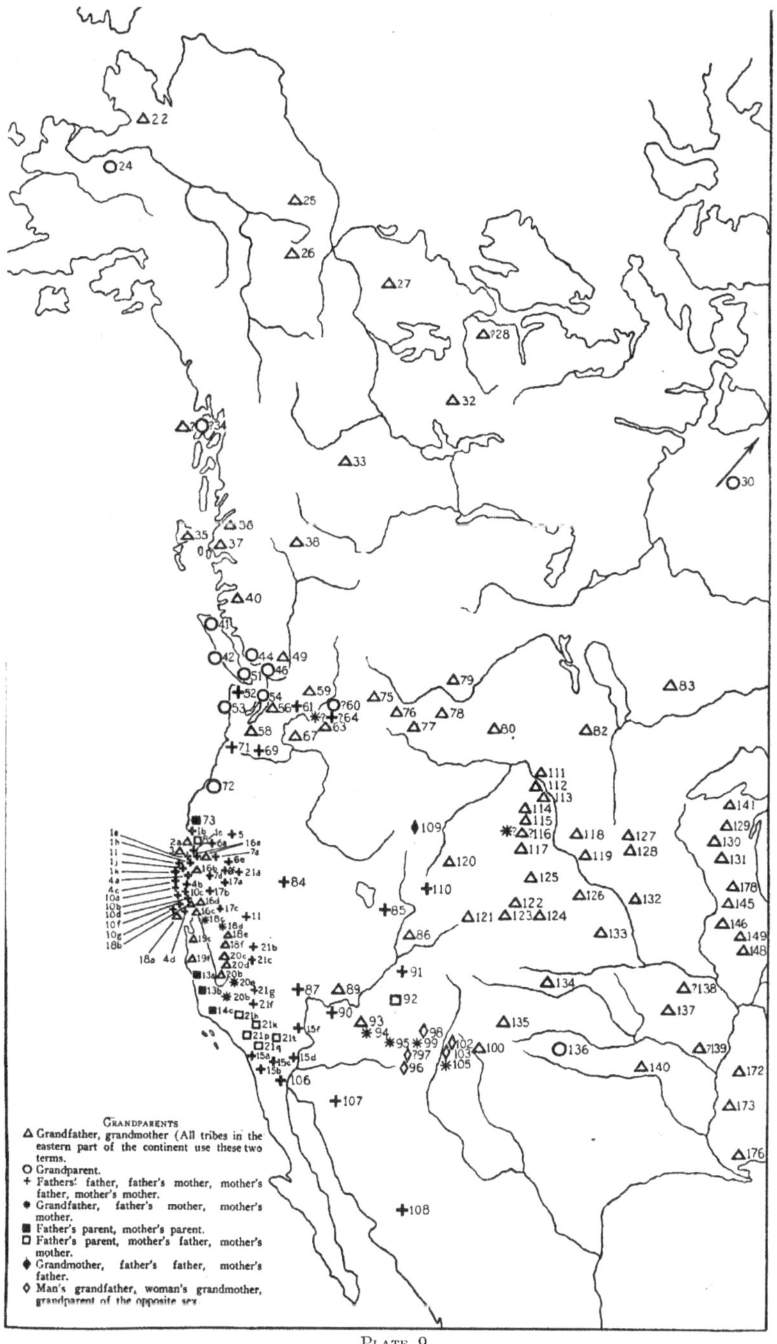



PLATE 9

and Cree, but includes Mohegan with them.[7] The Southern Siouans, Winnebago {HoChunk}, and western Central Algonkin form a group and are distinct from the Iroquois and Dakota. The Crow and Hidatsa are coupled with the Gulf nations and the Pawnee, and a resemblance of Laguna to this group is suggested.[8] Blackfoot is more like the Great Lakes Nations than the western Central Algonkins. Yellow Knife is like Hare. Delaware is recognized as a divergent type, but Munsi is nearest Delaware. The Greenland and Northumberland Island Eskimo are alike, and markedly different from the systems to the south. Spokan and Yakama are unlike the eastern groups, and resemble the Tabegwaches in the use of verbally reciprocal terms.[9]

On the whole this is in essential agreement with my classification. Morgan believes however that these resemblances are indices of biological relationship, Seneca is the typical system: the differences which occur in other systems show in what order they have diverged from the parent stock. He is more impressed with the merging of lineal and collateral relatives in the systems throughout the whole area than with resemblances of lesser range. Accordingly he is satisfied with establishing by this evidence that all the groups, excluding the Eskimo, belong to one biologic group, the "Ganowanian."[10]

---

[7] *Systems*, 166, 176, 204, 205, 222.

[8] *Loc. cit.*, 178, 179, 210-217, 188, 191, 198, 262.

[9] *Loc. cit.*, 226, 237, 221, 277, 245-252.

[10] *Loc. cit.*, 176, 192.

Lowie recognizes much the same groups. The Southern Siouans are grouped with some Central Algonkins: the Ojibwa, Cree, Wyandot, and Iroquois with the Dakota.[11] The similarity of cross cousin terminology among the Crow, Hidatsa, Hano, Hopi, Tlingit, Muskogeans, and Pawnee is pointed out. Another group exists in which paternal and maternal lines of descent are merged: Eskimo, Nootka, Quileute, Chinook, various Salish tribes, Kutenai, the Plateau Shoshoneans, and the tribes in a large section of California north and east of the Miwok. This is my Salish group with the important additions.[12]

Kroeber classifies the Californian tribes on the basis of twelve available [81] systems. These fall into three groups. Mohave and Luiseño are similar and show connections with the Southwest. Yurok is unique among Californian systems but bears resemblances to the Coast Salish and tribes of the eastern United States. This agrees with my assignment of the first two to the Yuman and the third to the Salish group. For the rest, Yaudanchi, Northern Paiute, Washo, Tubatulabal, Kawaiisu, and probably Yuki constitute a generic type distributed peripherally to Eastern Pomo, Central Miwok, and Southeastern Wintun. The latter have specialized inasmuch as their systems are simplified. This also corresponds to the present classification: these Pomo, Miwok, and Wintun systems are included in the Omaha type, the others are of the Mackenzie Basin type, except that I consider Tubatulabal and Kawaiisu similar to the Yuman systems.[13]

Gifford offers a general comparison of the Californian systems on the basis of the tripartite cultural division within the state. In such a form it is not altogether clear what relationship he sees between the northwestern systems, the southern, and those of central California. In the northwestern area Wiyot is noted as different from the Athabaskans, Yurok, and Karok. According to my scheme it is possibly to be classed with the Eskimo, the others being of Mackenzie and Iroquois type. Yurok is not recognized as exceptional. In southern California there is some difference between the Shoshonean and Yuman systems, the divergence increasing' with remoteness from the Yuma. This does not contradict my inclusion of all southern Californian Shoshoneans with the Yuman tribes, but it does not directly confirm it.[14]

Two groups are recognized in central California; a Sacramento-San Joaquin valley core with a peripheral mountain group. This corresponds fairly well with the present classification, at least so far as the valley group is concerned. All the tribes in the valley group shown in Gifford's Map 24, with two exceptions, have systems of the Omaha type. These two, Southern Pomo and Wappo, might be classed with the Crow or Yuma.[15] Elsewhere Gifford has suggested the resemblance of the Central Miwok to the Omaha.[16]

The mountain tribes are seen as a less homogeneous group. Yet the similarity of Shasta, Northeastern, Northwestern, and Southern Maidu, Lutuami, and Achomawi is noted. In this I concur, but I have separated the first three from the others on the basis of their cross cousin nomenclature, classifying them as of Iroquoian and Mackenzie type respectively. Gifford has

---

[11] This is not wholly independent corroboration for Lowie based his observations partly on the data assembled for the present paper.

[12] *Historical and Sociological Interpretations*, 296; *Kinship Systems of the Crow and Hidatsa*, 341; *Culture and Ethnology*, 124, 153, 167.

[13] *California Kinship Systems*, 378-382.

[14] *Californian Kinship Terminologies*, 199, 200.

[15] *Loc. Cit.*, 203.

[16] *Miwok Moieties*, 188.

also calculated the degree of inter-relation within the whole central Californian area.  If we take those systems having least resemblance, i.e. with less than fifty per cent of their categories in common, we have a series of systems which differ on the whole from the others.  These are Achomawi, Lutuami, Coast Yuki, Kawaiisu, Tubatulabal, Southern Pomo, Wappo, Southern Miwok, and Central Pomo. [82]

The first three belong to my Mackenzie Basin type; the others to the Crow, Yuma, and Omaha types.[17]

On the whole the present classification agrees with Gifford's in separating the southern Californians, the Wiyot, and the Interior valley systems from those of the mountain tribes.  I have gone further in classifying this remainder with the Salish, Iroquois, and Mackenzie Basin groups. [83]


## Bibliography

Barnum, Francis  *Grammatical Fundamentals of the Innuit Language* (Boston, 1901, 264-5).
   [Alaskan Eskimo; Nushagak to St. Michael's Is.]
Boas, Franz   *Second General Report on the Indians of British Columbia* (Report, British Association For the Advancement of Science, 1890, 688-692).
   [Bella Coola, Kalispel, Lillooet, Okanagan (61), Shuswap, Squamish.]
*The Vocabulary of the Chinook Language* (American Anthropologist, N.S., 6, 1904, 134-5).
*Tsimshian Mythology* (Thirty-First Annual Report, Bureau of American Ethnology, 1916, 489-495.)       [Kwakiutl, Tlingit, Tsimshian.]
*Kinship Terms of the Kutenai Indians* (American Anthropologist, N.S. 21, 1919, 98-101.)
Boas, Franz  and Goddard, Pliny Earle.  *Ts'ets'aut, An Athapascan Language From Portland Canal, British Columbia* (International Journal of American Linguistics, III, 1924, 15-16).
   [Ts'ets'aut (179).]
*Vocabulary of An Athapascan Dialect of the State of Washington* (*same*, 41).
   [Willapa ? (180).]
Chapman, John W.  *Manuscript of Tinneh Terms, Anvik, Alaska*, 1905.
Dall, W.H.  *Tribes of the Extreme Northwest* (Contributions To North American Ethnology, I, 1877, 117-119, 122, 137, 145).
   [Bellabella (39b), Eskimo of Cumberland Inlet, Baffin Land, Haida, Kadiak Eskimo (23), Kwakiutl, Nass, Tlingit, Tsimshian.]
Dorsey, J. Owen  *Omaha Sociology* (Third Annual Report, Bureau of Ethnology, 1884, 252-255).  See Riggs, Stephen R., xvii-xxiii.
   [Biloxi, Dhegiha, Hidatsa, Kansas, Mandan, Osage, Quapaw, Santee, Tciwere, Tutelo (171), Winnebago.]

---

[17]  *Californian Kinship Terminologies*: 202, 210.

Farrand, Livingston  *Notes on the Alsea Indians of Oregon* (American Anthropologist, N.S. 3, 1901, 244).

Frachtenberg, Leo  *Manuscript of Quileute Terms.*

Franciscan Fathers  *An Ethnologic Dictionary of the Navaho Language* (St. Michaels, Arizona, 1910, 435-6).

Freire-Marreco, Barbara  *Tewa Kinship Terms From the Pueblo of Hano, Arizona* (American Anthropologist, N.S., 16, 1914, 269-287). [84]
 *A Note on Kinship Terms Compounded With the Postfix 'E in the Hano Dialect of Tewa* (*same*, 17, 1915, 198-202).
   [Hano, Nambe, Santa Clara.]

Gibbs, George  *Tribes of Western Washington and Northwestern Oregon* (Contributions To North American Ethnology, I, 1877, 252-3, 270-1, 345).
   [Bella Coola, Colville ? (62), Coeur d'Alene (65a), Comox (43), Cowichan (47), Flathead (65b), Kalispel, Kuwalitsk, Lillooet, Nisqualli, Okanogan, Shuswap, Spokan, Thompson (48), Wakynakaine, Wenatchee (66).]

Gifford, Edward Winslow  *Miwok Moieties* (University of California Publications in American Archaeology and Ethnology, 12, 1916, 139-194).
 *Tubatulabal and Kawaiisu Kinship Terms* (*same*, 12, 1917, 244-7).
   [Uintah Ute, Kaibab Paiute.]
 *Californian Kinship Terminologies* (*same*, 18, 1922, 1-285).

Goddard, Pliny Earle  *Manuscript of Sarsi Terms.*

Goldenweiser, A.A.  *On Iroquois Work, 1912* (Summary Report For 1912, Anthropological Division, Geological Survey of Canada, 1913, 471).

Golomshtok, Eugene  *Manuscript of Atsugewi Terms.*

Grinnell, George Bird  *Blackfoot Lodge Tales* (New York, 1917, 210).

Gunther, Erna  *Manuscript of Duwamish, Klallam, Makah, and Wasco Terms.*

Haeberlein, Hermann K. {Haeberlin, Herman} and Gunther, Erna  *Ethnographische Notizen Uber Die Indianerstamme Des Puget-Sundes* (Zeitschrift Fur Ethnologic, 1924, 1-74).
   [Nisqualli, Snuqualmi.]

Harrington, John P.  *Tewa Relationship Terms* (American Anthropologist, N.S., 14, 1912, 472-498).
   [Tewa of San Ildefonso, Santa Clara, San Juan, and Nambe, Isleta, Taos, Jemez.]

Hawkes, E.W.  *Manuscript of Alaskan Eskimo Terms, 1916.*

Hill Tout, Charles  *Report on the Ethnology of the Siciatl of British Columbia, A Coast Division of the Salish Stock* (Journal of the Anthropological Institute of Great Britain and Ireland, 34, 1904, 80-1).
 *Report on the Ethnology of the Statlumh of British Columbia* (*same*, 35, 1905, 206-7).
   [Cowichan, Lillooet]
 *Report on the Ethnology of the South-Eastern Tribes of Vancouver Island, British Columbia* (*same*, 37, 1907, 352-4).
   [Songish.] [85]

Jenness, Diamond  *Manuscript of Sarsi Terms.*
 *The Life of the Copper Eskimos* (Report, Canadian Arctic Expedition, 1913-18, 12, 1922, 83-4).

Jones, William  *Kickapoo Ethnological Notes* (American Anthropologist, N.S., 15, 1913, 333-5).

Kroeber, A.L.  *The Arapaho* (Bulletin, American Museum of Natural History, 18, 1902, 9-10,

150).

    [Arapaho, Gros Ventre]

*Arapaho Dialects* (University of California Publications in American Archaeology and Ethnology, 12, 1916, 75).

*California Kinship Systems* (*same*, 12, 1917, 358-361).

*Zuni Kin and Clan* (Anthropological Papers, American Museum of Natural History, 18, 1917, 51-88).

    [Acoma, Laguna, Zuni.]

Lowie, Robert H. *Manuscripts of Yankton and Hopi Terms.*

*The Northern Shoshone* (Anthropological Papers, American Museum of Natural History, 2, 1909, 209).

*The Assiniboine* (*same* 4, 1909, 36-38).

*Social Life of the Crow Indians* (*same*, 9, 1912, 207-212, 248).

*Exogamy and the Classificatory Systems of Relationship* (American Anthropologist, N.S., 17, 1915, 223-239).

*Historical and Sociological Interpretations of Kinship Terminologies* (Holmes Anniversary Volume, 1916, 293-300).

*The Kinship Systems of the Crow and Hidatsa* (Proceedings, Nineteenth International Congress of Americanists, 1917, 340-343).

*Notes on the Social Organization and Customs of the Mandan, Hidatsa, and Crow Indians* (Anthropological Papers, American Museum of Natural History 21, 1917: 11-15, 26-42, 56-74).

*A Note on Kiowa Kinship Terms and Usages* (American Anthropologist, N.S., 25, 1923, 279-281).

*Notes on Shoshonean Ethnography* (Anthropological Papers, American Museum of Natural History 20, 1924, 287-291).

    [Moapa and Shivwits Paiute, Paviotso, Southern Ute, Wind River Shoshoni.]

Mason, J. Alden *Manuscript of Papago [Tohono O'odam] Terms.*

Matthews, Washington *Ethnology and Philology of the Hidatsa Indians* (U.S. Geological and Geographical Survey of the Territories, Miscellaneous Publications 7, 1877, 55-57).

Michelson, Truman *Notes on the Piegan System of Consanguinity* (Holmes Anniversary Volume, 1916, 320-334).

Morgan, Lewis H. *Conjectural Solution of the Origin of the Classificatory* [86] *System of Relationship* (Proceedings, American Academy of Arts and Sciences 7, 1868).

*Systems of Consanguinity and Affinity of the Human Family* (Smithsonian Contributions To Knowledge, 17, 1871).

    [Arikara (111), Cheyenne (120), Spokan (63), Tabegwaches (86), Tesuque (101), and Others.]

Morice, A.G. *The Western Denes – Their Manners and Customs* (Proceeding's, Canadian Institute, Third Series, 7, 1889, 120-1).

    [Carrier.]

Parsons, Elsie Clews *Manuscript of Acoma, Jemez, Laguna, and Navaho Terms.*

*Further Notes on Isleta* (American Anthropologist, N. S., 23, 1921, 149-153).

    [Isleta, Sandia (104).]

*Laguna Genealogies* (Anthropological Papers, American Museum of Natural History 19, 1923, 147-203).

[Acoma, Laguna, San Felipe, Santo Domingo.]
Petter, Rodolphe   *Sketch of the Cheyenne Grammar* (Memoirs, American Anthropological Association ,1905-7, 443-478).
Radin, Paul *Manuscript of Cochiti Terms.*
  The Winnebago Tribe (Thirty-Seventh Annual Report, Bureau of American Ethnology, 1923. 128-133).
Riggs, Stephen Return   *Dakota Grammar, Texts, and Ethnography* (Contributions To North American Ethnology, 9, 1893, 45, 203, 204, 207).
    [Santee.]
Rinaldini, Benito  *Gramatica, Diccionario Y Catecismo* (Mexico, 1743).
    [Tepehuane (108).]
Ross, Alexander  *Adventures of the First Settlers on the Oregon or Columbia River* (London, 1849, 326).
    [Okanagan of Washington (61).]
Sapir, Edward  *Manuscript of Nootka Terms.*
  *Notes on the Takelma Indians of Southwestern Oregon* (American Anthropologist, N.S., 9, 1907, 268-9).
  *Takelma Texts* (Anthropological Publications, University of Pennsylvania Museum, 2, 1909).
    [Takelma (73).]
  *A Note on Reciprocal Terms of Relationship in America* (American Anthropologist, N.S., 15, 1913, 132-8).
    [Kaibab Paiute, Uintah Ute.]
  *Terms of Relationship and the Levirate* (*same*, 18, 1916, 327-337).  [87]
  *Kinship Terms of the Kootenay Indians* (*same*, 20, 1918, 414-8).
  *Corrigenda to "Kinship Terms of the Kootenay Indians."* (*same*, 21, 1919, 98).
  *Nass River Terms of Relationship* (*same*, 22, 1920, 261-271).
  *A Haida Kinship Term among the Tsimshian* (*same*, 23, 1921, 233-4).
  *The Algonkin Affinities of Yurok and Wiyot Kinship Terms* (Journal De La Societe Des Americanistes De Paris, N.S., 15, 1923, 36-74).
Skinner, Alanson  *Manuscript of Bungi and Potawatomi Terms.*
  *Social Life and Ceremonial Bundles of the Menomini Indians* (Anthropological Papers, American Museum of Natural History 13, 1913, 32-4).
  *Notes on the Plains Cree* (American Anthropologist, N.S., 16, 1914, 73-4).
  *Societies of the Iowa, Kansa, and Ponca Indians.* (Anthropological Papers, American Museum of Natural History 11, 1915, 735-8, 766-9).
Speck, Frank G.  *Ethnology of the Yuchi Indians* (Anthropological Publications, University of Pennsylvania Museum, I, 1909, 68-70).
  *Notes on the Mohegan and Niantic Indians* (Anthropological Papers, American Museum of Natural History 3, 1909, 193-4).
  *Family Hunting Territories and Social Life of Various Algonkian Bands of the Ottawa Valley.* (Memoir, Geological Survey of Canada 70, 1915, 24-5).
    [Timagami (150).]
  *Kinship Terms and the Family Band among the Northeastern Algonkian* (American Anthropologist, N.S., 20, 1918, 143-161).
    [Abenaki, Malecite, Micmac, Montagnais, Passamaquoddy, Penobscot.]
  *Correction to Kinship Terms among the Northeastern Algonkian* (*same*, 22, 1920, 85).

Spier, Leslie  *Manuscripts of Havasupai, Kalispel, Nisqualli, and Wishram Terms.*
  *Blackfoot Relationship Terms* (American Anthropologist, N.S. 17, 1915, 603-7).
  *Wichita and Caddo Relationship Terms* (*same*, 26, 1924, 258-263).
Swanton, John R.  *Social Condition, Beliefs, and Linguistic Relationship of the Tlingit Indians.* (Twenty-Sixth Annual Report, Bureau of American Ethnology, 1908, 424-5).
      [Haida, Tlingit.]
  *Contributions to the Ethnology of the Haida* (Memoirs, American Museum of Natural History, 8, 1909, 62-6).
  Letters To R.H. Lowie  *Concerning Chickasaw, Choctaw, and Creek Terms*, May 9, 1914, Dec. 13, 1915.
  *Terms of Relationship in Timucua* (Holmes Anniversary Volume, 1916, 451-463).  [88]
  *Early History of the Creek Indians and Their Neighbors* (Bulletin, Bureau of American Ethnology, 73, 1922, 366-8).
      [Timucua.]
Swanton, John R. and Murie, James  *Manuscript of Skidi Pawnee Terms.*
Tolmie, W. Fraser and Dawson, George M.  *Comparative Vocabularies of the Indian Tribes of British Columbia* (Geological and Natural History Survey of Canada, Montreal, 1884, 14-109).
      [Bella Coola, Carrier, Chehalis (45), Chilcotin, Chinook, Haida, Kalispel, Klikitat (68), Kutenai, Kwakiutl, Kwantlen (50), Kyuquot, Lillooet, Nakuntlen, Nanaimo, Snohomish, Songish, Tiakluit, Tlingit, Tsimshian.]
Trumbull, James Hammond  *Natick Dictionary* (Bulletin, Bureau of American Ethnology, 25, 1903).
Uhlenbeck, C.C.  *Flexion of Substantives in Blackfoot, A Preliminary Sketch* (Verhandelingen Der Koninklijke Akademie Van Wetenschappen te Amsterdam, Afdeeling Letterkunde, n.r., 14, 1913).
      [Piegan.]
  *Some General Aspects of Blackfoot Morphology, A Contribution To Algonquian Linguistics.* (*same*, 14, 1914).
Walker, James R.  *Oglala Kinship Terms* (American Anthropologist, N.S., 16, 1914, 96-109).
Wells, Roger, and Kelly, John  *English-Eskimo and Eskimo-English Vocabularies* (Circular, Bureau of Education, Washington, 2, 1890).
      [Alaska Eskimo.]
Wissler, Clark *The Social Life of the Blackfoot Indians* (Anthropological Papers, American Museum of Natural History, 7, 1911, 14-6).

Leslie Spier  UWPA 1 (2): 69-88  August 1925

## OMAHA

MB > MBS = U  UD = M > M Ch = B Z  FZ + A > A Ch = ♂ ZS ZD  ♀S D Ch =GC
    Calif UD = MZ ~ MyZ


## CROW

FZ = A >FZD =A AS = F FCh = B Z MB = U > UCh = S D  Ch = GCh
    ♂B ♀Z Ch = S D  X Ch Np Nc


## SALISH

Fsb + Msb = U A  N  GP Ch GCh  o y B Z


## ACOMA

♂GF ~ GS  ♀GM ~ GD  xGP ~ xGCh  PZ = A  MB  FB = F ~ MB  ♂ZCh = MB  ♂B Ch = S D
U  ♀Sb Ch = A  ♂B  ♀Z  xSb
    Kutenai  ♀GM GD  GP ~ GCh


## YUMAN

FoB  MoZ  //Cz = B Z o / y by relative age of P  ♂BCh  ♀ZCh by age of P  oB oZ yB yZ
    //Cz = B Z  xCz  ♂Ch =S D  ♀Ch = Ch  GP > FF FM MF MM
    ♂SCh  ♂DCh  ♀SCh  ♀DCh


## MACKENZIE BASIN

Sb + x + // = oB oZ yB yZ  F M S D  FB FZ MB MZ  GF GM GCh


## IROQUOIS

xCz  Sb + //Cz  oB oZ yB yZ  F M S D  ♂BCh + ♀ZCh =Ch  GF GM GCh


## INUIT ESKIMO

Cz = // + x  o y yst Sb  N = ♂BCh + ♂ZCh + ♀ZCh ♀BCh  GF GM GCh

# George Gibb's Spokan Kinship Schedule to Lewis Henry Morgan

## Nations of the Columbia River and its tributaries

The section of the country thus defined can scarcely be paralleled on the face of the earth in the advantages which it affords to a people living without agriculture, and depending excluisvly upon natural subsistence. ... Its sea coasts, indented with numerous bays, one of which, Puget's Sound, has a shore-line fifteen hundred miles in length, afforded perpetual supplies ... But the crowning advantage of this favored area was found in the inexhaustible salmon fisheris of the Columbia [and Fraser], which, at stated season, filled the land with an abundance of food. ... [242] These natural advantages gave to the vally of the Columbia a permanent and controlling influence over all other parts of North America, and I think can be shown, over South America as well. ... The sum of the evidence from these several sources appears to be convincing and conclusive that the valley of the Columbia was the nursery of the Ganowanian family, and the source from which both the northern and souther divisions of the continent mediately and immediately were being replenished with inhabitants, down to the epoch of their discovery ...

Another remarkable fact connected with this area is the unprecedented number of stock languages spoken within it, and which have been found in no other of the same limited dimensions. Mr. Gallatin, whose reduction of dialects was founded upon the vocabularies of Hale and Dana, states the number at fourteen.' He adopts Hale's synopsis with a change in the orthography of a single name, and thus confirms its correctness. These languages were then (in 1841) spoken in a large number of dialects, of which twenty-six are represented in his tables.

Lewis and Clarke <ok> describe in their work and locate upon their map some thirty-four distinct nations, whom they found in 1805-1806, upon the Columbia River and its tributaries, and on the neighboring sea-coasts. Most of the nations visited by them have since been identified under different names.

Although a large amount of labor has been expended upon these languages, further investigations will probably reduce their number. A very considerable reduction would leave the number disproportionately large. These languages have recently been taken up anew by George Gibbs, Esq., of New York, who spent several years in Oregon and Washington Territory as a member of the Northwestern-Boundary Commission, and before that, of the Pacific Railroad Engineer Corps upon the northern parallel. From the rare facilities which he enjoyed, and from his high qualifications for linguistic investigations, we may expect in his forthcoming work a thorough elucidation of the philology of this area of Indian speech.

Mr. Gibbs has kindly furnished me with the following synopsis of the stock languages of this area as they are named and classified by him. –

1. Tinne (Athapascan, of Gallatin.). 2. Kootenay (Kitunaha, of Gal.). 3. Salish.
4. Makah (Wakash, of Gal.). 5. Sahaptin. 6. Kayuse (Waiilatpu). 7. Chinook. 8. Shoshonee.
9. Kalapuya. 10. Yakama (Jacon, of Gal.). 11. Kalawatset. 12. Lituami. 13. Shaste.[18]

---

[18]  1. Salish. 4. Kitunaha. 7. Litnami. 10. Jacon. 13. Athapascan.
  2. Sahaptin. 5. Waiilatpu. 8. Shaste. 11. Wakash. 14. Shoshonee.

It will be observed that three or four of the stock languages of Hale and Gallatin are consolidated with others, or disappear in the synopsis of Mr. Gibbs; and that the remainder, with one or two exceptions, are the same under the old or a new name.  Some of these languages are spoken in but one or two dialects, whilst others have a large number, one of them, the Salish, having upwards of fifteen.

The subdivision of the inhabitants of this area into such a large number of petty nations, which was their condition when first discovered, and which has continued to be the fact, notwithstanding their reduction in numbers, to the present time, was the inevitable result of their domestic institutions and mode of life.  But the present existence of such a number of stock languages in so inconsiderable an area [244] furnishes the highest evidence of its long-continued occupation.  It is explained by the hypothesis that it was the cradle land of the Ganowanian family.  Under the operation of the law which tended to the disintegration of particular nations, with their increase and spread, the several dialects thus formed would widen in the long course of ages until they become hardened by use into independent stock languages, all traces of identity in their vocables having disappeared.  The struggle for the possession of this area would tend to equalization by the failure of any single nation to acquire such a preponderance of numbers as would enable it to overmaster and expel the other nations.  The number of these stock languages necessarily implies an occupation of the Valley of the Columbia from an antiquity as great as can be assigned, from other considerations, to the Ganowanian family upon any part of the continent.  It is also a reasonable and a probable inference that the greater part of the stock languages found upon the North American Continent were indigenous within this area, or derived from such as were immediately traceable to this source.

Judging from the more recent instead of the older vocabularies, there are peculiarities in the dialects of this area which do not exist in the dialects spoken in other parts of the Continent, and which are difficult of reduction to equivalent sounds represented by the English letters.  This marked difference is surprising.  It suggests, at least, the supposition that an attempt has been made by means of an improved notation to preserve minute phonetic elements in these dialects which have been disregarded in other areas.  Unless great care is taken this new method will magnify and even create differences where none such to any great extent actually exist.

In 1855 the Indian nations in Washington Territory and Oregon were estimated at 27,000.[19]  At the time of Lewis and Clarke's visit they were several times more numerous.

II. Salish Nations.
1. Salish or Flathead. 2. Shoushwhap (Atna). 3. Samena. 4. Okinăken. 5. Schwoyelpi. 6. Sketunesh (Coeur d'Alene). 7. Piskwous. 8. Spokäne. 9. Sikatomlch (Upper Pend d'Oreilles). 10. Kälispelm (Lower Pend d'Oreilles). 11. Balhoolä 12. Kowooks, Sashalt, and Cowätahin.

---

3. Chinook. 6. Kalopuza. 9. Palaik. 12. Skittagets.
* The remaining stock-languages in British and Russian America along the northwest coast are named by him as follows: 1. Thlinkit, or Kolosh. 2. Haida. 3. Chimsyan. 4. Belbella, or Kailt. 6. Nootka, the last two probably related.

[19] Schoolcraft, Hist. Cond. and Pres., VI: 705.

13. Kwäntlan and Taieet.  14. Clallam, Lummi, Skagit, Chamakeem, Toanhook, and Nesqually.
15. Kwêlahyate, Kwanäwult, and Chehalis.  16. Kwäwaletsk.  17. Tellamooks.


The Salish stock language, spoken in the seventeen dialects above enumerated, has a wider spread than any other within the area under consideration.  Mengarini names ten nations speaking this language, most if not all whom are seated between the Rocky and Cascade Mountains;[20] but Mr. Gibbs has traced it west of the Cascade range, and quite down to the sea-coast.  The above list of nations speaking dialects of the Salish language was furnished by Mr. Gibbs.


1.  Spokan.  Out of this large list of nations, the Spokan and Okīnăken only [245] are represented in the Table.  The system of relationship of the former nation was furnished by Mr. Gibbs, that of the latter was obtained by the author from an Okīnăken woman {Mrs Ross} at Red River Settlement.  Both schedules are incomplete.  If an opinion may be formed from the limited portion of the system procured, it has been complicated by specializations to an extent unequalled in any form hitherto presented.  The Table contains two hundred and sixty-seven distinct questions descriptive of persons in the lineal and first four collateral lines.  Many of these questions are twice stated, once with *Ego* a male, and a second time with *Ego* a female, and some of them are in the alternative form of elder or younger, where relative age varied the relationship.  It was also found that in some cases a double set of terms existed for the relationships of the same persons, one of which was used by the males, and the other by the females.  With a schedule of questions elaborated to meet the most of these peculiarities it was found that all of the nations, whose dialects were sufficiently open and accessible to enable their system to be fully reached, answered these questions in full, the discriminations in frequent instances running beyond the compass of the schedule.  Wherever blanks occur in the Table it was for want of facilities to ascertain the relationships of the persons described, and not from a failure of the system to recognize them.  In other words, the Indians of all these nations know their kindred, near and remote, and preserve that knowledge by the usage of addressing each other by the term of relationship.  Now the Spokan recognition and classification of kindred undoubtedly extend to and include every person described in the Table, and their nomenclature furnishes the terms of relationship applied to each and all of them.  More than this, instead of leaving blanks to attest the failure of the system, a large number of the present single questions must be repeated, and some new ones added to develop the whole of the system.  The tendency to a double nomenclature, and consequently to a twofold system of relationship, one for the males and another for the females, is quite marked among the nations west of the mountains.  The incompleteness of the schedules, therefore, must be attributed to the inaccessibility of these dialects, and not to a failure of the system to recognize any relationship between *Ego* and the persons described.
There is one feature in the Spokan system that has not before appeared, namely, the use of the same term in a reciprocal sense, instead of correlative terms; for example, I call my father's father, *Is-hah'-pä*, and my son's son, *Is-hah'-pä*, consequently the relationship is reciprocal, as cousin and cousin, or brother and brother, instead of correlative, as grandfather and grandson.  This was carried into the first collateral line male, in the first Spokan schedule of Mr.

----

[20] *Salish or Flathead Grammar*: p. 120.

Gibbs, but in a subsequent and revised schedule the term was used in a modified form. According to the first I call my father's brother, *Is-se-mălt*, and my brother's son, *Is-se-mălt*, *Ego* in both cases being a male, which would establish between my brother's son and myself a reciprocal relationship expressed by a single term. In the revised schedule he is my son, *Kas-koo-să*, to which the other term is added for some explanatory purpose. It seems probable that the term *Is-se-mălt* is employed to indicate the relationship of these persons when speaking of their relationship to a third person; and that when they speak to each other they use the terms for father and son. The [246] opulence of the nomenclature is such as to favor this supposition. This is one of the questions with reference to the Spokan system that remains to be determined. It will be impossible to understand this remarkable form until it is more fully developed in its details, and its unascertained parts are procured. The system of the remaining Salish nations is also desirable, since some of them may not have adopted the refinements the Spokan displays, and may, therefore, be nearer the primitive form. Notwithstanding the imperfect presentation of the Spokan system about to be made, it will not be difficult to discover decisive traces of the common system of the family.[21]

In Mengarini's "Selish, or Flathead" Grammar, before referred to, he has collected the terms of relationship of the Flatheads, and given them with their Latin equivalents. They do not show the classification of consanguinei and marriage relations, which is the essential part of the system, and the use of some of the terms will probably be found to need correction; but the terms show the fullness of the nomenclature, and being in another dialect, may be useful to illustrate the Spokan form. Some of them will be referred to in connection with the corresponding terms in the Spokan. [247]

There are separate terms in this dialect for grandfather and grandmother. On the father's side *Is-hah'-pä*, and *In-kah'-no*, used by the males, and *In-chau'-wä* and *In-tchit-che-ä-ä*, used by the females; and for the same relationship on the mother's side, Is-see'-lä and In-chau-wä, used by the males and females. This is the first instance yet found of the discrimination of the ancestors on the fathers side from those on the mother's side, but this is limited to the maternal grandfather. There are also separate terms for father and mother, *En-le-ă'-u* and *E-sko'-i*, used by the males, and *En-ne-mes'-teem* and *En-tome'*, used by the females; for son and daughter *Is-kwoos-să* and *Is-tum-che-ălt*; and for grandson and granddaughter, namely, for son's son and son's daughter, *Is-hah'pä* and *In-chau'-wä*, and for daughter's son and daughter's daughter, *Is-se'lä* and *In-chit-che-ă*. It will be observed that three of these terms for grandchildren are applied equally to grandparents, showing them to be reciprocal.

There are terms for elder brother, *En-kat'-tch*, used by the males, and *En'l-kahk'-tsä*, used by the females; and a common term, *En'l-chit'-shä*, for elder sister; for younger brother, *Is-sin'-sä*, used by the males, and *Is-sis'-son-sä*, used by the females; and common term, *En'l-tsits-ă-opes'*, for younger sister. Beside these there are terms for brother and sister in the abstract, *En-se-lacht'*, and *Is-soo-sin-ăm'*; and for brothers and sisters in the plural. The great number of these terms, and the tendency to minute specializations throughout the Spokan system, increase the necessity for full details of the classification, as well as the whole of the nomenclature, to a right understanding of the system itself. The Spokan nomenclature is twofold to a greater extent than any previously presented.

---

[21] Corrected spellings are in John Alan Ross, *The Spokan Indians* 2011 ~ Appendix E: Spokan Conanguineal Kin Terms: 753-755.

*First Indicative Feature.* My brother's son and daughter, *Ego* a male, are my 'son' and 'daughter', *Kas-koo'-să*, and *Ka-stum'-che-ält.* To the first *Is-se-mălt* is added, as some kind of qualification. With *Ego* a female, I call my brother's son *In-tee'-kwl*, and he calls me the same. This is another instance of reciprocal relationship. In the Flathead the term *Ti-kul*, the same word dialectically changed, is applied by a female to her father's sister, and it seems probable that it is also applied by a woman to her brother's son, as in the Spokan. My brother's daughter I call [248]

## RELATIO CONSANGUINITATIS ET AFFINITATIS.

| | Relate ad viros. | | Relate ad mulieres |
|---|---|---|---|
| Sgelui. | Maritus. | Noganag | Uxor |
| L'eu. | Pater | Mestm. | Pater |
| Skoi. | Mater. | Tom. | Mater |
| Skokoi. | Amita (soror patris). | Tikul | Amita (soror patris) |
| Sgus'mem, | Soror. | Snkusgu | Soror |
| Tonseh | Nepos, neptis. | Skuselt | Nepos |
| Szescht, | Sororius (maritus sororis). | Sttmch'elt | Neptis |
| | RELATIO COMMUNIS | UTRIQUE SEXUI. | |
| Sgaepe, | Avus (ex parte patris). | Snkusgutelis, | Idem, de pluribus quam duobus. |
| Sile. | Arus (ex parte niatris). | | |
| Kene. | Avia (ex patre patria).* | K'ezch. | Frater natu maximus |
| Ch'chiez. | Avia (ex parte matris). | Ke'eus | Frater natu maior |
| Topie. | Abavus et abaria. | Sinze | Frater natu minor |
| Smel. | Patruus (frater patris). | St'tenti. | Frater natu minimus |
| S'si'i. | Avunculus (frater matris). | Lch'chochee. | Soror natu maior(diminutiva) |
| Kage, | Matertera (soror matris). | Ikak'ze | Soror natu minor (diminutiva) |
| Skusee, | Filius. | | Soror natu minor (diminutiva) |
| Sgusigult, | Filii et filiee, the children of. | Lzzups | Soror natu minima (diminutive) |
| Sk'kuselt, | Filiolus (generice). | | |
| S'schitemischlt, | Filius vel filia natu major. | Sgagee | Socer (pater mariti vel uxoris), beau pere |
| Sk'euselt, | Filius vel filia nata mijor. | | |
| St'eutelt, | Filiua vel filia, natu minimus | Lzesch, So | Socrus (mater mariti vel uxoris), belle mere |
| Stomchelt, | Filia. | | |
| Snkusguteus | Fratres vel sorores germani (de duobus) | Nluesta | Patruus. l'oncle (patre nepotism mortuo) |
| Sluelt | Nepos et neptia (patre | Nhoiztn | Lever et fratria (alterutro |
| Znechlgu | Gener. | Luestn | Vetricos et noverca |
| Zepu | Nurus | S'chelp | Nurus (filio mortuo),la veuve de son fils |
| Segunemt | Parentes matriironio junctorum | St'mels | Propinquus, affinis, etc. |

| Sestem | Levir vel fratria.  le mari de sa soeur, ou la femme de sou frere | Snkusigu | Patruelis sobrinus, consanguineus |
| | | Snkusgusigu | (Plur).  Les cousins, les cousines, les parens (generice), etc. |
| Ischeu | Uxor fratria uxoris.  le femme du frere de sa femme | | |
| Kolemnt | Cognatus le mari de la soeur de son mari ou la femme du frere de son mari | | |

*Grammar*, App. 117. [248]

*Is-see'-lä*, the same term I use to designate a grandmother.  Here the relationship again is reciprocal.

Second.  My sister's son and daughter, *Ego* a male, are my nephew and niece, for which a term in common gender, *In-toonsh'*, is employed.  With *Ego* a female, they are my son and daughter.  To the latter term, *Iri-kach'-ha* is added for some qualifying purpose.

Third.  My father's brother I call *Is-se-mălt*.  After the death of my own father I call him my step-parent, *Es-tlu-es-tin*.  The same is true in the Flathead, in which the word is *Nluestn*.

Fourth.  My father's brother's son is my brother, *Is-se-lqcht'*; and his daughter is my sister, elder or younger.

Fifth.  My father's sister, *Ego* a male, I call *In-kach'-ha*, and *Ego* a female, *En-tee'-kwl*. Both of these have before appeared as reciprocal terms.  The first I think is erroneously used.

Sixth.  My mother's brother is my uncle, *Is-să'*.

Seventh.  My mother's sister I call *In-kach'-ha*, in FIathead *Kage*.  After the death of my own mother I call her *Es-lu-es-tin* , my step-parent.

Eighth.  My mother's sister's son and daughter are my brother and sister, elder or younger.

Ninth.  My grandfather's brother is my grandfather.

Tenth.  The relationships of collateral descendants are not given, beyond those previously named.

The marriage relationships are in agreement with the typical form, e.g., the wives of my collateral sons and of my nephews, are my daughters-in-law; and the husbands of my collateral daughters and of my wives are my sons-in-law.  In like manner the wives of my several collateral brothers are my sisters-in-law; and the husbands of my several collateral sisters are my brothers-in-law.  There is one altogether novel marriage relationship recognized in a large number of Ganowanian nations, namely, between the parents of married pairs.  In Yankton-Dakota the fathers of a married pair call each other *O-mä'-he-to*, in Spokan *In-teh-tum-ten*, and in Flathead, *Segunèmt*.  Mr. Gibbs has furnished the signification of the Spokan term, "Dividers of the Plunder," i.e., the marriage presents.  It is probably a recent term, from the fact that it is still significant, and derisively bestowed.

With respect to the children of a brother and sister, they are brothers and sisters to each other.  Mengarini furnishes a term for cousin in the Flathead *Sakusiga*, which is probably the Spokan *Sin-kwa-seehw*, rendered "one like my brother;" but it is extremely doubtful whether the relationship of cousin has been developed either in the Flathead or Spokan system.

Notwithstanding the insufficiency of the materials to show this system completely, an opinion may be formed upon the question of its identity with the common form. In its incomplete state, as shown in the Table, it possesses the indicative relationships, although some of them are modified and obscured by the uncertainty that rests upon the modifications. It is at least supposable that the doubtful terms arc those used when speaking of the relationship, as before suggested, whilst the full terms may be employed when the particular persons are [249] addressed by *Ego,* by the term of relationship. The minute discriminations of the system, and its opulent nomenclature, tend to the inference that when produced in full, it will be found to contain all of the radical characteristics of the system, and that the special use of reciprocal terms will find a rational explanation.


2. Okinaken. The fragment of the Okinaken system was obtained from Mrs. Ross [Sally Timentwa, wife of Alexander Ross], a native of this nation, at Red-River Settlement. An absence of many years from her native country had rendered her so distrustful of her knowledge of the system that she would not undertake to give its details.


Lewis Henry Morgan  1871  *Systems of Consanguinity and Affinity of the Human Family.* DC: Smithsonian Contributions to Knowledge 17.  1997  University of Nebraska Press.  Elisabeth Tooker, ed. [242-3]

## Southern Puget Sound Salish Kinship Terms
Zalmai 'Zeke' *ʔəswəli* Zahir updates < Arthur C Ballard originals

### KINSHIP BY BLOOD

| A. Simple terms | | |
|---|---|---|
| xʷəlšucid | Plural | pasteducid |
| 1. bad < bad | | father |
| 2. sk̓ʷuy < skoi | | mother |
| 3. qəsiʔ < kasi' | qəsqəsiʔ < kaskasi' | brother or male cousin of speaker's father or mother |
| 4. pus[22] < pus | pupus < puspu's | sister or female cousin of speaker's father or mother |
| 5. scapaʔ < tsa'pa | scapcapaʔ < tsa'ptsapa | grandfather, brother or cousin of speaker's grandparent |
| 6. kayəʔ[23] < ka'ya | kaykayəʔ < ka'ikaya | grandmother, sister or cousin of speaker's grandparent |
| 7. sčabiqʷ < tca'biqᵘ | sčabčabiqʷ < tc a'btcabiqᵘ | great grandfather, great grandmother, etc.; reciprocally great grandchild, etc. |
| 8. kʷəliyiqʷ[24] < kwaliyɛ'qᵘ3 | | great great grandfather, etc. |
| 9. hikʷyiqʷ[25] < he'wɩlyɛ'qᵘ | | great great great grandfather, etc. |
| 10. bədəʔ[26,27] < bi'bda | bədbədəʔ < bɑ'dbəda | son, daughter: sex indicated by preceding demonstrative |
| 10a. bibdəʔ[28] < bi'bda | bibdəbədəʔ < bi'bdabəda | diminutive of preceding |
| 11. staləł < sta'lał | štaltaləł < sta'ltalał | nephew, niece, son or daughter of speaker's cousin |
| 12. ʔibac < e'bats | ʔibibac < e'byebats | grandchild |
| 13. sqa < ska' | txʷsqatəd < ᵗᵘˣska'təd | elder brother-sister, elder cousin |

---

[22]   *ʔəpus* (Northern Lushootseed)

[23]   *kiaʔ* (NL)

[24]   The term kʷəliliqʷ ~ ʔək̓ʷyiqʷ - t̓x̌ʷ < *kwaliyɛ'qᵘ* is said to mean "beyond;" hikʷyiqʷ ~ čəp̓yiqʷ - t̓x̌ʷ is said to be derived from hikʷ *"great"* and another word meaning "beyond."

[25]   *čəp̓yiqʷ* – TH

[26]   *bədaʔ* NL

[27]   *ʔubədab* ~ someone had a child

[28]   *bibdaʔ* NL

| 14. suq$^w$ə? < so'qwa | suq̓$^w$suq̓$^w$a? < s'qsoqwa | younger brother-sister, younger cousin |
|---|---|---|
| 14a. su?suq̓$^w$a? < so'soqwa | su?səsuq̓$^w$a? < sosəsoqwa | diminutive of preceding |
| 15. ?a?šəd < a'cɪd | ?ihišəd[29] < i'hicɪd | sibling, friend, sister brother: spoken by person of same sex |
| 16. ?alš < alc | ?alalš < a'lalc | sibling, friend, siste,r brother: spoken by person of opposite sex |
| 17. qaq$^{w30}$ < qɑq$^{hu}$ | | elder brother or sister: term of address |
| 18. yəlab < yɛla'B | yəɬyəlab < yɛlyɛla'B | brother, sister or cousin of deceased parent of speaker |
| 19. sqəlajutaɬ[31] < skʊla'djitaɬ | sqəlqəlajutaa < skʊlkʊla'djitaɬ | son or daughter of deceased brother, sister or cousin of speaker: reciprocal to preceding term |
| 20. syayə? < tsaya'ya | syayayə? < tsayai'aya | kinsman, kinswoman; general term, not clear whether restricted to kinship blood [relative, friend] |

| B. Derivative Terms | |
|---|---|
| x$^w$əlšucid | Pasteducid |
| 21. badalig$^w$əd < bada'ligwad | related on the father's side |
| 22. sk̓$^w$uyalig$^w$əd < skoi'a'ligwad | related on the mother's side |
| 23. čəxsəq̓$^w$u?ab[32] < $^{tcux}$sq'o'aB | having the same father and mother: "joined" ["split (two halves) are joined"] |
| 23a. ciɬəbsəu?abitag$^w$il[33,34] < tsi'ɬəBsq'oa bi'tigwɑl | preceding term amplified: precise meaning obscure, perhaps collective [half related to each other through parents] |
| 24. ciɬəbsbad < tsi'ɬəBsba'd | having the same father: "related through |

---

[29]  relatives, friends, one's own people (TH); Person or people with whom there is a close relationship.

[30]  George Gibbs gives qaq$^w$ ~ *older sibling* used by men, while sqaqaq$^w$ ~ *older sibling* is used by women

[31]  *sqəlaǰut* (TH)

[32]  prefix: *čəx̌- split;* root: *q̓$^w$u? gather, unite, collect.*

[33]  ciɬ ~ *half-sibling* (TH) əbs- (derivative of abs-) *to have* The ciɬəbs ~ *to have a relation via someone* prefix is rendered ciɬbəs- in *Lushootseed Dictionary.* bəs ~ *inherent right of ownership.*

[34]  *=bitag$^w$il ~ to one another*

| | |
|---|---|
| | the father" [half related brother or sister] |
| 24a. ciɫəbsbadbitagʷil < tsi'ɬəBsba'd bi'tigwɑ'l | preceding term amplified [related to one another, as brother or sister, through father only] |
| 25. ciɫəbsk̓ʷuy < tsi'ɬəBsko'i | having the same mother: "related through the mother" [half related brother or sister] |
| 25a. ciɫəbsk̓ʷuybitagʷil < tsi'ɬəBsjo'i | preceding term amplified [related to one another, as brother or sister, through mother only] |
| 26. ciɫəbsqəsiʔ < tsi'ɬəBskasi' | "related through the uncle" |
| 26a. ciɫəbsqəsiʔbitagʷil < tsi'sɬəBskasi' bi'tigwɑ'l | preceding term amplified [related to one another through an uncle] |
| 27. ciɫəbspus < tsi'ɬəBspu's | "related through the aunt" |
| 27a. ciɫəbspusbitagʷil < tsi'ɬəBspu's bi'tigwɑ'l | preceding term amplified [related to one another through an aunt] |
| 28. ciɫəbscapaʔ < tsi'ɬəBstsa'pa | "related through the grandfather" |
| 28a. ciɫəbscapaʔbitagʷil < | preceding term amplified [related to one another through a grandfather] |
| 29. ciɫəbskayəʔ < tsi'ɬəBska'ya | "related through the grandmother" |
| 29a. ciɫəbskayəʔbitagʷil < tsi'ɬəBska'ya bi'tigwɑ'l | preceding term amplified [related to one another through grandmother] |
| 30. sqabitagʷil < ska' bi'tigwɑ'l | elder brother, term amplified, perhaps collective [elder sibling, including cousins, to each other] |
| 31. təlix̌ʷ[35] sqa < tɪ'lix̠ᵘ ska' | elder brother, perhaps as distinguished from cousin [older sibling or cousin to whom there is a close affinity and is a relation by blood] |
| 31a. təlix̌ʷ sqabitagʷil < tɪ'lix̠ᵘ ska' bi'tigwɑ'l | combination of preceding terms [older siblings or cousins to each other. There exists a close affinity and is a relation by blood.] |
| 32. suq̓ʷaʔbitagʷil < so'qwa bi'tigwɑ'l | younger brother: term amplified, perhaps collective [younger siblings or cousins to each other] |
| 33. təlix̌ʷ suq̓ʷaʔ < tɪ'lix̠ᵘ so'qwa | younger brother, perhaps as distinguished from cousin [younger sibling or cousin to whom there is a close affinity and is a relation by blood] |
| 33a. təlix̌ʷ suq̓ʷaʔbitagʷil < tɪ'lix̠ᵘ so'qwa bi'tigwɑ'l | combination of preceding terms [younger siblings or cousins, to each other. There |

---

[35] *təlix̌ʷ ~ to be related by kinship (WAS/EB).  t̓əlixʷ ~ full-blooded brothers who are emotionally close to each other – ML.*

| | exists a close affinity between them and is a relation by blood.] |
|---|---|
| 34. ʔaʔšədbitagʷil < a'cɪd bi'tigwɑ'l | sibling or friend of same sex as speaker: term amplified, perhaps collective [sibling, friend, sister or brother to each other.  Both are of the same sex.] |
| 35. təlix̌ʷ ʔaʔšəd < tɪ'lix̲ᵘ a'cɪd | sibling or friend of same sex as speaker, probably indicating close relationship [sibling, friend, sister or brother of same sex.  There exists a close affinity between them and is a relation by blood.] |
| 35a. təlix̌ʷ ʔaʔšədbitagʷil < tɪ'lix̲ᵘ a'cɪd bi'tigwɑ'l | combination of preceding terms [sibling, friend, sister or brother to one another.  There exists a close affinity between them and is a relation by blood.] |
| 36. ʔalšbitagʷil < a'lc bi'tigwɑ'l | sibling or friend of opposite sex to speaker: term amplified, perhaps collective [siblings or cousins to one another of opposite sex.] |
| 37. təlix̌ʷ ʔalš < tɪ'lix̲ᵘ a'lc | sibling or friend of opposite sex to speaker, probably indicating close relationship [sibling or cousin of opposite sex.  There exists a close affinity between them and is a relation by blood.] |
| 37a. təlix̌ʷ ʔalšbitagʷil < tɪ'lix̲ᵘ a'lc bi'tigwɑ'l | combination of preceding terms [siblings or cousins of opposite sex to one another.  There exists a close affinity between them and is a relation by blood.] |

## KINSHIP BY MARRIAGE

| A. Simple terms | | |
|---|---|---|
| xʷəlšucid | Plural | pasteducid |
| 38. sčistxʷ[36] < tcistˣᵘ<br>sčištxʷ[37] < tcictˣᵘ | sčisčistxʷ < tcistcistˣᵘ<br>sčiščištxʷ < tcictcistˣᵘ | husband (Puyallup dialect)<br>husband (Snoqualmie) |
| 39. čəgʷəš[38,39] < tcɑ'gwac | čahagʷəš < tcɑ'hagwɑc | wife |
| 40. sx̌ax̌aʔ < sxa'xa | sx̌ax̌ax̌aʔ < sxa'xaxa | son-in-law, daughter-in-law of speaker, speaker's brother or sister [in-law]; reciprocally father-in-law, etc. |

---

[36] ʔučistxʷəb ~ *someone is looking for a husband.*
[37] Earnest Barr (Snoqualmie) used *sčistxʷ*
[38] *čəgʷas* (NL)
[39] *ʔučəgʷəšəb* (SL), *ʔučəgʷasəb* (NL) ~ *someone is looking for a wife.*

| | | |
|---|---|---|
| 41. x̌əɬtəd < xɑ'ɬtəd | x̌əɬx̌əɬtəd < xɑ'ɬxɑɬtəd | brother-in-law, husband of one's cousin, man speaking [only used by male speaking of brother-in-law or male cousin-in-law] |
| 42. sčəbəš[40] < stc'ɑbac | sčahabəš < stc'a'habac | sister-in-law, brother-in-law, woman speaking; sister-in-law, man speaking [used by female speaking of sister-in-law, brother-in-law or cousin-in-law. Used by male speaking of sister-in-law or female cousin-in-law.] |
| 43. q$^w$ilx̌$^w$ < kwel$^{xu}$ | q$^w$ilq$^w$ilx̌$^w$ < kwe'lkwe'l$^{xu}$ | related by marriage: general term |
| 44. sbalucid[41] < sba'lotsiD | šbalbalucid < sba'lbalotsiD | surviving marriage relative after death of spouse: reciprocal |

| B. Derivative Terms | | |
|---|---|---|
| x$^w$əlšucid < | | pastəducid |
| 45. ciɬəbsčistx$^w$ < tsi'ɬəBstcist$^{xu}$ | | co-wife, "related through the husband" |
| 46. čəɬbadəb < tcɪɬba'dəb | | step-father; husband of speaker's aunt |
| 47. čəɬtadəb < tcɪɬta'dəb | | step-mother, wife of speaker's uncle |
| 48. čəɬbədab < tcɪɬbɑda'b | | stepson, stepdaughter, son or daughter of husband's [or wife's] brother or sister: reciprocal to the two preceding terms] |
| 49. čəɬscapaʔəb < tcɪɬtsa'pa$^{aB}$ | | step-grandfather, husband of grandparent's sister |
| 50. čəɬkayəʔəb[42] < tcɪɬka'ya$^{aB}$ | | step-grandmother, wife of grand-parent's brother |
| 51. čəɬʔibacəb < tcɪɬe'pbats$^{aB}$ | | step-grandchild, grandchild of speaker's wife's (or speaker's husband's) brother or sister: reciprocal to the two preceding terms |
| 52. cix$^w$ʔibac[43] < tsix̱$^w$e'bats | | husband or wife of grandchild of speaker or speaker' brother or sister; term possibly reciprocal |
| 53. čəɬsx̌ax̌aʔəb < tcɪɬsxa'xa | | son-in-law or daughter-in-law of speaker's |

---

[40]  *čəbas* (NL). *čəbəš* (SL)

[41]  *ʔubalucidəb čəd ~ I married my sbalucid.*

[42]  *čəɬkiaʔəb* (NL)

[43]  *cix$^w$- ~ in-law* (TH)

| | |
|---|---|
| | wife's brother or sister, husband of speaker's stepdaughter: reciprocally uncle by marriage or stepfather of speaker's wife, etc. |
| 54. qʷilx̌ʷbitagʷil < kwel<sup>xu</sup> bi'tigwɑ'l | kin by marriage; term used in special sense to designate stepbrothers and stepsisters [literally: in-laws to one another] |
| 55. ciɬəbskayuʔ < tcɨɬəʙskayu' | "related through dead," previously related by marriage |
| 56. sq̓ʷuʔidup < sq'o'idup | persons whose wives are sisters; whose husbands are brothers; whose respective husband and wife are brother and sister: term derived from root syllable q̓ʷuʔ, "join" |
| 57. ciɬəbstubš < tsi'ɬəʙsto'bc | man whose wife is sister to the wife of another (?); "related through the man" |
| 57a. ciɬəbstubšbitagʷil < tsi' ɬəʙsto'bc bi'tigwɑ'l | preceding term amplified [related to one another through a man] |
| 58. ciɬəbsɬadayʔ < tsi'ʙsła'dai | woman whose husband is brother to the husband of another (?); "related through the woman" |
| 58a. ciɬəbsɬadayʔbitagʷil < tsi'ʙsła'dai bi'tigwɑ'l | preceding term amplified [related to one another through a woman] |
| 59. təlix̌ʷ sx̌ax̌aʔ < tɪ'li<u>x</u><sup>u</sup> sxa'xa | son-in-law related by blood to parent-in-law |

Arthur C Ballard  1935  Southern Puget Sound Salish Kinship Terms
*American Anthropologist* New Series, Volume 37, Issue #1: pages 111-116

THE UNIVERSITY OF CHICAGO

# A Study of Salish Kinship and Social Organization

A Dissertation Submitted To

The Facultyof the Division of the Social Sciences

In Candidacy for the Degree of Master of Arts

Department of Anthropology

## Iva Teruko Osasai /Schmitt/

CHICAGO, ILLINOIS

JUNE, 1941

## Table of Contests



## List of Tables

List of Illustrations




## Introduction

The Salishan-speaking peoples formerly inhabited the territory which now includes the southern portion of British Columbia, the eastern and southern coasts of Vancouver Island, the northern parts of the states of Washington and Idaho, and the northwestern corner of Montana, when found by the early explorers and fur traders of the Northwest in the latter part of the eighteenth century, these Indians were in full possession of their aboriginal culture; and this more or less continued to be the case while the white population was limited to explorers and traders.  As has so often happened in new areas of the world, however, the explorer, adventurer, and trader were followed by the missionary and the settler with their attendant disintegrative influences on native culture.  The 1840's and 50's saw a period of intensified missionary activity and white settlement, with the development of farming and the building of permanent homes.  As population increased, Indian-white relations became strained and a series of Indian wars marked the decade from 1850 to I860.  Lands were lost to the whites and Indian population was decreased through disease and war.  Finally, the lands and affairs of the Indian came under American and Canadian government supervision.  Today, remnants {!} of the once widely spread Salish stock are to be found on reservations in British Columbia and the American Northwest.

The Salish tribes were situated in that food area of North America which has been termed the "Salmon Area,"[44] and, as is implied [2] by the name, they subsisted chiefly upon salmon, supplemented by a diet of berries, vegetables, and wild game.  The nature of their subsistence required that the Salish live a life divided between a nomadic hunting, fishing, and gathering existence in the summer and settlement in villages in the winter.  Because of this, the tribes were all quite similar in type of local organization and in certain aspects of material culture, particularly those relating to the securing and handling of food.  Besides making the same kind of external adaptation to their environment, the Salish tribes shared the same kind of religion – a religion characterized mainly by a belief in guardian spirits capable of endowing individuals {families}, and groups with certain kinds of "power."  Furthermore, they all participated in the fcast- and gift-giving complcx typical of thc Northwcst rcgion.  In other aspects of culture, however, the Salish were quite different; and it is the purpose of this thesis to consider the tribes comparatively with respect to two such aspects of culture:  social organization and kinship.  The various tribes will be compared with the view of defining the type or types of social organization and kinship system from which variants arose.  The thesis will then attempt to determine the

---

[44] Clark Wissler, *The American Indian*, (2d ed; New York: Oxford University, 1922): p. 9.

nature of the changes which have taken place in social organization and kinship, how such changes may be correlated, and the factors responsible for the changes. Some contribution should be made to a better understanding of Salish kinship and social organization and the relationship between the two, and some light should be shed on the nature of social change on the Northwest Coast and its relation to environment.

<u>Geographical Regions and Tribal Distribution</u>

The greater part of the country formerly inhabited by the Salish is of a very rugged character, being cut by numerous rivers, [3] lakes, and streams, and traversed by several heavily forested mountain chains. Two major ranges of mountains extend in a north-south direction the length of the territory. The first of these includes the Coastal Range, which runs along the western coast of British Colombia, and its American counterpart, the Cascades of Washington. The other important range consists of the Rockies, which form the eastern boundary of British Columbia and then run astride the border line between the states of Idaho and Montana. Besides these two large ranges there exist several smaller groups of mountains such as the Olympics in the northwest corner of Washington and the Okanagon Highlands in the same state lying north of the Columbia and Spokan rivers and extending eastward from the Cascades. In British Colombia, three minor ranges are found just west of the Rockies; the Cariboo Mountains, the Columbia Mountains, and the Selkirk Range.

A number of the Interior Salish tribes lived in the intermontane valleys of these ranges. The Lakes and parts of the Okanagon and Shuswap tribes found their home in the Selkirks and the Columbia Mountains. The Methow, Sinkaietk, Sanpoil, Colville, Coeur d'Alene, Kalispel, Spokan, and Flathead lived in the region of the Okanagon Highlands and the American Rockies.

The rest of the Interior Salish resided in the plateaus lying between the Coastal-Cascade chain and the Rocky Mountains. The Canadian Plateau, called the "Fraser Area" by Kroeber,[45] was inhabited by the Thompson, Lillooet and Shuswap; while the Columbia Plateau, a rather open country in Washington lying south of the big bend of the Columbia River, was the home of the Columbia and Wenatchi. [4]

Kroeber places the Coast Salish in the physiographic area designated "Pacific Border.[46] This he divides into subareas, the first of which is a flat coast strip with ocean frontage lying just west of the Olympic Mountains. To this subarea he allocates the Quileute and Quinault, although the writer would also place here the Hoh, Queets, Copalis, Humptulips, Wynoche and Satsop. South of this subarea lies another coastal plain section where are found the Chehalis and Tillamook.

The coastal region of Washington, Kroeber points out, has an extension in the islands lying off the mainland of British Columbla – that is, Vancouver Island and the Queen Charlotte Islands. Salishan-speaking peoples in this second subarea are found on the eastern and southeastern parts of Vancouver Island and include the Comox, Pentlatch, Nanaimo, Cowichan, Sanetch, and other lesser groups.

---

[45] A.L. Kroeber, *Cultural and Natural Areas of Native North America*, ("University of California Publications in American Archaeology and Ethnology," XXXVIII [Berkeley, 1939]): 56.

[46] *Ibid*: p. 191.

The Puget Sound basin constitutes a third subarea of Kroeber's "Pacific Border." This is a broad, low alluvial plain lying between the Cascades and the Olympics, which extends northward to include the area between Vancouver Island and the mainland. The remaining Coast Salish tribes are placed in this section, these being the Indians of Puget Sound and the Gulf of Georgia, and the isolated Bella Coola. According to Spier, the following tribes should be included in the Puget Sound group: the Klallam, Twana-Skokomish, Nisqually, Squaxon, Puyallup, Muckleshoot, Suwamish, Suquamish, Snohomish, Stillaquamish, Snuqualmi, Skykomish, Skagit, Swinomish, Lummi, Swallah, Samish, Nooksak, and Somiahmoo.[478] As for the Gulf of Georgia tribes on the mainland, Barnett lists [5] the following: the Homalco, Klahuse, Slaiamun, Sechelt, Squamish and Muskwium.[48]

## Climate, Fauna, and Flora

The climate of the coast of British Columbia and Washington is milder and more humid than that of the Inland regions. The coastal mountains act as a barrier to the cold and hot land winds coming from the Interior and thus save the coast from extreme temperatures. They also stand in the way of warm moisture-laden winds coming from the Japan current and cause them to deposit most of their rain, on the coastal side. The coast is thus characterized by a high rainfall; consequently, the air is always damp and skies are often cloudy, especially during the winter which is the rainy season.

East of the Coastal Range in Canada and the Cascades in Washington the rainfall varies with the height of the land. On the whole, the climate is quite dry, the point of lowest rainfall being reached at the low plain of the Columbia River. Here there are also greater extremes in temperature; winters are cold and summers are hot.

The greater amount of rain on the coast produces a much heavier vegetation that is found in the interior. A geographer, J. Russell Smith, says:

> Continuous dampness makes the coast of British Columbia .... thick with trees and still thicker with undergrowth – some of it thorny, much of it yielding berries in great profusion, bush cranberries, wild raspberries, two or three varieties of huckleberries.[49]
> [6]

Trees are of the coniferous kind and include white pine, larch, spruce, Douglas fir, cedar, and hemlock; of these, the Douglas fir is by far the commonest. Besides the various kinds of berries mentioned above, there are other edible plants – ferns, horsetails, and wild vegetables such as the camas, onion, carrot, and potato.

In the intermontane plateaus of British Columbia and Washington, forests are sparser and the country is more open with less undergrowth. Grassland and steppe-land prevail and vegetation consists mostly of pine, sagebrush, and bunch-grass. According to Smith, ".... the

---

[47] Leslie Spier, *Tribal Distribution in Washington*, ("General Series on Anthropology," No. 3 [Menasha, 1936], pp. 53-39. See also list of tribes given in the article "Coastal Salish of Washington," by Marian W. Smith, *American Anthropologist* XLIII (1941): p. 204.

[48] H.G. Barnett, "The Coast Salish of Canada," *American Anthropologist* XL (1958): 119.

[49] J. Russell Smith, *North America*, (New York: Harcourt Brace & Co, 1925): p. 625.

lowest lands along the rivers are an expanse of sagebrush and poor pasture, with lakes of salt or alkaline water."[50] The same kinds of berries and vegetables that are found on the coast grow here, but not in such great abundance.

Several varieties of game are found in the interior, including the deer, elk, moose, goat, sheep, antelope, bear, and beaver. Land animals are fewer on the coast; but in the ocean water are to be found the whale, porpoise, and seal. The rivers of both the interior and the coast provide salmon, the food staple of the Salish. Some comments made by Smith on this fish, which is the main source of subsistence, are pertinent here. He says that the salmon

> .... has two habits that have made it an easy prey and a great resource to man. The first habit is that of being born in inland streams which have their sources in cold fresh water. The young fish remain here for only a few weeks, then they go out to sea where they stay until full-grown. The second habit which makes the salmon the easy prey of man is that of the adult fish, which returns to that same stream in which it was born to give birth to offspring and then to die.[51]

It was while the salmon were making the return trip to their native streams that the Salish did their principal fishing. Naturally, [7] since the Coast Salish were situated closer to the places where the salmon began their journey back they were able to make greater catches than were the Interior Salish. Other fish, besides the salmon, found in the Salish area are the suckers and trout of the inland streams and the halibut, herring, and cod of the coastal waters.

## Population

Evidently the greater abundance of food on the coast permitted a larger concentration of population than is found in the interior. An examination of Kroeber's table of tribal populations, taken after Mooney's figures, shows that, on the whole, population density is greater among the coastal groups.[52]

## Historical Background

The fact that there were differences in Salish cultures was early noted and remarked upon by ethnographers of the region. Thus, in the conclusion to Teit's monograph on the Thompson Indians, we find the following comments made by Dr. Franz Boas:

The Salish tribes .... are remarkable not only on account of their far-reaching linguistic differentiation and the diversity of physical types represented in the various groups, but also on account of the great variation in their cultural status. While the most northern Salish tribe, the Bella Coola, have absorbed all the important elements of the culture of the Northwest coast, which they have developed in their own peculiar way, we find that the tribes farther to the south have adopted this culture to a much less extent. The most northern tribe of this group are the

---

[50] *Ibid*: p. 523.

[51] *Ibid*: p. 625.

[52] Kroeber, *op. cit*: pp. 155-136.

Comox, who live on the central part of the east coast of Vancouver Island. While they still possess many of the characteristic features of the culture of the Northwest coast – such as totemism, highly developed plastic art, and a peculiar mythology – these decrease in number as we proceed southward, until on the coast of the state of Washington most of them are found to have disappeared. The most southern tribe of Salish affiliation, the Tillamook, who live in northern Oregon, have developed a culture which is strongly influenced by that of the tribes of northern California. East of the Cascade Range and [8] of the Coast Range of British Columbia we find Salish tribes who .... resemble in their culture, in many respects, the tribes of the Plains. The Lillooet .... are the only one among the Salish tribes of the Interior .... who have absorbed many elements of Coast Culture.[53]

### TABLE 1
### POPULATION RATIO BY AREA

| Tribes | Population | Area in 100 km | Density per 100 km |
|---|---|---|---|
| Bella Coola | 1,400 | 150 | 9.33 |
| Makah, Quileute, Quinault | 4,000 | 62 | 64.50 |
| Comox, Pentlatch, Cowlltz, Lkungen, Seehelt, Squamish, Lower Fraser | 20,500 | 607 | 55.70 |
| Nutsak, Lummi | 800 | 60 | 15.50 |
| Klallam, Chimakum | 2,400 | 58 | 41.50 |
| Skokomish, Nisqualli, Twana, Puyallup, Snoqualmi, Snohomish, Skagit | 6,000 | 357 | 16.80 |
| Lower, Upper Chehalis, Owilapsh, Cowlitz | 1,200 | 182 | 6.59 |
| Tillamook | 1,600 | 67 | 22*30 |
| Wenatchi, Sinkiuse, Peskwaus, Methow, Nespilim, Sanpoil, Colville, Spokan (part) | 5,500 | 513 | 11.20 |
| Wenatchi-Spokan group (part) | 2,400 | 208 | 11.50 |
| Kalispel, C. d'A., P. d'O., Flathead | 2,800 | 1,861 | 1.50 |
| Okanagon, Lake | 2,200 | 410 | 5.36 |
| Lillooet | 4,000 | 170 | 23.50 |
| Thompson, Nicola | 5,150 | 155 | 33.20 |
| Shuswap | 5,500 | 1,176 | 4.50 |

[9]

Similarly, Charles Hill-Tout, in several of his publications, including his book, *British North America*, pointed out the differences between the Interior Salish and Coast Salish as regards physical type, mode of life, habitation, social organization and religion. He contrasted the squat, thickset physical type of the coast with the slender, athletic type of the interior and attributed the difference to the fact that the coastal peoples lived a more sedentary life as

---

[53] James Teit, "The Thompson Indians," *Jesup North Pacific Expedition Publications* I (1900): p. 387.

fisherman while the interior folk lived a more active life in pursuit of land game. Hill-Tout also called attention to some differences in material culture, such as the fact that the Coast Salish lived in communal long houses made of cedar slabs while the Interior Salish dwelt in semi-subterranean huts {pithouses}. The outstanding contrast drawn by Hill-Tout was in regard to social organization. He pointed out, on the one hand, the simplicity of the interior social organization, and, on the other hand, the complexity of the coastal social organization with its gentes, associations, and division into castes. Lastly, he contrasted the individual guardian spirits of the inland peoples with the group totems of the Coast Salish.

Once the differences between interior and coast cultures had become apparent, students concerned themselves with the reconstruction of Salish history and asked such questions as: What were the characteristics of the original Salish culture and where was its home – in the interior or on the coast? Hill-Tout, considering the question of the original location of Salish culture, concluded that on the basis of relative simplicity and complexity the interior culture was the older; and hence the former home of all the Salish was in the interior. He pointed out the fact that if the Salish had at an earlier time lived as one group on the coast, we should expect to find among the modern interior peoples evidences of former contacts with the coastal culture. Instead, [10] we find simply "a well-defined and graduated decrease in complexity as we go inward."[54]

Boas also brought forth evidence for the hypothesis of migration to the coast. He asserted that if the former home of all the Salish had been on the coast, then the culture of the modern Coast Salish should be thoroughly "Northwest coast" in character. Then he pointed out that this was not the case, that there were a number of cultural features common to the more northern coastal tribes, including art and mythology, which were not shared by the Salish. Therefore, Boas concluded that the period of contact between the Coast Salish and the other coastal groups did not extend over an "excessively long time"; and hence at a not very remote time the Salish must have come from the inland region to the coast.[55]

It was further found that this conclusion was supported by a certain amount of linguistic evidence. Hill-Tout, for instance, pointed out that a comparison of the terms for "salmon" in the various Salish tribes indicated that "the earlier, undivided Salish stock did not live on the tidal waters of that part of the Pacific slope where the salmon is a conspicuous product."[56] Hill-Tout argued that if the salmon had been as important in the diet of the undivided Salish stock as it was among the modern Coast Salish – and certainly if the former home of all the Salish had been on the coast, one should expect just that – then the native terms for "salmon" in all the tribes should be cognates. But such, Hill-Tout found, was not the case. He found, instead, that all [11] the dialectic groups had different terms for the salmon, "which no method of linguistic equation" could "show to be the same or to have had a common origin."[57] The only reasonable conclusion in the light of this was that originally the Salish people lived elsewhere than on the coast.

Finally, the hypothesis of migration from the interior to the coast was given substantiation by archaeological evidence uncovered by Harlan I. Smith. During the years 1897-

---

[54] Charles Hill-Tout, "Report on the Ethnology of the Okanaken of British Columbia," *Journal of the Royal Anthropological Institute* XLI (1911): 133.

[55] 2/ Teit, *op. cit*: p. 389.

[56] Hill-Tout, *op. cit*: p. 135.

[57] *Ibid*: p. 134.

1899, Smith carried on archaeological investigations in the southern interior of British Columbia, on the Columbia River in Washington, and on the coasts of Washington and British Columbia. While working in the Thompson River region, Smith excavated a burial ground at Lytton and village sites at Kamloops and Spences Bridge, all of which sites pre-dated the coming of the white man. At all three places he found that the material culture – hunting implements, household utensils, habitations – was very similar to that of modern natives of the region. This he took to indicate that the mode of life and culture of the Indians had changes{d} very little from prehistoric times, a fact supported by the uniformity of physical type and language of the modern Interior Salish.

When Smith excavated the shell heaps on the shores of Puget Sound and the Gulf of Georgia, however, he did not find the uniformity of strata which characterized the interior sites. The upper layers contained a material culture resembling that of the modern Coast Salish, but the lowest strata showed an absence of Salish culture and the presence of another culture. Middle layers contained a mixture of non-Salish and Salish traits (the latter being essentially the same as those of the interior).

The combined findings of Smith in the interior and on the [12] coast pointed again to a movement of interior peoples to the coast – a movement which carried with it traits of interior culture including, probably, the art of stone chipping, use of tubular pipes and geometric decorative art, and the custom of depositing artifacts with the dead. When the people reached the coast, they mixed physically and culturally with the groups there.

With a tentative conclusion reached as to the direction of the spread of Salish peoples and culture, there remained for the students of Salish ethnology the question of what the original culture was like. No actual reconstruction was undertaken but it was suggested by Hill-Tout and Boas that since the migration of peoples had been from the interior to the coast, it appeared only reasonable to suppose that the culture of the interior Indians (which archaeological findings had shown to have undergone very little change), was close to the parent type. A recent study by Verne Ray makes this appear all the more likely. Having considered the cultural relationships and influences in the Plateau area, he comes to the conclusion that

> the Southern Okanagon, Colville, Sanpoil, Lower Spokan, and Columbia may with reasonable safety be viewed as most representative of older levels and fundamental aspects of Plateau culture.[58]

Thus, the culture of the central Interior Salish appears to be typical of not only the primitive Salish but of all the early Plateau peoples as well.

## Problems and Procedures

To date, the students of Salish culture, aside from producing purely ethnographic monographs on specific tribes, have been concerned primarily with problems relating to the reconstruction [13] of Salish history. This thesis continues to deal in part with problems of an historical nature, containing as it does an attempt to define the "original" types of Salish social

---

[58] Verne Ray, *Cultural Relations in the Plateau of Northwestern America*, ("Publications of the Frederick Webb Anniversary Fund" III [1939]): 149.

organization and kinship system and to determine the variations or changes from these types.  A further goal of the thesis, however, is to examine more closely than has been done heretofore the *nature* of the changes in social organization and kinship and to find how these changes are interrelated.  It is hoped, too, that the consideration of this latter problem will lead to some determination of the basic principles which underlie social change on the coast.

In view of the hypothesis of migration from the interior to the coast and the tentative conclusion that the culture of the Interior Salish approaches most nearly that of the early undivided Salish stock, the defining of the "original" type of social organization is coincidental with the defining of the Interior Salish type of social organization.  Accordingly, the first chapter of the thesis contains a comparative description of Interior Salish social organization.  The elements shared in common by the tribes and the variations due to the influence of other cultures are noted, and from this the type is established.  Differences from this Interior Salish type of social organization found among the coastal tribes are indicated in a descriptive account of Coast Salish social organization given in the third chapter.

In establishing the primitive Salish kinship type, the systems of all the Salish tribes (i.e., those for which information is available) are compared.  Again common features are noted and considered to be features of the early system.  To aid in the reconstruction, native vocabularies are also compared and cognate forms determined – but this to only a very limited extent because of the writer's lack of linguistic knowledge.  The comparative [14] analysis of Salish kinship leading to the establishment of the primitive type is preceded by descriptions of the interior and coast systems in the second and fourth chapters.

The reconstruction of early Salish kinship and social organization and the changes which have taken place in those aspects of culture should increase our historical knowledge of the Salish.  Also, in connection with the defining of the kinship type and its variations, some suggestions are offered as regards the re-classification of Salish kinship with reference to other North American systems.

The thesis should also make some contribution to sociological knowledge of the Salish.  It should give a better understanding of Salish kinship – the relation of terminology to behavior and of kinship as a whole to the rest of the social structure – and should indicate some of the functional interrelationships existing between the different aspects of the social organization.  Finally, the thesis offers some suggestions as to the "explanation" of social change on the coast. [15]

# CHAPTER I
## THE SOCIAL ORGANIZATION OF THE INTERIOR SALISH

### Tribal Locations

Salishan-speaking peoples of the interior include the Shuswap, Lillooet, Thompson, Okanagon, Sinkaietk,[59] Sanpoil, Nespelem, Lake, Colville, Wenatchi, Columbia, Spokan, Kalispel, Coeur d'Alene, and Flathead.  These tribes formerly inhabited, the territory extending from Quesnel Lake in British Columbia southward to the middle section of the Columbia River in Washington and corresponding latitudes in Idaho and northwestern Montana.  The country for the most part was bounded on the west by the Coastal-Cascade range and on the east by the Rocky fountains; however, the Lillooet and Thompson did spill over into the heart of the Coastal Range and the Flathead extended beyond the Rockies into the level region of Montana.

Southernmost of the tribes were the Shuswap who lived in the territory extending from the Fraser River to the Rocky Mountains and including the valleys of the Fraser, North Thompson, and South Thompson rivers.  They were bounded on the west and north by the Athabaskan tribes and on the northeast by the Sarsi and Cree.  The northern part of their country offered a good supply of wood, water, and grass, but the southern portion was semi-arid and covered [16] mostly with bunch-grass.  The Lillooet were situated to the southwest of the Shuswap in a region which included a small section of the Fraser River and a narrow valley stretching "from Cayuse Creek through the mountains first in a westerly and then in a southerly direction, to Harrison Lake."[601] The topography of this area was more rugged than that of any other interior tribe.

East of the Lillooet and south of the Shuswap were their cultural brethren, the Thompson.  The Thompson were located on the Fraser, Thompson, and Nicola rivers.  Their country was mountainous but less so in the northern portion than in the southern part.  Rainfall and forestation were heavier and game scarcer in the Lower Thompson region than in the upper country.

The Southern Okanagon were found on the Okanagon and Similkameen rivers in British Columbia; and their southern neighbors, the Sinkaietk, lived in the "…. entire territory from about six miles east of Condon's Ferry on the Columbia River, down that river to the mouth of the Okanagon River and up the Okanagon River to Tonasket."[61] The Sanpoill and Nespelem were located on the rivers of the same names, and the Colville were situated to the north of the

---

[59]  In earlier writings of Hill-Tout and Teit, the Sinkaietk or Southern Okanagon are grouped with the Northern Okanagon, Walters, however, prefers to differentiate the two groups of Okanagon, pointing out that the Sinkaietk have complete political independence, possess a name of their own, and are as culturally distinct from the northern Okanagon as are the Sanpoil or Colville, L.V.W. Walters, "Social Structure," *The Sinkaietk or Southern Okanagon of Washington.* ed. by Leslie Spier, ("General Series in [16] Anthropology, " No. 6 [1938]): p. 73.

[60]  James Teit, "The Lillooet Indians," *The Jesup North Pacific Expedition Publications*, II, (1900): p. 195.

[61]  Walters, *op. cit*: p. 73.

Sanpoil and to the east of the Sinkaietk in the region of the north Columbia River.  According to Teit,

> in climate, natural features, flora and fauna the territories inhabited by the Okanagon, Sanpoil, and Colville are very similar to those of the upper Thompson and neighboring Shuswap.  The climate is slightly moister ...., the valleys are wider, and the surrounding country less mountainous.[62] [17]

The Lakes {tribe} were located north of the Colville and east of the Okanagon and Shuswap in the heart of the Selkirks.  Their territory was very rough, being covered by heavily forested mountains.  In the valleys were numerous connected lakes and rivers, which greatly facilitated intratribal travel and intercourse.  The uniqueness of their habitat made for greater tribal solidarity than existed in the other tribes of the interior.

The Wenatchi and Columbia were situated in the valley of the Columbia River from Priest's Rapids, or points even farther south, northward to the Okanagon country.  They were surrounded on the southwest, south, and southeast by various Sahaptin tribes.

Most eastern of the interior tribes were the Spokan, Kalispel, Coeur d'Alene, and Flathead.  The Spokan were located on the Spokan and Little Spokan rivers.  The Kalispel and Coeur d'Alene inhabited the heavily forested and mountainous area of northern Idaho and northeastern Washington.  The Flathead were east of them in the northwest section of Montana.  The western part of their country was mountainous with fairly good rainfall but the eastern half consisted of semi-arid plains.

The various Interior Salish tribal territories thus varied somewhat in topographical and climatic characteristics.  On the whole, however, and as was pointed out in the Introduction, it can be said that the inland country was of a rugged character with a rather low rainfall.  This limiting nature of the environment, as will be shown later, is an important factor in explaining the rather undeveloped character of interior social organization as compared with the complexity of coastal social organization.

<u>Linguistic and Cultural Relationships</u>

The Interior Salish tribes have been grouped into the following [18] linguistic dialects by Hodge:[63]
1.  Lillooet.
2.  Thompson.
3.  Shuswap.
4.  Okanagon.
    a.  Okanagon proper.
    b.  Sinkaietk[64]

---

[62]  James Teit, "The Salishan Tribes of the Western Plateaus," *45th Annual Report of U.S. Bureau of American Ethnology*, (Washington, 1927/28): p. 203.

[63]  F.W. Hodge, *Handbook of the American Indians*, Bulletin of Bureau of American Ethnology, XXX (Washington, 1907, 1910): 417.

[64]  Added to Hodge's list by the writer.

    c.  Colville.
    d.  Lower Spokan.[652]
    e.  Sanpoil and Nespelem.
    f.  Lakes.
5.  Flathead
    a.  Upper and Middle Spokan.[66]
    b.  Kalispel.
    c.  Flathead.
6.  Coeur d'Alene.
7.  Columbia.
    a.  Wenatchi.
    b.  Sinkiuse.
    c.  Methow.

As a group, the Interior Salish tribes are sufficiently different in culture from tribes of the surrounding areas of Coast and Plains, and sufficiently similar to their northern and southern neighbors, the Athabaskans and Sahaptins, to be placed together with the latter groups in a separate culture area which has been called the Plateau. Of the four linguistic groups found in the Plateau area, the Salish are said to be the most "typical." that is, as exhibiting fewer traits characteristic of other areas. Furthermore, of the Salish themselves, the central groups – the Okanagon, Sinkaietk, Sanpoil, Nespelem, Colville, Lakes – are considered to have the most unadulterated culture. On the other hand, the more western tribes, the Thompson, Shuswap, and Lillooet, have a number of cultural traits which are characteristic of the [19] Northwest Coast; and the eastern groups – the Kalispel, Coeur d'Alene, Spokan, and Flathead – and the Middle Columbia Salish have been considerably influenced by the historic Plains {horse} culture.

## Territorial Organization

The Interior Salish were arranged on the basis of territorial habitation and special distribution into several different social groupings. The largest of these territorial groups was the tribe, which extended over a comparatively large and continuous area. The tribe was divided into a number of bands and each band in turn consisted of one or more village units. The basic constituent of the village was the house group.

The Tribe. – The tribe, as found among the Interior Salish, may be defined as a body of people inhabiting the same general geographical area, speaking the same dialect, sharing in the same culture, and recognizing themselves to be one people bound by ties of blood and mutual interests. There was no formal organization to the tribe. So far as political organization is concerned, it can be said that most of the tribes had no tribal government at all, and such as did exist in others was of little importance. Hill-Tout, for instance, mentions a tribal chief in the case of the Lillooet but describes him as being "rather a patriarch than a ruler."[67] The Salish did not

---

[65]  Added to Hodge's list by the writer.

[66]  Added to Hodge's list by the writer.

[67]  Charles Hill-Tout, "Report on the Ethnology of the Stlatlumh of British Columbia," *Journal*

convene in tribal assemblies or hold large tribal-wide ceremonial affairs such as were typical of the Plains tribes.

It must be added that among some of the more eastern tribes, such as the Spokan, Kalispel, Coeur d'Alene, and Flathead, a radical change took place in the social organization in [20] the seventeenth and eighteenth centuries due to the advent of the horse {!} and consequent adoption of much of Plains culture. The acquisition of the horse facilitated intratribal intercourse and made hunting in large groups possible. This had its effect upon the social organization. The importance of local bands and villages faded and they became overshadowed by the larger tribal structure. Political authority became centralized in the tribal chief and council, and the members of the tribe gained a national consciousness, acting together as a unit. It must be remembered, however, that the tribe as it formerly existed among these eastern groups, as in the other Interior Salish groups, was not a political unit, but rather an informal union of the local bands and villages on the basis of common habitat, language, and culture.

The division. – Several of the Interior Salish tribes, according to Teit, were divided into bodies called "divisions." Thus, the Thompson were separated into Upper and Lower divisions, the Shuswap into seven divisions, and the Coeur d'Alene into three. Traces of the division were also found among the Spokan, Kalispel, Columbia, and Wenatchi. The division, however, seems to have been little more than a geographical grouping of bands, its area being delimited by natural boundaries.

Seasonal dichotomy in territorial organization. – Band and village structures functioned only in the winter portion of the year. During the summer months the people were dispersed in small family groups wandering about over the bands' territories, engaged in fishing, hunting, and gathering wild foods.

As soon as the spring of the year rolled around the people began breaking up winter camp and left for the root-digging grounds and the nearer hunting and fishing places. At this season most of the fishing was for suckers and trout, and in the Northern Okanagon [21] tribe, at least, hunting took the form of a communal hunt for deer and sheep. With the coming of summer, the salmon season began and the people were busy spearing and trapping the fish which was the main item of their diet. Salmon fishing continued to be the major occupation of the people during the late summer and early fall months, although root-digging and berrying were also important. There was very little hunting done at this time; however, that which was done was of the individual pursuit type. The salmon season ended around October and the late fall months found the people gathering the last roots and berries. Hunting loomed important again, and in a number of tribes deer hunts were held in which the whole band participated.

In late fall the people returned to their winter homes. Salmon and other foods collected during the summer and dried for winter use were stored away, houses were rebuilt, and village life was resumed. During the winter season some hunting was done and in some tribes band hunts were held for deer and sheep. Game for the most part, however, was scarce during the cold months, and the people lived almost wholly on the results of their summer endeavor.

During the summer months life was largely of a nomadic character. Since the people were on the move most of the time, camps were only of a temporary nature with families living in rude shelters made of poles covered with mats or branches. The actual duration of summer camps varied. The Sinkaietk, we are told, sometimes stayed at one place for several weeks when

---

fishing for salmon or hunting deer, but for a much shorter time when collecting other foods.[68]

It appears that in most of the tribes, members of the same [22] band usually went to the same general vicinity to hunt, fish, and gather roots and berries.  There was nothing rigid about this, however; some families wandered over a much wider territory and members of different bands were free to enter upon each other's land.  Not infrequently several different bands, and even different tribes, would be found represented at the larger, more important sites.  At such times opportunities for intercourse between bands were numerous and the peoples visited and traded with each other and participated in games and sports together.  Teit says that the two greatest fishing places of the Okanagon tribe, Okanagon Falls and Kettle Falls, were also the two greatest trading centers.[69]

With bands and village groups broken up and intermingling in a casual fashion, and with camps being only of a temporary nature, band and village organizations could not function.  Apparently, even when a camp was composed entirely of people belonging to one band, the band organization was not in effect.  Walters says that when a large group of Sinkaietk people, all members of the same band, were camped together at the same site there was .... no reflection of their winter affiliations in the arrangement of the camp."[70]

In winter an entirely different life was lived by the people.  Instead of wandering about in the pursuit of food, they settled in villages and occupied themselves with work about their houses.  Band and village organizations were in effect and group life of the people, i.e., as members of the same band or village, became important.  The people gathered together on cold winter evenings for games, story-telling, and other past-times.  Public [23] ceremony, practically non-existent during the summer season, came to life and became most intense at midwinter when a series of dances and shamanistic performances were held.  Ray's words concerning the Sanpoil at this period no doubt apply to all the Interior Salish: "Emotion was built up and released.  At the end of the series of dances all were more content, to await the coming of spring."[71]

The band. – At the time they were studied, most of the Interior tribes were found to be divided into local groups which in the literature have been termed "bands."  Information given by the various writers as to how the band was constituted is not very explicit.  It appears, however, that the band was a grouping of people on a purely territorial basis, consisting of families who generally wintered in the same locality.  Some families were more nomadic than others and did not always settle with the same group, but, as Teit has pointed out in the case of the Coeur d'Alene,

> each family, no matter in what part of the tribal territory it might temporarily be living, belonged to some particular band and therefore had a locality that was considered to be its home, and which it claimed as such.[72]

---

[68] Richard H. Post, "The Subsistence Quest,"' *The Sinkaietk or Southern Okanagon of Washington,* ("General Series in Anthropology," No. 6 [1938]): p. 11.

[69] Teit, "The Salishan Tribes of the Western Plateaus," *op. cit:* p. 252.

[70] Walters, *op. cit.,* p. 88.

[71] Verne Ray, *The Sanpoil and Nespelem,* ("University of Washington Publications in Anthropology," V, [1932]: 28.

[72] Teit, "The Salishan Tribes of the Western Plateaus," *op. cit:* p. 150.

The component families of a band were usually related, most of them being descended from people who had made the band's territory their winter headquarters for many years.  The band was not primarily a kinship group, however; for membership in it was determined, not by birth, but by residence.  An individual, especially if a male, often remained a member of the band in which he was born but he was free to change his local affiliation if and when he so chose.  Thus, band membership was flexible.  Though a [24] certain core within the band would remain unchanged from year to year, members were lost through marriage, because of inability to get along with others, or for other reasons.

Besides being knit together by kinship bonds, the members of a band were unified by a common political structure and territory.  Each band had a chief who looked after the general interests of the group and saw to it that peace and order were kept.  Also, each band had associated with it a territory commonly recognized as being its property.  Here, its winter headquarters and its fishing, hunting, and food gathering grounds were located.

The number of villages in a band varied with the different tribes.  In the Coeur d'Alene tribe, the band ordinarily formed a single village community although occasionally there might be one or two outlying villages.  In other tribes, such as the Sinkaietk, a band included as many as four or five villages with headquarters at the principal village.

The band organization just described was not found among all the tribes.  Ray informs us that the Sanpoil were characterized by a strict village autonomy with no bands at all, and that the band found among the Wenatchi, Columbia, Spokan, and Kalispel was of a different type, being rather an "....  embryonic tribe, developing under direct influence from the plains."[73]  Ray believes that bands of the type found in the other Interior Salish tribes (i.e., the type described above) were but expanded forms of the autonomous village group, and developed when individual settlements "....  joined together in a mutually advantageous union."[74]  He considers the independent village of the Sanpoil to typify the [25] original situation throughout the Plateau.  This appears to be a reasonable conclusion, especially in view of the fact that in several tribes studied by Teit he found that bands had not been nearly so well marked a number of years previously and that independent villages had been more numerous.

The village. – The villages of the Interior Salish were situated in the valleys of the Thompson, Fraser, and Columbia rivers.  The essentials of a good village site were described by Dawson as being " ....  a warm southern exposure as much sheltered as possible from the wind, particularly the cold down-river wind of winter; a dry, sandy or gravelly soil, and convenient access to water."[75]  Walters also cited the importance of a supply of firewood in determining the choice of a site.[76]

The size of villages varied.  Some were small, including only two or three families while others wore large, being composed of several hundred individuals.  At the time the Interior Salish were studied, a normal-sized community was found to contain the following:  at least one long house used for public dances, meetings and ceremonies, and for the housing of visitors; several long mat houses, each used as living quarters for two or more families; other smaller

---

[73]  Verne F. Ray, *Cultural Relations in the Plateau of Northwestern America*: p. 14.

[74]  *Ibid* : p. 15.

[75]  George M. Dawson, Notes on the Shuswap People of British Columbia," *Royal Society of Canada, Transactions* (1891): p. 8.

[76]  Walters, *op. cit*: p. 87.

dwellings housing individual families; several sweat houses and menstrual huts.  The lay-out of the typical village was probably very much like that described by Walters for the Sinkaietk:  the houses were built parallel to the water's edge, usually in a north-south direction " .... In order to afford the greatest security from the strong north winds."[77]

Since the village group was either identical with or a [26] component of the band.  It shared most of the latter's characteristics.  Its members were usually related, but village membership was a matter of residence rather than birth.  If for any reason a person wished to change his village affiliation, he could do so by taking up residence with another community.

There seems to have been little economic specialization within the village.  Each family was quite independent and provided for its own sustenance?  It secured its own food and manufactured its own technical equipment.  There was, however, a definite cooperative spirit among the people of a village.  This was demonstrated, for example, in the fact that all worked together in constructing the chief's house and probably each other's homes as well.  Furthermore, poorer members of the village who did not have enough food to sustain them and their families for the winter were assisted by more fortunate citizens of the village.  Walters, in speaking of this fact among the Sinkaietk, says:

> In case of famine and extreme conditions, the wealthy assist the poor.  Even a man who is poor because of laziness is not permitted to starve.  He is cared for by his more enterprising and therefore more affluent relatives.[78]

Though there were few economic specialists in the village, there were individuals who held certain specialized social positions such as war leader, house leader, shaman, hunting leader, dance leader.  These individuals were elected to these positions because of certain abilities acquired from guardian spirits which especially fitted them for such roles.  And so they were the leaders of the village activities:  the war leader because of his military prowess led his people in battle; the dance leader because of his knowledge of spirit songs and dances figured prominently in the winter ceremonial; the hunting leader because of his [27] ability in the hunt was organizer and head of village hunting parties.

At the head of the village was the village chief.  He ruled the community independently of the band chief; but it appears that if a band chief wished to exercise his authority concerning some village matter, the village headman had to submit to it.

The members of a village enjoyed together a certain social and ceremonial life.  One of the communal ceremonies observed by them was that which followed the rebuilding of winter camp. Walters describes this ceremony as follows:

> When all the houses are finished, and then only, individuals move into their private dwellings and store their provisions.  The following day the chief's wife selects women to prepare food for a feast to be eaten in the middle of the day.  The chief ..... makes a speech and then the men eat.  There is no singing or festivity .....
>
> That evening everyone returns to the chief's house for 'the washing of the house', a ceremony at which all adolescent children are whipped ceremonially by a chosen man

---

[77] *Ibid.*

[78] *Ibid*: p. 87.

to strengthen them.[79]

The chief ceremonial event was the winter guardian spirit dance which was held usually during the month of January or February in the village meeting house.  Given by a single individual {or family}, the dance presented all the members of the village, as well as neighboring communities, with an opportunity to give vent to their own power songs as well as those of the host.  Cline points out in his discussion of the Sinkaietk dance that through this general participation lesser individuals were able to unite themselves .... for a moment with the most influential members of their society.

> To the possessors of great power they made their most vital wishes known, and from them they received some hope of aid, if not the promise of fulfillment.  It was the one time at which the religious resources of the group and its friendly [28] neighbors were pooled for the common good.[80]

Furthermore, the power sing and dance, together with the feasts and distribution of gifts by the host, afforded everyone a good time.  Thus, in both its religious and social aspects, the winter ceremonial was an important unifier of the local group.

<u>The household</u>. – Houses among the Interior Salish were of three types: a long mat-covered lodge, a mat-covered tipi, and a semi-subterranean house.  Houses of the first type held more than two families while those of the latter two types contained only one or two families.  The usual case was for several families to live under one roof, and generally they were related.  Thus, due to the custom of patrilocal residence, a typical house group might consist of a man and his wives, perhaps his parents, his unmarried daughters, his married sons and their families, and perhaps a cousin or two.

The house was divided into sections, each with a fireplace, occupied by the separate families making up the larger house group.  There seem to have been no set rules concerning the composition of the individual family groups.  Walters says that in the Sinkaietk tribe a young couple might share a section with the man's parents or might live separately.

> If the mother-in-law was stingy, they might have separate households in the same house, keeping their supplies separate and eating apart.  But ordinarily since they managed to maintain pleasant rotations, they lived as a single family.[81]

The families of brothers, however, lived separately as did also the families of non-related wives.

Each family kept its supplies separate, thus symbolizing [29] its economic independence, and ate alone except in cases of large formal feasts.  Yet there was a certain closeness and co-operative feeling existent between house members, especially if they were related.  During the summer months they frequently traveled together while fishing, hunting, and gathering food.  At the beginning of the winter season they labored together in building the house in which they

---

[79] *Ibid*: pp 87-88.

[80] Walter Cline, "Religion and World View," *The Sinkaietk or Southern Okanagon* ("General Series in Anthropology," No. 6 [1938]): p. 146.

[81] Walters, *op. cit*: p. 118.

were to live, and in the early spring they all helped dismantle it. They were further unified by the wintertime social life of the household consisting of games and story telling by campfire, and by the existence of a house leader. The latter individual was usually the owner and oldest member. His authority, associated with a certain "power" given him by his guardian spirit, was respected by the other members of the house, and he generally succeeded in maintaining amicable rotations among them.

As in the case of the village group, the composition of the house groups though usually not changing much from year to year, was not a rigid thing. According to Walters, two important factors governed stability of the house group among the Sinkaietk: "the compatibility of personalities and the manner in which individuals treat each, other's children."[82]

<u>Political Organization</u>

As has been mentioned above, the tribe as it existed among the Salishan peoples (with the exception of the more eastern Plains-influenced groups) was not a political entity. The government of the people lay in the hands of band and village chiefs. Walters, in discussing the relation of village headman to band chief among the Sinkaietk, says:

> Should the band chief wish to use his authority, it must be followed by the headman. The headman is not appointed by the [30] chief, and acts freely on his own judgment without consulting the chief, directing the communal hunting and fishing of the village, and the summer and winter camping.

If Ray's contention is correct, at one time the band was non-existent and there was no larger political group than the autonomous village unit.

Verne Ray has classified Plateau chieftainships, on the basis of the way in which they are acquired, into three types:

(1) strictly hereditary chieftainship, (2) loosely hereditary chieftainship, and (3) chieftainship based on personal achievement.[83] The first of those was characteristic of the Lillooet, among whom there was a definite chiefly lineage with the office passing in strict succession down the male line. Ray comments thus upon the relationship between the Lillooet type of chieftainship and that found among the Coast Salish:

> The strict inheritance of chieftainship among the .... Lillooet .... is quite obviously a reflection of coastal heredity minus any great emphasis upon wealth. Geographical considerations suggest this, but it is further apparent in the associated emphasis upon lineages ....[84]

Ray's second type, the loosely hereditary chieftainship, was found among all the other Interior Salish tribes except the ones most influenced by the Plains, and probably existed among

---

[82] *Ibid*: p. 87.
[83] *Ibid*: p. 88.
[84] Verne Ray, *Cultural Relations in the Plateau of Northwestern America*: p. 190.

the latter at one time.  In the Thompson, Shuswap, and Sanpoil tribes, chieftainship descended in the male line; in case there was no son, the office was inherited by the former chief's brother or brother's son.  While there seems to have been a preference for the eldest son among the Shuswap, such was not the case among the Sanpoil.  It was customary in the latter tribe if there were several sons or candidates who could fill the chieftainship, for the [31] assembly to select one of them; and if there were no candidates, the assembly elected the new chief.  Thus, Ray points out, the Sanpoil made a compromise between succession by inheritance and election by popular vote.  Among the Sinkaietk and Thompson the chief theoretically was chosen by the people; actually, however, chieftainship was hereditary, the newly selected chief always being a son, brother, or close relative.

Selection on the basis of personal achievement was characteristic of the Columbia, Flathead, Coeur d'Alene and other eastern tribes, and can clearly be traced to Plains influence.  Chiefs among the Columbia were elected because of their wealth or war exploits such as stealing horses and killing enemies.  Says Teit:

> They took scalps, and kept count of the number.  They counted coup, and at dances related their deeds in war and how many persons they had struck, wounded, killed, or scalped.  A man who had killed many enemies, or a man who had become a great warrior and was known to be brave, was made a chief by the people.  The man who had killed the greatest number was considered the greatest chief and became the head war-chief and leader of large war expeditions.[851]

Political organization among the Flathead was centralized in the tribe and authority was given to the tribal chieftain, who was assisted in his various functions and duties by the sub-chief and "small chiefs."  We have two conflicting reports concerning the acquisition of chieftainship among the Flathead.  According to Teit, though in former times the son usually succeeded his father, in more recent times chiefs were elected.  He says:

> Chiefs were generally superior men, and before election were distinguished for qualities such as wisdom, social influence, oratory, truthfulness, or bravery.  Dignity, wealth, renown for warlike exploits, and striking physical appearance were also considered.[86]

[32]

Turney-High, however, says that the tribal chieftainship was considered hereditary and descended to the eldest son.  "In this the Flathead chieftainship was stable and rather dynastic."[87]  Turney-High is probably describing the old type of chieftainship here, evidently.  Ray, in citing the Flathead as exemplary of his third type of chieftainship, must have used Teit's material.

The Plains origin of a chieftainship based on personal achievement is quite obvious.  That the Flathead once possessed a social and political organization much like that of the other

---

[85]  James Teit, *The Middle Columbia Salish*, ("University of Washington Publications in Anthropology" II, [1931]): p. 126.

[86]  Teit, "The Salishan Tribes of the Western Plateau," *op. cit*: p. 376.

[87]  Harry H. Turney-High, *The Flathead Indians of Montana*, ("Memoirs of the American Anthropological Association" XXXIX [1937]): 49.

interior tribes is indicated by the presence of vestiges of the old system.  Teit points out that the "small chiefs" who assisted the tribal chief were probably originally band chiefs.  Further, the people who followed the "small chief" on his summer food gathering expeditions were no doubt descendants of the old local band.

Ray, upon comparing the principle of hereditary chieftainship found in the Plateau with that found on the Coast, finds that they are quite different.  On the Coast, heredity in chieftainship is correlated with and probably an outgrowth of the wealth-rank complex.  In the Plateau, however, wealth and rank are of scarcely any importance and, besides, the heredity principle there seems to be quite old.  Ray says:

> In view of these considerations the reasonable conclusion is that the principles of heredity are independent in the two areas.  Or, very possibly, the principles as phrased in the Plateau may at an earlier time have characterized both that area and the Coast.[88]

The duties of a chief among the Interior Salish were of several different sorts.  First of all, the chief looked after the [33] general welfare of the group and organized the collective activities having to do with food-getting.  He often directed the hunting, fishing, and gathering expeditions participated in by the band or village as a whole.  He supervised the reorganization of the band or village and the readjustment of sedentary life which took place in the fall.  He also regulated the food supply, looking after, for instance, the maturing of berries so that none would be picked before they were ripe.  The second category of chiefly duties was of a judicial nature.  The chief acted as arbitrator in petty disputes and rendered decisions.  He also served as mediator in feuds between families, attempting to bring about reconciliation or acting as representative in cases in which an indemnity was to be paid by one of the parties.  He was judge in criminal cases, announced verdicts, and administered penal sanctions.  Thirdly, the chief exerted an important moral influence upon his people.  He himself was expected to be of an exemplary character and he exhorted his people to good moral conduct.  Teit says he "admonished the lazy and quarrelsome."[89]

The chief also presided over council meetings, advised his people on all matters, and acted as host to visitors from other neighborhoods.  He was in no sense a despot; actually, he possessed no power to enforce his decrees other than that which stemmed from the support of popular opinion.  Writers on the Interior Salish frequently describe the chief as being much like a "father" to the group.

The chief did not act as war leader,[90] as that position was held by a specially qualified war "chief," a man noted for his [34] bravery or deeds in war and elected to the position on that basis.  Of the Sinkaietk war leader, Walter says:

> A man with power from a strong animal such as a cougar or eagle may be the war leader .... He was considered immune to wounds and directed the tactics of all his men.

---

[88]  Verne Ray, *Cultural Relations in the Plateau of North America*: p. 21.

[89]  James Teit, "The Shuswap Indians," *Jesup North Pacific Expedition Publications* II (1900): p. 570.

[90]  Except in the eastern tribes where, as we have seen, the chief was usually a man known for his military exploits.

Such an individual is supposed to be able to dream of an approaching evening attack, so it is always desirable to winter with him .... He has no proper title or position, but is much respected as a strong fighter and a man who has saved his people.[91]

There was also a special hunting chief, chosen because of his expertness as a hunter. He led the group hunting expeditions and saw that the game was equally divided. His actual authority, however, lasted only during the hunt.

The chief was advised and assisted in ruling the community by the house leaders and elders of the group, who composed a sort of informal council. Occasionally, meetings of this council were held and presided over by the chief. They were open to the public and anyone had the right to voice an opinion. Only matters of major importance were considered at council meetings; these included war, major movements of the group, elections, and other matters which involved the whole group.

## Social Stratification

Social stratification did not exist among the central Interior Salish tribes – the Sanpoil, Nespelen, Sinkaietk, and Northern Okanagon. There was no nobility in any sense of the word and no slavery. In connection with the chief's family, it is true, there was some conception of "good birth." Because of their ancestry the chief's relatives were given a certain prominence. They did not, by any means, constitute a specially privileged group, however. According to Walters, the chief's wife worked just as did other women, though her suggestions were respected by them and [35] usually followed.[92] There was also no class structure based upon wealth. Actually, there were only a few wealthy persons within a community. They were given a certain amount of respect because of their ability to accumulate wealth, and people looked to them for protection and care in times of adverse circumstances, but they too possessed no organized body of privileges.

Other persons besides the wealthy and members of the chief's family who enjoyed a certain amount of prestige were the various "leaders" mentioned above. Every person in the society received a certain amount and kind of "power" from his guardian spirit, but these individuals, because of their special "powers," were given positions of authority in various spheres such as war, the hunt, and the dance. However, though granted the respect of the people and authority in their respective fields, again it can be said they were not accorded special privileges and did not constitute a class.

In the central tribes, everyone was free to live where and as he pleased. Walters says that in the Sinkaietk tribe if a man did not like a certain chief, he could, if he wished, change his residence.[93] Everyone could speak freely in the village assembly. Furthermore, there was no real poverty, for food was shared with the less fortunate persons. In short, the society was quite a democratic one characterized by the feeling that all men should possess the same rights and privileges.

In the other Interior Salish tribes we find either a definite stratification of society or a

---

[91] Walters, *op. cit*: p. 79.

[92] *Ibid*: p. 95.

[93] *Ibid*: p. 87.

suggestion of such.  In the Flathead, Columbia, and Coeur d'Alene tribes there was no specially privileged class or nobility, but there was a ranking of [36] "braves" on the basis of their war deeds.  The men who possessed the most outstanding war records were accorded a great deal of prestige and became "chiefs."

The Thompson and southeastern Shuswap recognized no hereditary nobility, but did rank persons on the basis of wealth and personal abilities, such as wisdom, oratory, and prowess in war.  According to Teit, wealthy persons were important figures in the life of the society, and their prestige increased as their liberality became greater.  An individual who gave public feasts and distributed presents was highly esteemed

Among the western Shuswap and Lillooet there was a definite cleavage of the society into three classes; nobility, commoners, and slaves.  Members of the Shuswap nobility were known as "chiefs," "chief's offspring," or "chiefs descendants."[94]  The Lillooet noble class included a "nobility of rank," composed of hereditary chiefs, and a "nobility of merit," composed of persons who had not been born to nobility but who had achieved it through their liberality or other personal qualities.[95]  Nobles were accorded special privileges and usually married within their class. Slaves were war captives.

That we have a definite foreshadowing of coastal rank structure in the case of the western Shuswap and Lillooet seems clear.  As Ray has pointed out, the spread of the coastal rank structure with its privileged hereditary nobility and slavery must have been comparatively recent for its distribution is limited.  This recency, says Ray, is also shown by the "existence of the 'nobility of merit', an anomaly in any class society .... [37] obviously a concession to persisting Plateau social standards."[96]

It appears, then, that the rank structure found in the western Interior Salish tribes spread from the coast, and that ranking on the basis of military achievements, existent among the eastern tribes, was due to Plains influence.  Again, the situation found among the central Interior Salish seems to represent the original one.  We can thus conclude that in the early type of Interior Salish social organization {any} social stratification was non-existent.  All persons were of equal status so far as rights were concerned, and there existed no hereditary nobility, no class distinctions on the basis of wealth, and no slavery.

## Formal Organization

Formal lineage groups or clans were totally absent from the Interior Salish social structure.  Teit, however, speaks of "clans" in connection with the Shuswap and Lillooet, and so it is necessary that we consider these groups briefly.

It is difficult to determine precisely what was the nature of the "clan," as information is rather vague.  We can be certain, however, that this grouping, at least among the Lillooet, was not a clan in the now accepted sense of the term, i.e., a body of relatives who consider themselves to be descended in _one_ line from a given pair of ancestors.  It is true that members of the Lillooet "clan" were supposed to be descendants of a common ancestor, and there were traditions concerning such an origin, _but_ membership descended in both male and female lines.

---

[94]  Teit, "The Shuswap Indians," _op. cit_: . 576.
[95]  Teit, "The Lillooet Indians," _op. cit_: p.255.
[96]  Verne Ray, _Cultural Relations in the Plateau of Northwestern America, op. cit_: p. 28.

The Shuswap "clans," according to Teit, were hereditary crest groups to which the nobles belonged.[97] The groups appear to [38] have been exogamic. A person marrying a member of a crest group was not considered a member of it, but his children were.

There were other groups which cross-cut Shuswap society and included both nobles and commoners. They were not of a particularly hereditary nature but seem rather to have been more like the associations of the coast. Membership was acquired, not by birth, but through a period of training, and the neophyte underwent an initiation ceremony in which he "had to dress and act like the protector of the group he had chosen to enter."[98] The group's only hereditary aspect lay in the fact that a son generally joined the group to which his father belonged.

Teit himself recognizes the fact that the Shuswap and Lillooet {totemic} "clans" were foreign to the original Plateau culture, and must have come from the coast. He believes that they were introduced to the Shuswap by the Carrier, Chilcotin and Lillooet, "who themselves have borrowed these customs from their neighbors of the coast – the Carrier chiefly from the Tsimshian, the Chilcotin mainly from the Bella Coola [Nuxalk] and the Lillooet principally from the Squamish."[99] [39]

---

[97] Teit, "The Shuswap Indians," *op. cit*: p. 576.
[98] *Ibid*: p. 577.
[99] *Ibid*: p. 581.

## CHAPTER II
## THE KINSHIP SYSTEM OF THE INTERIOR SALISH

Information on the kinship systems of most of the interior tribes is of a fragmentary nature.  For some of the groups, namely, the Lakes, Sanpoil, Columbia, and Coeur d'Alene, we have no published kinship data whatsoever; and the terminologies and accounts of kinship behavior given us by Boas, Hill-Tout, and others for the Thompson, Shuswap, Lillooet, Wenatchi, Spokan, and Kalispel are appallingly incomplete.  Indeed, truly satisfactory material is available for only the Sinkaietk and Flathead tribes.  The following analysis of Interior Salish kinship, then, cannot rest upon an entirely solid foundation and is subject to correction and addition when and if new material appears.

In the following pages there will be given first a comparative description and analysis of Interior Salish kinship terminology.  This will be followed by a discussion of kinship behavior.

<u>Kinship Terminology</u>

Consanguineal Terminology

A comparison of the Salish kinship schedules leads to the following summary description by generations of the consanguineal terminology:

<u>Second ascending generation</u>. – the Shuswap,[100] Thompson,[101] [40] and Lillooet[102] kinship terminologies give two terms, <u>grandfather</u> and <u>grandmother</u>, for members of this generation. The Northern Okanagon, Sinkaietk,[103] Kalispel,[104] and Flathead[105] schedules, however, show that a differentiation is made between maternal and paternal grandparents.  Four terms are used, these being <u>father's father</u>, <u>father's mother</u>, <u>mother's father</u>, and <u>mother's mother</u>; and these are extended to the grandparents' siblings.

Among the Spokan, according to the schedule recorded by Gibbs, the following native grandparental terms are used:  for mother's father, <u>is-see-lä</u>; for grandfather (probably father's father, though Gibbs does not state as much definitely), <u>is-hah'-pä</u>; for grandmother, <u>in-chau-wä</u>

---

[100] For Shuswap kinship terminology see Franz Boas, "Second General Report on the Indians of British Columbia," *Report, Sixtieth Meeting of the British Association for the Advancement of Science* (London: John Murray Co 1891): p 659.

[101] For Thompson kinship terminology see Charles Hill-Tout, "Notes on the N'tlaka'pamuQ, of British Columbia," *Report, Sixty-ninth Meeting of the British Association for the Advancement of Science* (London; John Murray Co 1900): p. 505.

[102] For Lillooet kinship terminology see Boas, "Second General Report on the Indians of British Columbia," *op. cit.*, p. 689.  Also cf. schedule in Charles Hill-Tout, "Report on the Ethnology of the Stlatlumh of British Columbia," *Journal of the Royal Anthropological Institute* XXXV (1905): 148.

[103] For Northern Okanagon and Sinkaietk kinship terminology see Walters, *op. cit.*, pp. 88-90.

[104] For Kalispel kinship terminology see Boas, "Second General Report on the Indians of British Columbia," *op. cit*: p. 692.

[105] For Flathead kinship terminology see Turney-High, *op. cit*: pp. 57-61.

(male speaking); <u>in-kah'-nä</u> (also male speaking), and <u>in-tch-te-a</u> (female speaking).[106] Inasmuch as <u>in-kah'-nä</u> resembles the Northern Okanagon, Sinkaietk, Flathead, and Kalispel terms for father's mother (<u>ka'kena</u>, <u>ka'qEna'</u>, <u>k'enE</u>, <u>kene'</u>, respectively), we can probably safely assume that it applies only to father's mother among the Spokan. Furthermore, the term <u>in-tch-te-a</u> is similar to the Flathead term for mother's [41] mother and probably applied, to that relative. The remaining term is mystifying; it may be an alternative for <u>in-kah'-nä</u> or may be the term used by the male for mothers mother. At any rate, though the data are confusing, it can probably be assumed that the Spokan system of terminology for grandparents was like that of the Sinkaietk and Flathead.

<u>First ascending generation</u>. – The Shuswap, Thompson, and Lillooet do not make a terminological distinction between the mother's siblings and the father's siblings. Mother's brother and father's brother are called by the same terms, as are also mother's sister and father's sister. In the northern Okanagon, Sinkaietk, Flathead, Kalispel, Wenatchi, and Spokan tribes, four terms are used: <u>father's brother</u>, <u>father's sister</u>, <u>mother's brother</u>, and <u>mother's sister</u>. The Northern Okanagon, Sinkaietk, and Flathead schedules show those terms to be extended to the parents' cousins.

<u>Ego's generation</u>. – In the interior tribes we find the use of four (or three) sibling terms: <u>older brother</u>, <u>older sister</u>, <u>younger brother</u>, <u>younger sister</u> (or, instead of the latter two, <u>younger sibling</u>, as is the case in the Lillooet and Shuswap tribes). These terms are extended to the speaker's cousins, both parallel and cross, and on both his father's aide and his mother's side. The terms given in the Spokan schedule for cousins appear to be somewhat different from those for siblings, but in his text Morgan says that children of brothers and sisters call each other "brother" and "sister."[107]

<u>First descending generation</u>." – There is considerable divesity among the various Interior Salish tribes as to nepotic terms. The Shuswap call *ego*'s siblings' children "son" and "daughter." [42] The terms which the Thompson and Lillooet use for nephew and niece are phonetically similar to the Shuswap terms for son and daughter. (We do not have specific son and daughter terms for the Thompson and hence cannot make a direct comparison.) The Kalispel terms used by a female speaker for nephew and niece closely resemble the terms for son and daughter, but an entirely different term with no differentiation as to sex is used by a male speaker. The Northern Okanagon and Sinkaietk have one general term for ego's siblings' children, with no differentiation as to sex.

The Flathead, in the main, make use of self-reciprocals between uncles-aunts and nephews-nieces. A woman, however, calls her sisters daughter, "daughter," and uses a distinct term for her sister's son. In the Spokan tribe, a man's brother's son and daughter are his "son" and "daughter." He may also use as an alternative for his brother's son the self-reciprocal. His sister's son and daughter are called by a separate nepotic term with no sex differentiation. With a female *ego*, the use of a reciprocal term exists between her and her brother's son, while her sister's son and daughter are called "son" and "daughter."

---

[106] See Spokan kinship schedule in Lewis H. Morgan, *Systems of Consanguinity and Affinity*, ("Smithsonian Contributions to Knowledge," XVII [Washington: Smithsonian Institution, 1871]): pp. 291-582. {herein pp 39-45}

[107] Morgan, *op. cit*: p. 245.

In summary: The Shuswap apply son and daughter terminology to nepotic relatives. The Thompson, Lillooet, and Kalispel (♀ female speaking) use terms which are separate from but very similar to the son and daughter terms. The Northern Okanagon, Sinkaietk, and Kalispel (♂ male speaking) apply a generalized term, with no distinction as to sex or as to whether the relative in question is *ego*'s brother's child or his sister's child. The Flathead, for the most part, use only self-reciprocal terminology. The Spokan terminology appears to be a mixture of all these usages.

Second descending generation. – Most of the tribes seem to [43] have a general term "grandchild," applied not only to the speaker's own children's offspring but to the children of his sibling's children as well. Among the northern Okanagon, Sinkaietk, Flathead, Spokan, and perhaps other tribes, we also find the use of self-reciprocal terms. For instance, in the Sinkaietk tribe, a man and his son's child call each other by the term for father's father, *sxa'xba.*

## Affinal Terminology

In all the tribes, except the Lillooet (who call father-in-law and mother-in-law by the same term), two terms, father-in-law and mother-in-law, are applied to *ego*'s parents-in-law and, according to our data on the Sinkaietk and Flathead, to their siblings. Similarly, all the tribes term the spouses of *ego*'s children son-in-law and daughter-in-law, and in some of the tribes, at least, these terms are extended to the spouses of *ego*'s siblings' children.

Among the Northern Okanagon, Sinkaietk, Flathead, Spokan, and probably also Kalispel, brother's wife and wife's sister are called by the same term, here translated "sister-in-law"; and sister's husband and wife's brother are called by the same terra, "brother-in-law." Similarly, in the case of a female speaker, brother's wife and husband's sister are "sister-in-law" and sister's husband and husband's brother are "brother-in-law." Among the Sinkaietk, wife's sister's husband is also called "brother-in-law"; however, wife's brother's wife is not called "sister-in-law" but by a different term. Whether this is true in the other tribes is not clear, due to incompleteness of the terminologies.

In the Thompson tribe, the same term *cea'dEm* is applied, to all siblings-in-law, regardless of their sex. In the case of the Lillooet, we learn that brother's wife is equated with wife's sister [44] and sister's husband with wife's brother, as in the above tribes. However, our information on the terminology used by a female speaker among the Lillooet is confused, as is all the information on the affinal terminology of the Shuswap.

The Sinkaietk call the spouse's siblings' children by the nepotic term. Again, we cannot state whether this holds in the other tribes.

A reciprocal term is used between the two sets of parents-in-law involved in the marital union of two persons. The native terms used in the different tribes are all cognate: Flathead, segunɛmt; Sinkaietk, ntimtn; Lillooet, cqunāmt; Kalispel, segunemt.

## Additional Terminology

First of all, it should be mentioned that in most of the tribes a different {decedence} terminology was employed for certain relatives after the death of intermediary relatives. For the most part, these included affinal relatives; however, in the Spokan, Kalispel, and Flathead tribes, the terms for certain blood relatives were also changed after the connecting relative's death. In the latter tribes, after the death of a person's father, he called his father's brother by a term meaning "step-father"; similarly, his mother's sister would become "step-mother" in the event of his mother's death.  In these tribes, also, the terms for a person's sibling's children were changed after the death of his sibling.  These practices clearly reflect the sororate and levirate customarily found among the Salish people.  Among the Flathead, grandparents and grandchildren were also called by different terms following the connecting relative's death.

In all of the Interior Salish tribes, affinal relatives were given different terms after the death of the intermediary [45] relative.  The Lillooet had a term ck'a'lpaa which, was used by a person for all relatives by marriage after the spouse's death.  In the Kalispel, Flathead, Northern Okanagon, and Sinkaietk tribes, a special term was applied to sons-in-law, daughters-in-law and parents-in-law following the decease of the connecting relative.  Native terms used in this case by the various tribes were:  Kalispel, s'chēlp; Flathead, s'tcɛɛlp; Sinkaietk, cqīɪ'lp.  Similarly, in these tribes, an individual employed a special term for siblings-in-law after his spouse's death.  The native terms were:  Kallspel, nhoi'ztn; Flathead, nkʍitsətən; Sintealetk, nqō'ɪtstēn.

Mention should, perhaps, also be made of the fact that in the Lillooet tribe, according to Boas, it was customary in addressing certain relatives to use terms different from the ones used in speaking of those relatives.  Such usage of both vocative and non-vocative terms may have occurred in the other tribes also but was overlooked by the writers in describing the terminologies.

Lastly, it should be pointed out that the use of different native terms for certain relatives by speakers of different sex also occurs among the Interior Salish.  This is practically universally true so far as the parental terms, mother and father, and the affinal terms, brother's wife and sister's husband, are concerned.  We also find that speakers of different sex call the following relatives by different terms in the following tribes:  aunts and uncles, Shuswap; father's sister, Sinkaietk, Flathead, Spokan, Kalispel; mother's brother, Flathead; siblings, Flathead Spokan; grandchildren, Sinkaietk, Flathead, Spokan.  This usage in connection with the father's sister, mother's brother, and sibling's children among the Flathead is consonant with the combined facts that a distinction is made between mother's siblings and father's siblings, and that verbal reciprocity occurs between [46] aunts or uncles and their nephews or nieces.  Verbal reciprocity also accompanies the use of different terms by different sexes for grandchildren among the Sinkaietk, Flathead, and Spokan.  But why different terms should be used by male and female speakers for uncles and aunts among the Shuswap and for father's sister in the Sinkaietk and Kalispel tribes is not clear.

Extension of kinship. – Information on the extension of kinship is given us only by the writers on the Sinkaietk and Flathead.[108]  In the case of the other tribes, we have scarcely more than terms for members of *ego*'s lineage.

In the Sinkaietk and Flathead tribes, the four grandparental terms are extended to the grandparents' siblings and cousins and to other of *ego*'s blood relatives belonging to this generation.  According to our Flathead data, the affinal term for grandparent-in-law is also applied to siblings and cousins of this relative.

In the parental generation, the four terms for *ego*'s aunts and uncles are extended to their cousins, near and distant.  Mandelbaum says that the term "mother's sister" is also used for *ego*'s step-mother and his father's other wives.[109]  The affinal terms "mother-in-law" and, "father-in-

---

[108] Walters, *op. cit*: pp. 88-91; Turney-High, *op. cit*: pp. 56-61.

[109] May Mandelbaum, "The Individual Life Cycle," *The Sinkaietk or Southern Okanagon of*

law" are applied to their siblings and cousins.

The sibling terms, according to Walters, are extended to all of *ego*'s cousins and, indeed, to all collateral relatives of that generation:  his step-brothers, step-sisters, half-brothers, half-sisters, and adopted siblings.[110] [47]

Nepotic terms are probably extended to the children of all of *ego*'s siblings.  Among the Sinkaietk, *ego*'s spouse's sibling's children are also called by the term for nephew and niece.  In the Flathead and Spokan tribes, the spouses of *ego*'s collateral "children" or "nephews and nieces" are called "son-in-law" and "daughter-in-law."

Lastly, the terms for *ego*'s direct descendants in the second descending generation appear to be applied to his collateral relatives of that generation.

On the whole, it probably can be said that through the comparatively simple mechanism of extension just described, all of the Interior Salish kinship systems were wide-ranged.  Kinship in most of the tribes appears to have been reckoned {via hereditary names} to the sixth or seventh generation vertically and to an indefinite extent laterally.

Differences in Interior Salish Kinship

A comparative analysis of Interior Salish kinship shows there to be two types of systems: (1) that found among the Thompson, Shuswap, and Lillooet, and  (2) that found among the Northern Okanagon, Sinkaietk, Kalispel, Spokan, and Flathead.  Within the latter type, the Flathead appear to represent a variant.

The kinship systems have been charted on pages 48, 49, and 50.  It should be pointed out here that the Thompson-Shuswap-Lillooet system has been partially reconstructed upon the charts, due to the incompleteness of the original terminologies.  For example, we do not actually have terms for grandparental siblings, but on the chart the grandparental terms have been extended to them following the general pattern of extension characteristic of all Salish systems (coast and interior).  Then, on the basis of [48] > [51] the rule of uniform descent,[111] children of the grandparents' siblings should be termed "uncle" and "aunt," offspring of *ego*'s cousins should be given terms for *ego*'s sibling's children, and the grandchildren of *ego*'s cousins should be called by the term for grandchild.

---

*Washington*, ("General Series in Anthropology" No. 6 [1938]: p. 118.
[110] Walters, *op. cit*: pp. 89.
[111] See Sol Tax, "Some Problems of Social Organization," in *Social Anthropology of North American Tribes*, Fred Eggan, ed (Chicago: University of Chicago Press 1937): p. 20.

## Lillooet ~ Shuswap ~ Thompson

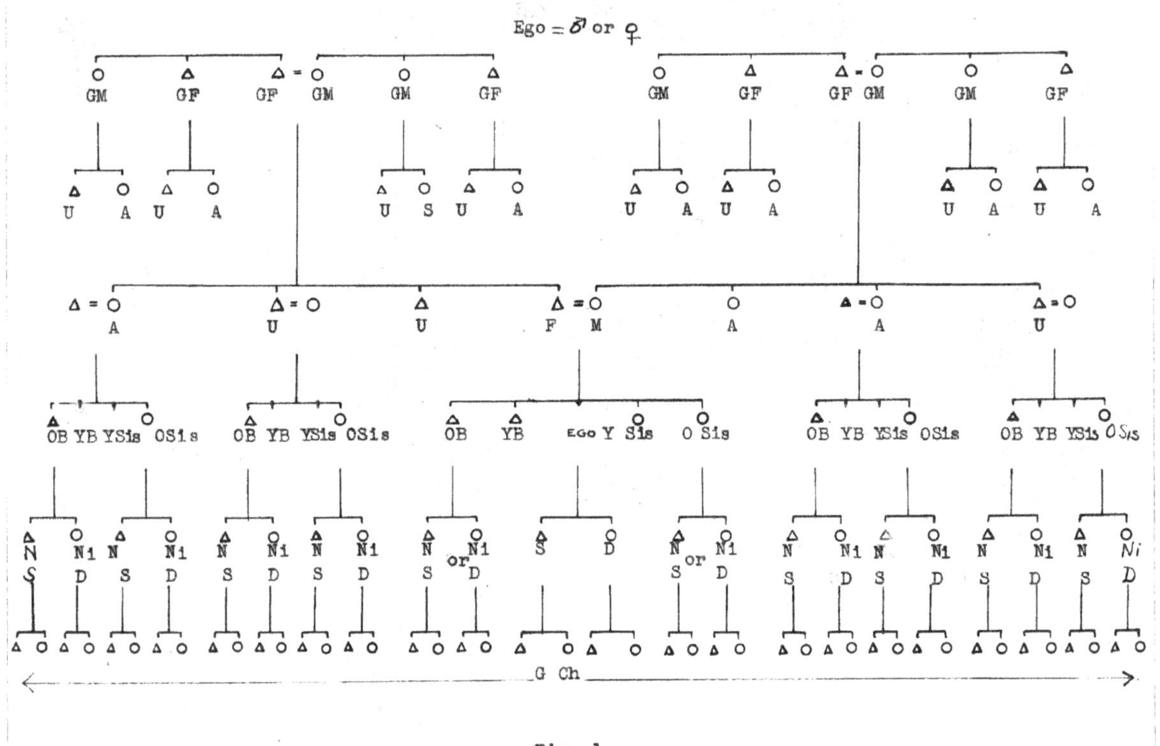


Fig. 1.

## Okanagon Kinship System

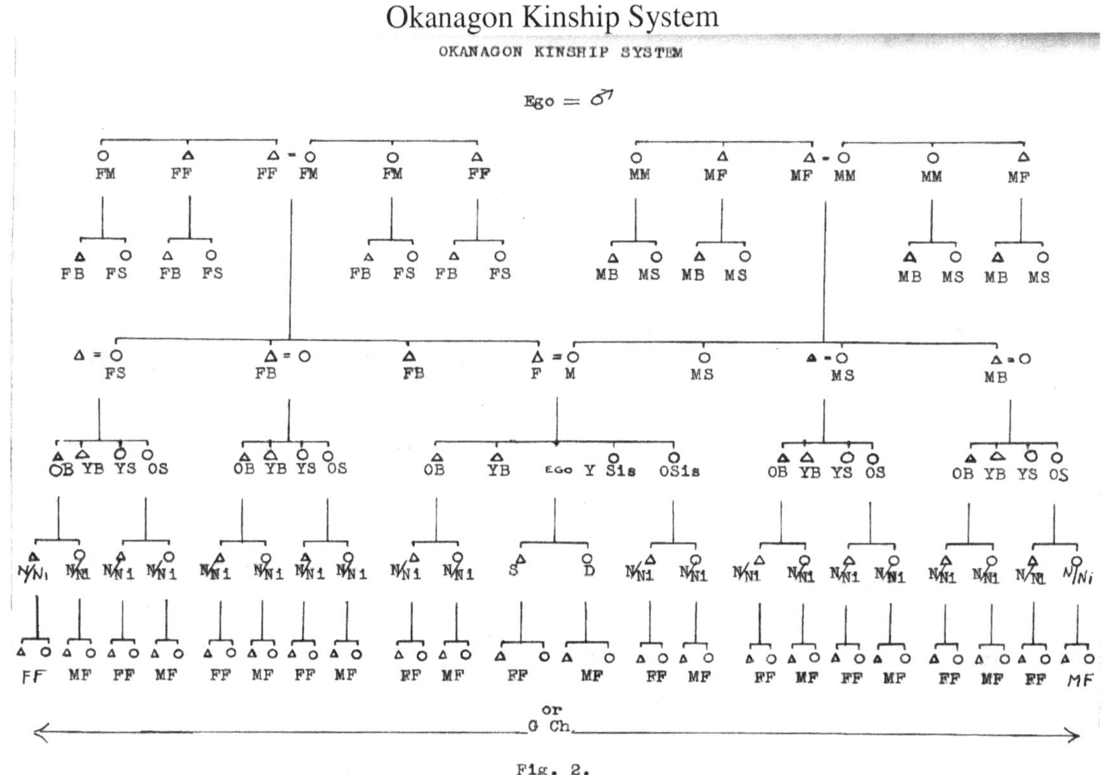


Fig. 2.

## Flathead Kinship System

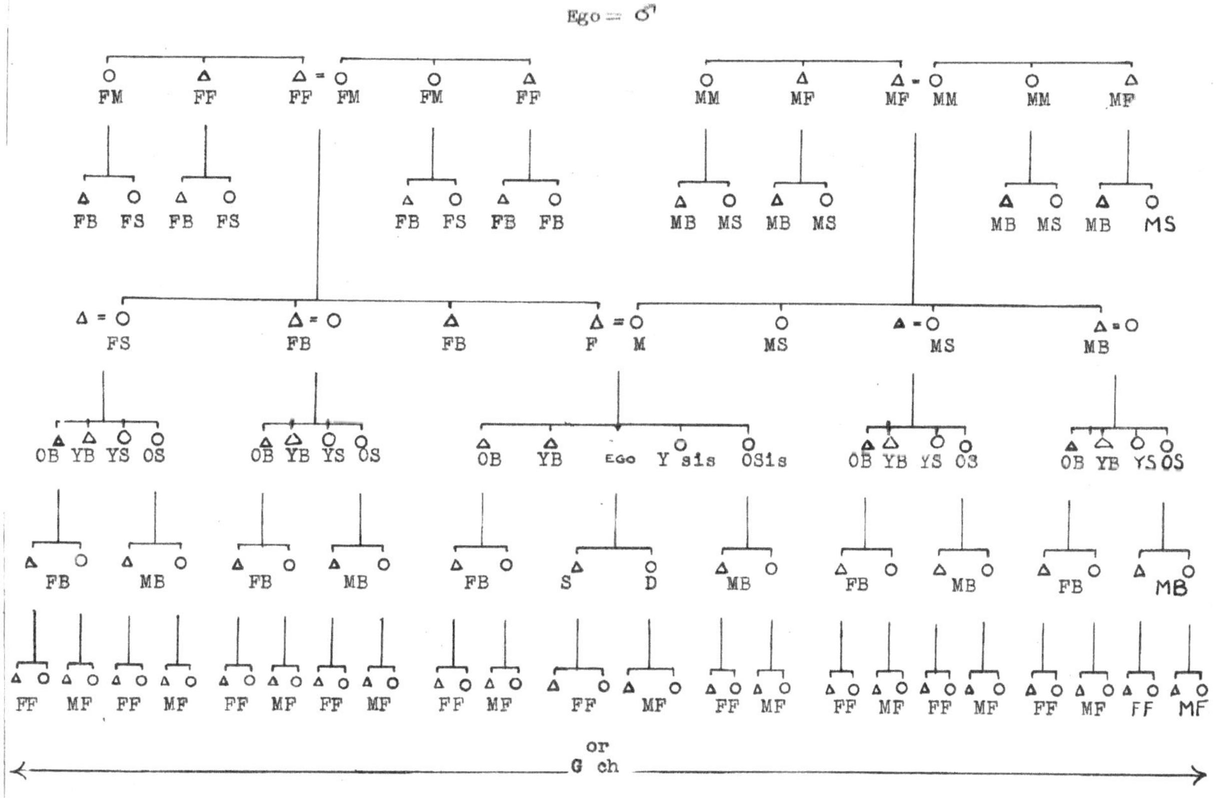

Fig. 3.

The systems are similar in the following logical features:

1. The terminological distinction of generation.
2. The distinction of sex in the first and second ascending generations and in *ego*'s generation (except for the use of the term "younger sibling" among the Shuswap and Lillooet).
3. The differentiation of lineal relatives from collateral relatives in the parental generation.
4. The use of sibling terms in which relative age is denoted and the extension of these sibling terms to all cousins.
5. The use of one term "grandchild," with no sex distinction, for members of the second descending generation.

Though we cannot ascertain as much, the systems are also alike, no doubt, in the manner in which kinship is extended to collateral relatives and in separating affinal relatives from consanguineal.

The chief point at which the two systems differ is the treatment of relatives in the generation above *ego*'s. Whereas the Sinkaietk, Northern Okanagon, Flathead, etc., tribes distinguish between maternal and paternal relatives, the Thompson, Shuswap, and Lillooet do not. The system of the former tribes also differs from that of the latter tribes in that it is characterized by the use of self-reciprocal terms between grandparents and grandchildren.[112] [52]

So far as nepotic terminology is concerned., there is great variation throughout all the tribes.  It is at this point that the Flathead system differs from the Sinkaietk system, its distinguishing characteristic being the use of verbally reciprocal terminology between the members of the first ascending and first descending generations.

## Kinship Behavior

### The Life Cycle

In studying kinship behavior, it is of value to consider the individual life cycle.  The reason for this is that in connection with the customs and practices associated with the various phases of the life cycle, the individual's relatives play important roles; and a study of these roles aids in establishing the patterns of behavior which characterize the different kinship relationships.  Accordingly, in the paragraphs below, a description is given of the various stages in the life of an individual among the Interior Salish.

Birth. – In the Sinkaietk and Flathead tribes, and perhaps in the other groups as well, it was customary for a pregnant woman to go to her mother's house to give birth to her child.  She was attended by her mother, aunt, grandmother, mother-in-law, or some other matron, and during the actual birth no males were allowed to be present.  Following a safe delivery, in most of the tribes, the father gave a feast to a small gathering of relatives and neighbors.  Mandelbaum, describing the affair among the Sinkaietk, says that it was quite informal and simple.

The child was passed about among the assembled company and each person present held it, greeting it with some such common formula as .... 'You are here'.[113] [53]

Naming. – An infant remained a social non-entity until its naming, which usually took place at the close of or some time within the first year.  A ceremony was held in which the name of either a recently deceased relative or a more remote ancestor was formally bestowed by one of the grandparents or by some other elderly and influential relative.  Except in the Flathead tribe, among whom it was customary to inherit names from the maternal side, the name could be taken from either side of the family.  In the Sinkaietk tribe, according to Mandelbaum, "there was a strong feeling against duplication of names by two individuals at the same time.  This was a situation favorable to the development of family ownership of particular names."[114]  The naming was followed by a feast given by the child's parents and close relatives.  Later in life, at puberty or some other time, the individual might change his name, a feast being given in connection with the changing of the name.

---

[112]  It is possible that this usage of self-reciprocal terminology between grandparents and grandchildren also occurred in the Thompson, Shuswap, and Lillooet tribes and simply was not recorded.

[113]  Mandelbaun, *op. cit*: p 104.

[114]  Mandelbaum, *op. cit*: p. 106.

<u>Childhood</u> – This was a period of both play and training.  For the first five or six years of life, children spent most of their time playing, though even then a child was taught such things as "to avoid the fire and snakes, not to molest the food, and to conduct himself decently when he was with older people."[115]  Such training in these very early years was largely in the hands of the mother and grandmother as the father was not at home during the day.[116]

When they were older, boys accompanied their fathers on hunting and fishing trips and were instructed in the various manly pursuits by their fathers, uncles, and grandfathers.  Girls, in the meanwhile, were trained in the women's duties such as cooking, [54] beadwork, and the manufacture of basketry mats, and clothes.  They also went with their mothers to pick berries and dig up roots and took care of their younger sisters and brothers.  It seems that in the Sinkaietk tribe there were special girls' houses to which girls began to go when they were seven years old for instruction in the women's crafts.[117]  {cf Psk$^w$aws weaving lodge}  Boys and girls spent the remainder of their time in play, in which they participated together; games were usually imitations of adult occupations.

Children were expected to give strict obedience to their elders; if they did not, they were punished, generally by being whipped.  They were supposed to devote part of their time to learning the traditions and moral values of their culture.  Mandelbaum says that in the Sinkaietk tribe household lectures wore given morning and evening by an old man, and that these "contained injunctions to be industrious, honest, clean, liberal, and respectful."[118]  Children were also expected to rise early and take a swim each morning, and once a year they went through a "whipping ordeal."  This strict physical training was supposed to make them hardy adult individuals of good character, and to prepare them for their guardian spirit experience.

The several years before puberty were characterized by the seeking of a guardian spirit.  At some time during this period, the boy or girl went to some isolated spot, perhaps a mountain top, and spent a time in seclusion.  During the seclusion period, the child fasted, prayed, slept very little, and concentrated upon his goal.  Sometimes he danced and took sweatbaths, and, by doing this, according to Cline, put himself in "the proper nervous state."[119]  Finally, in a vision, his spirit appeared to him and [55] bestowed power upon him.  In the Sanpoil tribe, he also received a name from the spirit which was symbolic and connected with the spirit in some way.  He could not use this name, however, until after the winter dance in which he was initiated upon reaching maturity.[120]

While he was on his quest, the child had to provide for himself.  However, he was given the moral support of his parents and relatives, who advised him and supervised his quest.  In regard to the part played by the parents and relatives in the Sinkaietk tribe, Cline says:

> Parents or other older relatives supervised the child's quest, withdrawing a short distance from the rest of the community and camping separately .... Parents warned the

---

[115]  *Ibid*: p. 107.

[116]  *Ibid*.

[117]  *Ibid*.

[118]  *Ibid*: p. 108.

[119]  Cline, *op. cit*: p. 138.

[120]  Verne Ray, *The Sanpoil and Nespelem*: p. 114.

child against sleeping, cowardice, and failure to concentrate during the venture, against bring{ing} back a false report of conduct or success, and against the approaches of an evil power.  They advised him to receive a guardian spirit cautiously, since it might be a bad one and play him false ....

Though the parent did not tell the child what spirit he would meet he equipped him with the power emblem which he had cherished for many years, and the child, wearing or carrying this during his search, had a better chance of receiving the power which it represented.[121]

<u>Puberty</u>. – The Interior Salish tribes vary somewhat as to practices observed directly at puberty.  Apparently, in some tribes, puberty was marked specifically by the guardian spirit quest.  In the Sinkaietk tribe, however, where usually the spirit quest was undertaken several years previous to puberty, another rite was observed.  According to Mandelbaum, when a Sinkaietk boy's voice changed he was told by his father to leave camp and go to a mountain top and remain there for several days.[122]  The boy spent his time there running, fasting, and taking sweatbaths morning and evening, followed by plunges in the cold mountain stream.  [56]

A pubescent girl was isolated in a separate hut or in a screened-off portion of the house for a period varying in the different tribes.  During her first menses, she fasted, observed certain menstrual tabus, and, at the end of the period, took a sweat-bath.  There followed a purification period during which she took sweatbaths frequently, swam every morning and occupied herself with women's crafts such as making basketry.[123]  While in seclusion, the girl was attended and instructed by her mother, aunt, and grandmother.

After puberty, boys and girls were expected to put away their childhood pursuits and to participate seriously in adult life.  Boys assisted their fathers with their hunting and fishing and other men's tasks, and the girls helped their mothers with the various household duties.  The young women were now considered ready to be spoken for in marriage.  The two sexes were no longer allowed to associate freely.  In fact, girls were supposed to stay at home most of the time, and whenever they went any place they were closely chaperoned by an older female relative.[124]  Since the young folk were now considered to be adults, they were permitted to participate in the religious life of the community and join in the power sings and dances.

<u>Marriage</u>. – Marriage theoretically was prohibited between all blood kin; actually, distant collateral relatives sometimes married.  Since wealth and class distinctions were not important among these people, there were no restrictions concerning marital unions between rich and poor or between persons of different status.

In most of the tribes, marriage appears to have been of the three types described by Teit for the Coeur d'Alene:  [57]  (1) marriage by proposal of the man's family, followed by their giving gifts to the girl's family,  (2) marriage by betrothal, the girl's family frequently taking the initiative, and  (3) marriage by "touching" or direct choosing.[125]  The commonest and preferred

---

[121]  Cline, *op. cit*: p. 137.
[122]  Mandelbaum, *op. cit*: p. 110.
[123]  *Ibid.*
[124]  *Ibid*: p. 112.
[125]  Teit, "The Salishan Tribes of the Western Plateaus," *op. cit*: p. 170.

type was that in which the father, uncle, or some older male relative of the boy asked the parents of the girl for her hand in marriage.

There seems to have been a good deal of variation among the Interior Salish as to the kind of ceremony. Mandelbaum says that in the case of the Sinkaietk, marriage was usually quite informal, announced by a feast given by the parents of either bride or groom, with "no ceremonies, no gifts, no special clothing."[126] In a more elaborate type of ceremony, the relatives of the couple gathered, and the parents of the boy distributed gifts to the bride's kin and then gave a feast.[127] The marriage ceremony of the Lillooet described by Hill-Tout had two important features:

> first, the formal offering of firewood by the youth to his prospective father-in-law. This act signified that the younger man was subject to his father-in-law

and secondly,

> the union of the bridegroom with the bride's family by the formal invitation to sit among them. This inclusion of the son-in-law within the family circle gives him all the rights of sonship and his offspring are regarded as belonging to his wife's family just as much as to his own.[128]

Though a young married couple might live with the girl's parents for a short period immediately following marriage, in most cases they eventually took up permanent residence with the groom's folk. Sometimes a man and his wife did not reside with either set [58] of parents, but lived alone.

The levirate and sororate were practiced in all of the Interior tribes, but were not absolutely obligatory. Usually, however, a widow married her husband's brother and a widower his wife's younger sister. If no immediate siblings of the dead spouse were available, the custom was extended to cousins (i.e., distant "siblings"). Co-wives shared the food brought by their husband and took turns sleeping with him and cooking for him. Each had her own section of the house and took care of her own children; whether actually related or not, they were "mother's sister" to each other's children.[129]

<u>Death</u>. – Relatives mourned the death of an individual, prepared the corpse for burial, and took charge of the interment. The deceased's property was divided among his immediate relatives. The widow did not receive very much as, due to the operation of the levirate, she usually became her husband's brother's wife and shared in his property.

## Kinship Behavior Patterns

From the data on the individual life cycle, the patterns of behavior characterizing the

---

[126] Mandelbaum, *op, cit*: p. 115.

[127] *Ibid.*

[128] Hill-Tout, "Report on the Ethnology of the Stlatlumh," *op, cit*: p. 131.

[129] Mandelbaum, *op. cit*: p. 118.

various kinship relationships can be partially abstracted.  They are briefly described in the paragraphs below.

The relationship between parents and children, as in all societies, was an exceedingly important one.  Parents were responsible for the social, as well as physical, nurturing of their children.  They had, first of all, to instruct them in the different economic pursuits necessary for securing and maintaining a living.  Fathers taught their sons how to fish and hunt, and how [59] to make the appliances used in those occupations.  Mothers instructed their daughters in cooking, sewing, weaving, and the manufacture of mats, bags, baskets, clothing.  Parents also educated their children in the traditions, customs, and religious beliefs of the society.  They were chief discipliners of their children's behavior; they lectured to them on morals, and when a child misbehaved they reprimanded him and inflicted punishment.

Parents encouraged their children when the latter went on their power quest and assisted in whatever way they could.  They also figured prominently at the time of their children's marriage.  The father, aided by other older male relatives, would frequently propose for the boy, and, if accepted, would present the girl's family with gifts.  After marriage, the girl was instructed by her mother or mother-in-law in how to be a good wife.

Children, in turn, respected and obeyed their parents.  When the parents became old and enfeebled, they took care of them.

The relationship between brothers seems to have been a very close one.  Older brothers helped their parents in the instruction of their younger brothers.  Brothers played, hunted, and fished together when they were young; and even after they had grown up and married, they were frequently in the same household, due to the custom of patrilocal residence, and continued to be in a close, co-operative relationship.

Older sisters looked after and instructed their younger sisters.  Sisters, too, often continued to be members of the same house group after marriage, because of the customs of the sororate and sororal polygyny.  Sisters treated each other's children much as they did their own.

Brothers and sisters played together until puberty, but after that they were expected to maintain a certain reserve toward each other.  Tickling or any other "sort of intimate trifling" was [60] frowned upon, and boys were supposed to refrain from obscenity in the presence of their sisters.[130]  This behavior also held between cousins, who were considered to be distant siblings and treated as such.  Sexual intercourse was strictly forbidden between "siblings."  Brothers watched over their sisters' sexual conduct.

The relationship between husband and wife was an impotant economic one.  The division of labor involved in this relationship was basic to the whole economic life of the group.  A man's duties were to hunt, fish, fight, make tools and weapons, fell trees, and build the winter houses.  Women did the cooking and other house work, made household utensils, constructed temporary residences, and gathered vegetables and berries.  A husband expected strict obedience and faithfulness from his wife.  If she failed in these respects, he might inflict actual physical punishment upon her.

Uncles and aunts assisted the parents in their duties toward their children.  The uncle helped the father train his sons, and the aunt helped the mother instruct her daughters.  During a girl's isolation at puberty and again later during her confinement at childbirth, the aunt was one of her attendants.  The uncle went with the father when be proposed marriage for his son.

---

[130] Mandelbaum, *op. cit*: p. 112.

Similarly, an individual's duties and behavior toward his aunts and uncles were of the same category as those involved in his relationship with his parents. The writer could not determine from the available material whether there was any behavioral differentiation between maternal and paternal siblings, other than that brought about by differences of sex.

A very close, friendly relationship existed between grandparents and grandchildren. Grandparents assisted in the training [61] of children and had a good deal of influence over them. They seem to have had much part in disciplining, however, and the following description of the grandparent-grandchild relationship among the Sanpoil would no doubt apply in all the tribes:

> Grandparents customarily defended children and seldom criticized them. They petted them and played with them more than their parents. As a result, children were often .... more fond of their grandparents than of their parents.[131]

One of the grandparents usually conferred a name upon the child in the naming ceremony which took place during the child's first year. Grandfathers were closer to boys, and grandmothers to girls. There seems not to have been much difference in the behavior of maternal and paternal grandparents.

The Coeur d'Alene appear to have been the only tribe in which a mother-in-law tabu existed. There, according to Teit, man was forbidden to speak to his mother-in-law, and, in many families, women did not speak to their fathers-in-law.[132] Teit rejects the possibility that these customs came from the Plains, as they were "said to have been in vogue long before the tribe commenced to go to the plains."[133] Even so, contacts with plains tribes may be one factor involved.

In the other tribes, however, the relationship between children-in-law and their parents-in-law was of a different nature. According to Mandelbaum, a Sinkaietk individual behaved toward his sons-in-law and daughters-in-law much as he would toward his own sons and daughters. Mandelbaum says:

> If a man liked the wife of his son, he would treat her as he would his own daughter. 'He would sit near her and tell her stories.' Similarly, a woman and her son-in-law were like [62] mother and son. If the son-in-law or daughter-in-law was lazy, the mother-in-law (but never the father-in-law) might beat him, or her. Unless there were some untoward personality difficulty, young married people got on perfectly well with the parents of their spouses.[134]

There is scarcely any information on the relationship between siblings-in-law. Among the Flathead, a joking relationship existed between a man and his wife's sister, but whether this was true in the other tribes cannot be stated.

Turney-High describes the relationship between the two groups of parents-in-law in the

---

[131] Verne Ray, *The Sanpoil and Nespelem*: p. 132.
[132] Teit, The Salishan Tribes of the Western Plateaus," *op. cit*: p. 172.
[133] *Ibid.*
[134] Mandelbaum, *op. cit*: p. 118.

Flathead tribe as one of "mutual friendship and aid."[135] This was true in the other Interior Salish groups, also. A self-reciprocal term was used between them, and this reciprocity manifested itself at the time of marriage, as well as afterwards, in the exchange of gifts and visits.

In the various accounts of kinship behavior among the Interior Salish no mention is made of a behavioral difference between maternal and paternal relatives. It appears that relatives on the two parental sides behaved in much the same way toward an individual, and vice versa, although actually in the everyday relations of life, the individual's paternal relatives must have been more actively concerned because of the greater frequency of patrilocal residence. There also seems to have been no differentiation in <u>type</u> of behavior between lineal and collateral relatives. Thus, uncles and aunts had the same kinds of duties and obligations toward *ego* (though to a lesser degree) as did his parents. Similarly, *ego* extended the same respectful, obedient behavior toward his uncles and aunts as he did toward his mother and father. Furthermore, he was in a friendly relationship with all members of his grandparents' generation, and treated all blood relatives of [63] his own generation as though they were siblings. The chief differential of kinship behavior, then, was generation. There was a certain well-defined way in which, *ego* behaved toward members of each generation; differences within this pattern of behavior were attributable to sex differences and to the varying degrees of relationship, the pattern of behavior becoming more tenuous the more remote the relative. [64 III]

---

[135] Turney-High, *op. cit*: p. 87.

## CHAPTER III
## THE SOCIAL ORGANIZATION OF THE COAST SALISH

### Introduction

### Dialect Groups, Tribes and Locations

The Coast Salish lived west of the Coastal-Cascade range in the coastal areas of British Columbia and Washington, and on the eastern and southern shores of Vancouver Island. Their physical environment differed from that of the Interior Salish in that the country was flatter, the rainfall greater, the climate more even-tempered, the vegetation more luxuriant, and the rivers more plentiful with salmon.

A complete list of the Coast Salish tribes is given in F.W. Hodge's *Handbook of American Indians*.[136] Since the tribal names are very numerous and of difficult spellings, only the better known tribes will be mentioned in the list below, which is taken after Hodge, but not in exact quotation. The dialect groups, their locations, and the more important tribes belonging to each, then, are as follows:

1. The Bella Coola, on Dean's Inlet, Burke Channel, and the Bellacoola River. The Bella Coola {Nuxalk}, most northerly of the Coast Salish groups, were separated from the other coastal tribes by the Kwakiutl Indians. Two different but seemingly equally plausible conjectures have been made as to where the Bella Coola were formerly located and as to how they became isolated from the rest of the Salish stock. Boas and Hill-Tout believe that they originally lived farther south and at some moved northward, while Swanton considers them a branch of Interior Salish who migrated to where the Bella Coola are presently located and were later cut off from the [65] Shuswap of the interior by an intruding wedge of Chilcotin Indians.[137]

2 The Comox group, in the northern part of the Gulf of Georgia, on Vancouver Island, and the mainland. It includes the
    a) Comox proper
        1) Comox
        2) Homalco
        3) Seechelt
        4) Sliammon
    b) Puntlatsh

3. The Cowichan group. "in the neighborhood of Nanaimo on Vancouver Island, and in the Fraser delta." More important tribes are the
    a) Nanaimo
    b) Kwantlen

---

[136] Also cf. map in Barnett, "The Coast Salish of Canada," *op. cit*: p. 120.

[137] John R. Swanton, "Origin of the Bella Coola," *American Anthropologist*, VI (1904): 743; "The Development of the Clan System and of Secret Societies among the Northwestern Tribes," *American Anthropologist* VI (1904): 485.

c) Musqueam
d) Scowlitz

4. <u>The Squamish group</u>.  It includes the
    a) Squamlsh of Burrard Inlet and Howe Sound
    b) Nooksak of northern Washington (probably)

5. <u>The Songish group,</u> "on Juan de Fuca Strait, San Juan Island, and parts of the coasts of Washington and British Columbia."  It embraces the
    a) Clallam
    b) Lummi
    c) Samesh {Samish}
    d) Sanetch
    e) Semeahmoo
    f) Songish
    g) Sooke

6. <u>The Nisqualli group,</u> "embracing all the tribes east of Puget Sound and south to Mount Tacoma {Rainier}, and, on the west side, the region up to Olympia, except Hood Canal."  It includes the
    a) Nisqually proper
    b) Dwamish {& Suquamish}
    c) Puyallup
    d) Skagit {& Swinomish}
    e) Snoqualmu or Snoquamish
    f) Squaxon

7. <u>The Twana group</u>, "on Hood canal, Puget Sound."

8. <u>The Chehalis Group</u>.  It includes six dialects:
    a) Quinault and Quaitso of northwestern Washington
    b) Humptulips of northern Gray's Harbor
    c) Lower Chehalis of Gray's Harbor and Shoalwater Bay
    d) Satsop, east and northeast of Gray's Harbor
    e) Upper Chehalis, east of Shoal water Bay [66]
    f) Cowlitz, on the Cowlitz River

9. The Tillamook, on the coast of Oregon.

## Cultural Groupings

All of the Coast Salish tribes have been placed in the Northwest Coast major culture area by both Wissler and Kroeber.[138]  According to Kroeber's classification, they further fall into four sub-areas:  (1) Central Maritime, (2) Gulf of Georgia, (3) Puget Sound, and (4) Lower Columbia.[139]  The Salish tribes included in the Central Maritime subarea are the Bella Coola, Quinault, and Quileute, all of whom have been culturally influenced by the Kwakiutl – the Bella Coola directly and to a greater degree, the other two indirectly via the Nootka and Makah, and to a lesser degree.  The Bella Coola together with the Kwakiutl and Heiltsuk tribes, Kroeber points

---

[138]  See Wissler, *op, cit*: p. 227, and Kroeber, *op. cit*: 28-29.
[139]  Kroeber, *op. cit*: p.29.

out, have a more developed art, ritual, and social organization than the Quinault and Quileute. The latter tribes, on the other hand, together with the Nootka and other seaward tribes of Washington, participate in whale hunting, whereas the Bella Coola, who are situated on protected water, do not.[140]

The Canadian tribes of the Gulf of Georgia subarea have been further subdivided by Barnett into the following groupings:  (1) the Comox proper, with "a decided bear <ok> toward the Kwakiutl," and the related Pentlatch;  (2) the Homalco, Klahuse, and Slaiamun, having been only moderately (and lately?) influenced from the north and exhibiting now and again features suggesting interior contacts," and the related Sechelt;  (3) the Nanaimo, Cowichan, and Sanetch, who "are in pronounced cultural agreement [with the tribes of the second group], except for a few traits which have filtered [67] around the tip of Vancouver Island from the Nootka," plus perhaps the Muskwium and Squamish.[141]  Tribes in Washington which probably should be placed in the Gulf of Georgia subarea, being most closely related to the groups of southeastern Vancouver Island, are the Klallam, Lummi, and Nutsack.  The culture of these latter tribes, however, is not as developed as that of the other Gulf of Georgia tribes and, in a number of respects, is closer to the culture of the Puget Sound groups.

Features typical of the more northern coastal tribes, such as a highly developed caste system, an emphasis on wealth, potlatches, and secret societies, are greatly toned down among the Puget Sound groups.  Traits of culture seem to have traveled down the open coast of Vancouver Island much more easily and farther than they did in the Gulf of Georgia and Puget Sound areas.  Olson, in commenting upon this fact, says:

> It may be that something inherent in Salish temperament or culture acted as a barrier which, at the southern limit of Kwakiutl territory, slowed down those currents of culture which on the west coast of Vancouver Island flowed the length of Nootka territory and across the straits to the Makah.[1422]

<u>Territorial Organization</u>

Seasonal dichotomy. – The Coast Sallsh, like their brothers of the interior, depended mainly upon salmon, roots, berries, and wild vegetables for their subsistence, though their diet also included various sea foods such as clams, mussels, halibut, cod, porpoise, seal, and whale. Since these foods were of a seasonal nature, the people spent a large portion of the year away from the villages following the various runs of salmon, gathering berries [68] as they ripened, and collecting the other items of their diet at the appropriate times.  Each village, it is true, was located near fishing place; however, not all streams had the same kinds of salmon in them and runs took place at different times in different places.  Thus, the people traveled back and forth between fishing rounds, moving with the salmon runs.  Gunther, describing such movements in the Klallam tribe, says:

---

[140]  *Ibid.*

[141]  Barnett, *op. cit*: p. 121.

[142]  Ronald L. Olson, *The Quinault Indians*, ("University of Washington Publications in Anthropology" VI [Seattle, 1936]): 12.

People from Washington Harbor and Dungeness often go to Port Discovery Bay because it is famous for its spring salmon. Then, when the spring salmon runs up the Dungeness River, the people from Discovery and Washington Harbor go there.[143]

The people usually traveled, in small family groups. Sometimes, however, the members of a whole village moved together. Entire Klallam villages, for instance, migrated each year to Hood Canal for the dog salmon run.

Summer camps lasted for varying lengths of time. The Klallam stay at Hood Canal was quite an extended one, lasting for several months, but camps usually were much shorter. Villages were not entirely abandoned during the summer. Old people commonly stayed there throughout the entire year. Then, too, parties would return to the village off and on during the summer to store the food they had obtained. They never remained, however, always starting off again on another trip.

The mode of life during the summer differed a great deal from that of the winter. Village organization lay dormant and household structure was greatly relaxed during the warmer months. The whole life was less formal and contacts between members of tribe and village were of a more casual nature. According to Smith, meetings of people at lesser known fishing and gathering places were rather sporadic, but meetings at good, popular sites [69] "were annual, anticipated occurrences." Smith adds:

Individuals looked forward to them as to periods of holiday, a social, festal atmosphere prevailed and rigid rules of conduct maintained at the home sites ware relaxed.[144]

The assembling of people at food gathering grounds or fishing places offered opportunities for trading. Taking advantage of such opportunities, the Indiana exchanged certain foods for other foods, or food for products such as baskets. Gunther remarks,

In all this trading each individual has in mind not only the securing of food or materials for working, but also gathering things suitable for potlatch giving and food for entertainment. If a man or woman excels in the production of any one article, he or she can rapidly acquire wealth through trading this product.[145]

As in the interior, winter months were spent in living a sedentary life in villages. During this season, village and household groups were quite compact units, economically and socially. The more formal aspects of social organization were revived. The political organization, consisting of rule by village chiefs assisted by the group elders, functioned more actively again. The rules of behavior governing relations between the classes or castes were more closely observed; and potlatches, the chief mechanism through which the class structure was maintained, were important winter events. Secret societies also became active in those tribes which had

---

[143]    Erna Gunther, *Klallam Ethnography*, ("University of Washington Publications in Anthropology," VI [Seattle, 1927]): 200.

[144]    Marian W. Smith, *The Puyallup-Nisqually*, ("Columbia University Contributions to Anthropology," XXXII (New York, 1940]): 26.

[145]  Gunther, *op. cit*: p. 213.

them, and the climax of the winter ceremonial life was reached with the initiation of the secret society neophytes.

Thus, we find that the Coast Salish were characterized by the same seasonal dichotomy in life and territorial organization that was found among the Interior Salish. In the summer, life was [70] nomadic and the people were broken up into family groups; in the winter, life was sedentary, and the people were collected in localized communities.

Tribal organization. – Like the peoples of the interior, the Coast Salish appear to have possessed no formal tribal organization. The individual villages were not united by a larger political structure, and though some village chiefs might have been more influential than others, there was no head chief who ruled over the entire tribe. The members of the tribe were unified territorially, culturally, linguistically, and through kinship bonds.

The village. – Coastal villages were located along and at the mouths of the various rivers found in the area. River mouths were especially choice locations for sites, and other places along the rivers were chosen on the basis of "feasibility of erecting a salmon weir."[146]

Villages were of different sizes. We are told that a Quinault village might include only one house with one or more families, or as many as eight or ten such houses. Ten was also the top number of dwellings found in the Klallam village. In the Puyallup-Nisqually community there were from one to three large houses and several smaller dwellings, each village containing twenty to fifty inhabitants. Large villages always had at least one large structure where potlatches and other important affairs could be held, this structure sometimes also serving as living quarters for the chief and his family.

Houses generally were built in one row along the water's shore. According to Hill-Tout, among the Squamish and other tribes of the Lower Fraser, the chief's house was placed in the center of the village, which was the most protected spot. Nearest [71] it were his brothers' houses, then come the houses of other nobles, and finally, on the outer edges were the commoners' dwellings.[147] Gunther says that in the Klallam villages, too, the upper class people were spacially separated from the lower class people, the latter being made to occupy a small group of huts {!} built in an unprotected place, "so that they would bear the brunt of an attack in war."[148]

Though half of the year was spent away from these permanent habitational sites in a nomadic existence, every individual as affiliated with some village to which he returned each winter and which he considered to be his true home. The village in which a individual claimed membership usually was the one in which he was born, but if he wished, he could change his village connections at any time. In the Puyallup-Nisqually tribes, however, according to Smith, the village was a very compact unit, which "closed its doors" against a person taking up residence in another community,[149] Smith says that in such instances "return was difficult" and that also newcomers to a village were regarded with suspicion and required to go through a

---

[146] Olson, *op. cit*: 14.

[147] Charles Hill-Tout, "Ethnological Studies of the Mainland Halkomelem," *Report, Seventy-second Meeting of British Association for the Advancement of Science*, 1902, [London: John Murray Co., 1903]): p. 360.

[148] Gunther, *op. cit*: p. 184.

[149] Smith, *The Puyallup-Nisqually*: p. 56.

probationary period.[150]

Due to the custom of patrilocal residence, in both the village and household, the males constituted the stabilizing element, the women marrying out into other villages.  Barnett says:

> Not infrequently brothers or cousins owned adjacent houses, and in all probability the principle of kinship through males governed the formation of village and even the aggregates of villages ....[151] [72]

A goodly number of the local group were thus related, but as in the interior, the village was not primarily a kinship group.  Village solidarity was based on association with a certain, geographical locality and its fishing places.  Each Puyallup-Nisqually village, for instance, was connected with a certain drainage; through habitual use of and association with this drainage the people became more or less identified with it.[152]

The coastal village seems to have been characterized by a more complex economic life than was found among the interior groups.  There was more specialization in economic tasks and a greater exchange of economic goods and services.  Hunting was not important on the coast.  There was {a} tendency for each village to have one person who specialized in hunting and who supplied the rest of the people with game.  Similarly, in those tribes which participated in whaling and sealing, there usually was one whaler and one sealer to each village.  Furthermore, persons who excelled in certain crafts such as canoe-making, basketry, net-making, etc., would spend most of their time in those occupations and would exchange their products for such goods and services as they desired.

The village was a political and social unit.  Each community had its own chief and was subject to no higher authority.  It also had its own social and ceremonial life, which culminated in the midwinter secret society initiation with its associated feasting and gift-distribution.

The household. – The type of habitation found throughout all the coastal tribes was the communal long house, a structure with walls of cedar planks and a roof of either the gabled or shed type.  It was usually a large building holding two or more families, and each family had its own living section with sleeping [73] bench, storage place, and fire for cooking and heat.  If there were only two families, the fires were built one at each end; if there were four families, there was one in each corner.  Among the southern Puget Sound tribes, where the house groups seems often to have consisted of more than four families, the fires were built in two rows extending the length of the house, and the families occupied the spaces between the fires and the side walls.  If a man had several wives, each wife had her own living quarters and fire.  In the Quinault tribe, the head of the house occupied the rear wall and his wife had her fire in the northeast corner; there was no special placing of secondary wives.[153]

According to Smith, residence was about equally matrilocal and patrilocal among the Puyallup-Nisqually;[154] in all the other coastal tribes, however, residence was predominantly

---

[150]  *Ibid.*

[151]  Barnett, *op. cit*: p. 130.

[152]  Smith, *The Puyallup-Nisqually*: p. 56.

[153]  Olson, *op. cit*: p. 64.

[154]  Smith, *The Puyallup-Nisqually*: p. 32.

patrilocal.  Olson, in discussing the composition of the house group among the Quinault, says:

> A man and his married sons, a group of brothers, uncles and nephews, cousins, or combinations of these were the commonest relationships between the heads of families. Wives, children, parents-in-law, slaves, and hangers-on completed the household group.[155]

In most of the tribes, one man, usually the eldest and builder of the house, or descendant of the builder – and probably also the wealthiest and most influential member – was considered the "owner" of the house.  The right of ownership passed from this individual to his eldest son, or to his brother, cousin, or nephew.  In the southern Puget Sound tribes and among the Quinault, the whole house did not always belong to one person; sometimes each section was owned individually, and the "head of the household was [74] regarded as 'owning' only the end or corner which he occupied."[156]  Among the Strait of Georgia tribes, a man, his sons, and his brothers were thought of as a sort of owning unit.

The owner or eldest member of the household was generally considered to be its head. He controlled the collective interests and economic activities of the group as a whole.  He was looked to for guidance and protection by the others, and, in turn, as Barnett says, "he was granted their respect and allegiance on the score of his prestige and influence."[157]  Barnett, in continuing his description of the house owner's authority and prestige among the Strait of Georgia Salish, says:

> By virtue of his aristocratic birth he owned or exercised a controlling interest in certain property rights and ceremonial privileges.  His brothers and housemates were not entirely excluded from them and in order to validate his birth right he was expected to improve upon it by industry, generosity, and dignified behavior.  Through an intelligent exercise of these qualities he was able to maintain an appreciable control over his retainers.  It was power of an informal sort, implicit in the kinship bond which linked him in some way with almost every member of his extended household.[158]

The house group was an important economic unit.  Despite the fact that there was some economic specialization in the village, each household was a self-sufficient unit.  According to Smith, however, the individual families within the larger house group were not economically independent (as they were in the interior) but tended to specialize in certain economic tasks. Smith says that each family's "effort was expended in keeping up its share of the total economy rather than in any attempt at self-sufficiency."[159] [75]

Smith points out also that in the Puyallup-Nisqually house group there was specialization in purely social activities, so that each house had its own story teller, gambler, etc.[160]

---

[155] Olson, *op. cit*: p. 95.

[156] Olson, *op. cit*: pp. 92-95.

[157] Barnett, *op. cit*: p. 150.

[158] *Ibid.*

[159] Smith, *The Puyallup-Nisqually*: p. 54.

[160] *Ibid.*

In accordance with the laying of emphasis on wealth and prestige among the coastal tribes, household "spirit" was much more important there than it was in the interior. House groups were rivals, vieing for social and economic prestige, and each individual was expected to contribute toward raising his house group's status.[161]

## Political Organization

Political authority was vested in the village chief, who, like the chief among the interior peoples, was principally advisor and "father" to his village. He admonished the lazy and shiftless, settled disputes, arbitrated feuds, and acted as judge in criminal cases. His actual executive authority was very limited, however.

In most of the tribes there was a strong tendency for the chieftainship to be hereditary, passing to a man's eldest son, or in case there was no son or he was unsatisfactory, to a brother, cousin, or nephew. Among the Songish and other tribes of the Strait of Georgia, chieftainship was very strictly hereditary, and great care was taken in preserving the chiefly family pedigree.

Barnett 's statement that "political power was coincident with social status" seems to apply in all the tribes.[162] In the Strait of Georgia tribes, the chief was the person holding highest rank and he was also head of the leading family or sept. Invariably, in all the groups, the chief was a very wealthy man. Olson [76] says that among the Quinault "it was assumed that to be a chief was to be a rich man, to be a rich man was to be a chief."[163] Thus, the Quinault chief owned the largest house, the most wives and slaves, and the greatest amount of property in general. The same was true of the Klallam chief, who also possessed the fish trap nearest the mouth of the river, a most cherished piece of property. A good Puyallup-Nisqually chief could hardly help being rich, for according to Smith, if he filled his position well, the people literally "showered him with gifts."[164]

## Social Stratification

Social stratification, whereas practically non-existent among the interior peoples, was an important aspect of Coast Salish social organization and one of the chief means of regulating social behavior. The different coastal tribes varied, however, in the degree of rigidity and formality characterizing the system of social stratification. The most strictly defined class structure was found among the Bella Coola and other tribes of the Strait of Georgia, where society was divided into four social strata: chiefs, nobles, commoners, and slaves. Class membership here was a matter of birth – one had to be born next. Family histories and genealogies were thus carefully kept and a person of blue blood would point proudly to his pedigree. Commoners were those persons who could not so boast of their ancestry.

In these groups where noble status was ascribed there was very little mobility in the larger class structure; commoners [77] could not through any means become members of the nobility. Within the commoner class itself, however, individuals could rise through the

---

161 *Ibid.*

162 Barnett, *op. cit*: p. 150.

163 Olson, *op. cit*: p. 95.

164 Smith, *The Puyallup-Nisqually*: p. 50.

acquisition of wealth, and for this reason a middle class developed in some of the tribes such as the Songish.  It included people who were not of noble birth, who had no "grandfather" and no "pedigree of honorable descent," but who had gained a certain amount of prestige through the accumulation and displayal <ok> of property.[165]

Inasmuch as nobility was determined by birth in these tribes and marriage was strictly within class boundaries.  It would seem that the term "caste" could be more appropriately applied than the term "class."  Barnett, however, has pointed out that it would be incorrect to speak of a caste structure as existing among the Strait of Georgia peoples, for one reason:  Though a person had to be the child of a nobleman to be himself a member of the nobility, not all descendants of nobles were of high rank.  This was due to the fact that, as among the Kwakiutl, the children of a nobleman were not all of equal status but were ranked according to their order of birth, the eldest thus being given the highest social standing and the larger part of the inheritance.  From the line of eldest sons there was a "gradual shading off .... so that the youngest son of a youngest son received precious little of the original patrimony," and evidently was not of noble status.[166]

Be that as it may, however, there did exist among the Strait of Georgia Salish a definite noble class with an organized body of privileges and distinguished by certain characteristic [78] modes of behavior.  Hill-Tout, in describing the behavior of members of the Songish nobility, says:

> The family pride and exclusiveness of the privileged classes was .... illustrated in every social function which they held and of these there were a goodly number, such as naming-feasts, marriage-feasts, mortuary-feasts, and the 'potlatch' or gift-feasts.  On these occasions the chiefs put on lofty and condescending airs, conversed only with one another, and formed a group apart by themselves.[167]

In none of the other tribes was class structure so rigidly defined and so absolutely hereditary.  Olson says that a Quinault chief and family were noble in that they were of "good blood" but this emphasis on blood he describes as "ill-defined."[168]  In this tribe it appears that wealth was about as important in determining rank as good birth.  There was no clear-cut line dividing nobility from commoners, but a series of intergradations.  Between the persons who were definitely noble and those who were definitely common, i.e., "from not of good Blood," there were:  (1) the rich man, not of noble birth,  (2) the newly rich, also not of noble birth,  (3) "people of good blood, but not nobles,"  (4) poor people, but not of poor blood.  A person through the acquisition of wealth could climb this social scale, and "in time even lowly origin would be overlooked or forgotten."[169]

In the Klallam tribe, also, wealth and blood were about equally important as determinants of rank.  Chieftainship was hereditary, but the successor of a chief had to justify his inheritance through the displayal <ok> of property.  A chief was one who could give big potlatches, and the

---

165    Charles Hill-Tout, "The Salish Tribes of the Coast and Lower Fraser Delta," *Annual Archaeological Report, 1905* (Toronto, 1906): p. 226.

166    Barnett, *op. cit*: p. 151.

167    Charles Hill-Tout, "The Salish Tribes of the Coast and Lower Fraser Delta," *op. cit*: p. 227.

168    Olson, *op. cit*: p. 95.

169    *Ibid.*, p. 90.

renown he got through this caused him to be recognized by the people as leader.  The upper class included [79] besides the chief and his family, persons not necessarily related to the chief, and hence not of especially good birth, but who possessed and exhibited much property.  The low class was composed of individuals who had never been able to acquire wealth, together with freed slaves and their children.

Among the Puyallup-Nisqually, according to Smith, there was practically no inheritance of rank.  Smith says that here "the culture .... conferred the patent of nobility not as the insignia of social caste but as a sort of judgment of worth."[170]  People with certain abilities and who because of them held positions of authority were considered "noble."  Such leaders, Smith points out, could be classified into three types:  (1) the professionals, including hunters, harpooners, canoe makers, and gamblers,  (2) the political leaders, and  (3) the warriors.[171]  All of these could, through their various abilities, acquire wealth.  The professionals could accumulate wealth by the exchange of their products and services for different kinds of property.  The political leaders and warriors could acquire property through gifts from the people in recognition of their services.

Smith states that practically all of the Puyallup-Nisqually people were of the high class since it included "any man or woman who took his place in the society by producing, procuring or manipulating property, or who participated in its affairs with any show of intelligence or arrogance."[172]

The closest approach to the hereditary nobility existent among the other coastal peoples lay in the case of the house leaders and village chiefs and their families, who tried to perpetuate their authority and prestige.  Low class people among the [80] Puyallup-Nisqually were known as "no-accounts" and were persons who were without village affiliation and thus filled no position in the life of the community, or who "shifted marital relations" frequently.[173]  A class structure similar to this of the Puget Sound tribes was also found among the Halkomelem groups of the Lower Fraser.

The lowest stratum in all the tribes was composed of slaves.  These were usually individuals who had been taken captive in war and made subservient to their captors.  Generally speaking, they were treated well and did about the same kind of work as did their masters.  They were excluded, however, from participation in most of the social life of the community.  They were not allowed to become members of the secret societies, scarcely ever married into the free classes, and could not seek to climb the social scale.  They were important as an index to wealth; in the words of Olson, ".... slaves were as important for ostentatious purposes as for the services they performed."[174]

Wealth was the symbol of rank in all of the Coast Salish tribes.  Among the Strait of Georgia groups, as we have seen, the inheritance of rank was accompanied by the inheritance of property, and all members of the nobility were at the same time owners of much wealth; the chief, who was highest in rank was also the richest person.  In the Quinault and Klallam tribes, too, high status was linked with the possession of wealth; to be of upper rank was to be rich, and

---

[170]  Smith, *The Puyallup-Nisqually*: p. 48.
[171]  *Ibid*: p. 49.
[172]  *Ibid*: p. 51.
[173]  *Ibid*: p. 52.
[174]  Olson, *op. cit*: p. 114.

vice versa.  As for the Puyallup-Nisqually tribes, Smith states: "The degree to which a man was well known and the amount of property he was capable of accumulating were the outward sign of his prestige."  Smith hastens to explain, however, that [81] the actual amount of property was not as important as "the way in which that property had been obtained, the ease with which it had been obtained and the manner in which it might be used."[175]

The mere possession of wealth in the form of canoes, slaves, houses, shell money, surplus food, etc., was not enough to maintain a person's prestige in any of the coastal groups.  He was obligated as a person of high status to exhibit his wealth through the distribution of gifts at potlatches.  The latter events were held in connection with a number of occasions such as the initiation of novices into the secret societies, the holding of guardian spirit sings and dances, the receiving of a name, and the death or reburial of an individual.  Gift distributions varied in elaborateness from the simple giving of presents to show one's gratitude for some act of service by another, to the immense potlatch affairs of the type held among the Kwakiutl, in which huge amounts of property were given away with the expectation of later receiving gifts of greater value from the donees.

## Secret Societies

Several of the Kwakiutl secret societies {guilds} spread to the Coast Salish tribes.  The Songish possessed the Tcyeyī'wan and QEnqanī'tEl societies, the latter corresponding to the Kwakiutl Tlokoā'la (Black Tamanous) and NōntlEm societies; and the Comox, Pentlatch, and Sanetch also had the NōntlEm.[176]  The secret societies of the Bella Coola (Sisau'kH and Kū'suit) and of the Quinault (Klo'kwalle and Tsa'jak) were equivalent to the northern Kwakiutl [82] Tlōola'qa (Black Tamanous) and Ts'ētsa'ēk•a.[177]  The Klallam had only one society, the xūnxanē'te, as did also the Puyallup-Nisqually (Black Tamanous).  These societies seem to be but attenuated forms of the more elaborate Kwakiutl societies, becoming increasingly paler reflections of the latter, the more distant the tribe from the Kwakiutl.

The Salish secret society, like that of the Kwakiutl, was thought to have its origin in the appearance of a certain spirit to the ancestor of the group, bestowing him with "power" and giving him certain songs and dances.  These secret rites were passed down to the individuals who came to make up the society.

The Nuxalk Bella Coola secret societies resembled the Kwakiutl societies more than did those of any other Coast Salish tribe.  Each sept {kindred} of the Bella Coola tribe had rights to certain secrets and dances of the Sisau'kH and Kū'suit societies and had its own masks or carvings which its members used in the secret society ceremonies.  It seems, however, that though the sacred objects and dances connected with the Sisau'hH society were owned by the various *septs*, they had to be acquired by each individual wishing to belong to the society.  As regards this, Boas says:

.... every free person has the right to acquire a certain group of carvings and names,

---

[175] Smith, *The Puyallup-Nisqually*: p. 49.

[176] Franz Boas, "Third Report on the Indians of British Columbia," *Report, Sixty-first Meeting of the British Association for the Advancement of Science* (1891): p. 579.

[177] Franz Boas, "Second Report on the Indians of British Columbia," *op. cit*: p. 412.

according to the gens to which he or she belongs ..... A person cannot take a new carving, but must wait until it is given to him by his relatives – father, mother, or elder brother.[178]

Apparently a person acquired secret society secrets at potlatch events, and when he was given a new secret, he also changed his name. Boas says:

> Each person has two names, a Kū'suit name, which remains the [83] same throughout life; and a Qē'mtsioa name, which is changed at these festivals .... These names are also the property of the various gentes, each gens having its own names."[179]

A man distributed his Sisau'kH secrets among his sons and daughters and might also give one or several to his daughter's husband.

The various dances connected with the *Ku'suit* were also owned by the septs. These too were given to individuals by their relatives but could not be presented to a son-in-law, or anyone else who was not a blood relative. When the individual was given his *Ku'suit* dance at some time following puberty, he went through an initiation ceremony in which he was also presented with his *Ku'suit* name.

A person wishing to join the Songish Tcyeyī'wan society went to the woods where he stayed until he finally dreamed of the dance he was to perform and the song he was to sing. He went back to the village and taught these to the members; the dance was performed and he was considered a member. Only wealthy individuals could belong to the Songish NōntlEm society, as very great payments were required. If an individual's father could not afford to make the payment he was sometimes assisted by his other relatives.

The Quinault did not ask heavy initiation payments. Indeed, according to Olson, "friends and relatives of members were often taken in without any initiation fee."[180] The Klallam society, however, exacted large fees from the initiates. For this reason there were usually more non-members than members in a village, and membership in the society was considered to be an indication of "high class."[181] [84]

The activities of a secret society centered around the initiation of new members, which in all of the tribes except the Klallam took place in the winter following the solstice. The usual procedure seems to have been to segregate the novices in a certain place, often the village potlatch house, for several days. During that period, they were taught the traditions of the society, its secrets, dances, songs, and other rites, none of which was ever divulged to non-members. While this was going on, the novices were supposed to have been killed and to have gone to the world of the supernatural where they communed with the spirit of the society. Then they were thought to return to life, being able as well as obliged to participate in the secret society dance. The dance itself was of a public nature and performed in the presence of non-members. Smith, in describing the Puyallup-Nisqually ceremony, says: ".... its rites were

---

[178] Franz Boas, "Third Report on the Indians of British Columbia," *op. cit*: p. 414.
[179] *Ibid.*
[180] Olson, *op. cit*: p. 121.
[181] Gunther, *op. cit*: p. 281.

characterized by a horrific and maniacal aspect meant to impress its beholders."[182]   A large potlatch was always held in connection with the secret society ceremony.

## Sept Organization

The people of the Squamish, Songish, Bella Coola, and other Strait of Georgia tribes were divided into kinship groups which have been variously designated by Boas and Hill-Tout as "clans," "gentes," and "septs."  Since in no case do these groups conform to the present definition of clans and gentes, we have chosen to call them septs.

A sept was composed of families who claimed descent from a common ancestor.  The sept's "first man" {first couple} supposedly was an individual "who was sent down from heaven by the deity, and who, in [85] some way or other, obtained his crest from a spirit."[183]   Each community consisted of several septs, although originally each sept was thought to have been coextensive with a single village.

Descent was in both the male and female lines of the sept; a child could belong to either parent's sept, the comparative rank and wealth of his parents probably being an important factor in determining his choice.  There seems to have been a preference for patrilineal descent, however, this perhaps being correlated with the facts that the sept was localized and residence was patrilocal.

The septs were exogamous, but it appears that members of septs located in the same village were permitted to marry, provided they were at least third cousins.  The Bella Coola had two pairs of intermarrying septs.

We have only scattered bits of information on the septs, but we can probably safely assume that in their most developed form they were much like the Kwakiutl *numayms*:  that is, they each possessed a tradition of origin, a body of names to be applied to children, specific rights in the secret societies, certain houses, etc.  As among the Kwakiutl, the septs of a village were no doubt ranked with the oldest one being the leading one and its head man being the village chief. [86 IV]

---

[182]  Smith, *The Puyallup-Nisqually*: p. 92.

[183]  Franz Boas, "Preliminary Notes on the Indians of British Columbia," *Report, Fifty-eighth Meeting of British Association for the Advancement of Science* (London: John Murray Co 1889): p. 237.

## CHAPTER IV
## THE KINSHIP SYSTEM OF THE COAST SALISH

In considering Coast Salish kinship the same plan of discussion will be followed as was used in the section on Interior Salish kinship.  The kinship terminology will be described first, and this will be followed by a discussion of the variant types of Coast Salish kinship and a description of kinship behavior.

### <u>Kinship Terminology</u>

#### Consanguineal Terminology

<u>Second ascending generation</u>. – The coastal tribes do not distinguish between maternal and paternal grandparents.  Instead, we find either the use of two terms, <u>grandfather</u> and <u>grandmother</u>, as in the Quinault,[184] Bella Coola,[185] and Puget Sound tribes,[186] or the use of one term, <u>grandparent</u>, as among the Klallam[187] and tribes of the Strait of Georgia.[188]  These grandparental terms are extended to [87] the grandparents' siblings and in the Puget Sound tribes, at least, to the grandparents' cousins and other relatives of the grandparental generation.

<u>First ascending generation</u>. – Relatives on the father's side are not differentiated from relatives on the mother's side.  Either two terms, uncle and aunt, are applied to parental siblings, as among the Bella Coola, Quinault, and Puget Sound tribes, or one term is used for all siblings of the parents, regardless of sex, as in the Klallam and Strait of Georgia tribes.  In the Klallam tribe, an age distinction is made in the terminology for the parents' siblings, these relatives being called <u>parent's older sibling</u> and <u>parent's younger sibling</u>.  In the southern Puget Sound groups, and probably in the other tribes as well, the terms for parents' siblings are extended to the parents' cousins and other members of the first ascending generation.

<u>*Ego*'s generation</u>. – Two terms <u>older sibling</u> and <u>younger sibling</u> are used by most of the coastal tribes, and, as in the case of the Interior Salish, these terms are applied to cousins, both parallel and cross.  The tribes differ, however, in the ways in which sibling terms are extended to

---

[184]  For Quinault kinship terminology, see Olson, *op cit*: pp. 91-92.

[185]  For Bella Coola kinship terminology, see Boas, "Second Report on the Indians of British Columbia," *op. cit*: p. 689.

[186]  For kinship terminology of the southern Puget Sound tribes, see Smith, *The Puyallup-Nisqually*: pp. 173-175.

[187]  For Klallam kinship terminology, see Gunther, *op. cit*: pp. 258-259.

[188]  For kinship terminology of the Strait of Georgia tribes, see Boas, "Second Report on the Indians of British Columbia," *op. cit*: p. 688; Charles Hill-Tout, "Report on the Ethnology of the Southeastern Tribes of Vancouver Island," *Journal of the Royal Anthropological Institute*, XXXVII (1907): 352-354; Charles Hill-Tout, "Report on the Ethnology of the Siciatl of British Columbia," *Journal of the Royal anthropological Institute*, XXXIV (1904), 80-81; Barnett, *op. cit*: p. 155.

cousins.  Among the Strait of Georgia and Lower Fraser tribes,[189] children of parents' older siblings are called "older siblings" and children of parents' younger siblings are called "younger siblings."  In the Puget Sound tribes, the terms are applied to cousins according to whether the cousins are older or younger than *ego*.

The Quinault call siblings <u>older brother</u>, <u>older sister</u>, and <u>younger sibling</u>; however, these terms are not applied to cousins [88] but rather a general term <u>sibling</u> is used for the latter.  It is not clear from the data whether the Klallam terms <u>older sibling</u> and <u>younger sibling</u> are extended to cousins; we do know that two other sibling terms which denote sex, but not age, difference are used for cousins.

<u>First descending generation</u>. – All the tribes for which we have terminologies use one general term for nephews and nieces, on both sides.  In the Puget Sound tribes the nepotic term is extended to the children of cousins and all reciprocals of "aunts" and "uncles."  This is probably the case in the other tribes, also.  The Klallam distinguish between children of *ego*'s older sibling and younger sibling.

<u>Second descending generation</u>. – Most of the coastal tribes call members of this generation by the term <u>grandchild</u>.  The Tcil'qeuk use the self-reciprocal term <u>se'la</u>.

Affinal Terminology

In all the tribes, except the Quinault, one term with no differentiation as to sex is used for parents-in-law.  This term is extended to siblings of the parents-in-law in the Puget Sound tribes, and probably in the other groups also.  The Puget Sound tribes call the spouses of parents' siblings "uncle" and "aunt."  The other tribes give these affinal relatives a distinctive term and make no sex differentiation.

A self-reciprocal term is used between all siblings-in-law in the Squamish, Kwantlen, and Quinault tribes.  In the Puget Sound and Songish systems, wife's brother is differentiated from wife's sister; wife's sister and brother's wife are called "sister-in-law" and wife's brother and sister's husband are "brother-in-law."  There are separate terms for spouse of wife's siblings.  Wife's siblings' children are called by the nepotic terra.  The [89] Klallam distinguish between younger brother's wife and older brother's wife.

Comparing the Puyallup-Nisqually affinal system with that of the Interior Sinkaietk, we find that differences are not very any.  The Sinkaletk make a sex differentiation in the case of the parents-in-law while the Puyallup-Nisqually do not.  The Sinkaietk and Puyallup-Nisqually both call wife's brother and sister's husband by the same term, but the Sinkaietk also extend this term to wife's sister's husband while the Puyallup-Nisqually do not.  In all other respects the systems are alike.  As in consanguineal terminology, so in affinal terminology there seems to be less differentiation as to sex in the Strait of Georgia tribes than in the Puget Sound and Quinault tribes.

---

[189]  For kinship terminology of the Lower Fraser tribes, see Charles Hill-Tout, "Ethnological Studies of the Mainland Halkomelem," *Report, Seventy-second Meeting of the British Association for the Advancement of Science* (London:  John Murray Co 1903): pp. 366sq.

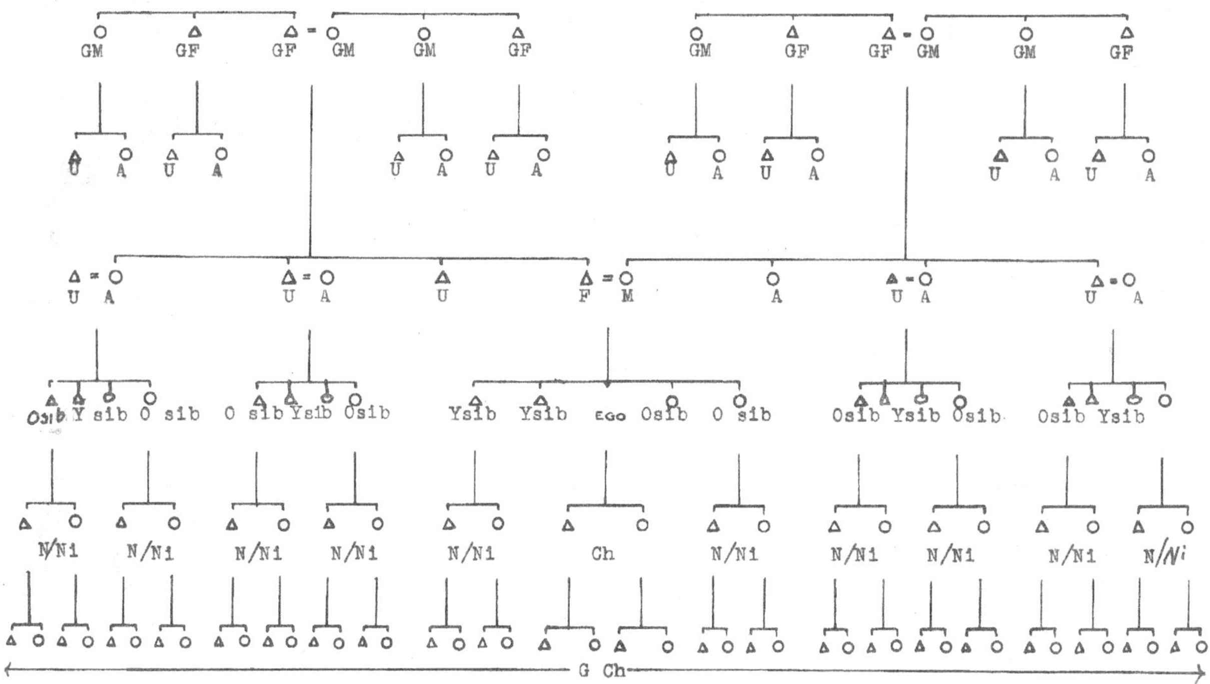

Fig. 4.

KLALLAM KINSHIP SYSTEM

[91]

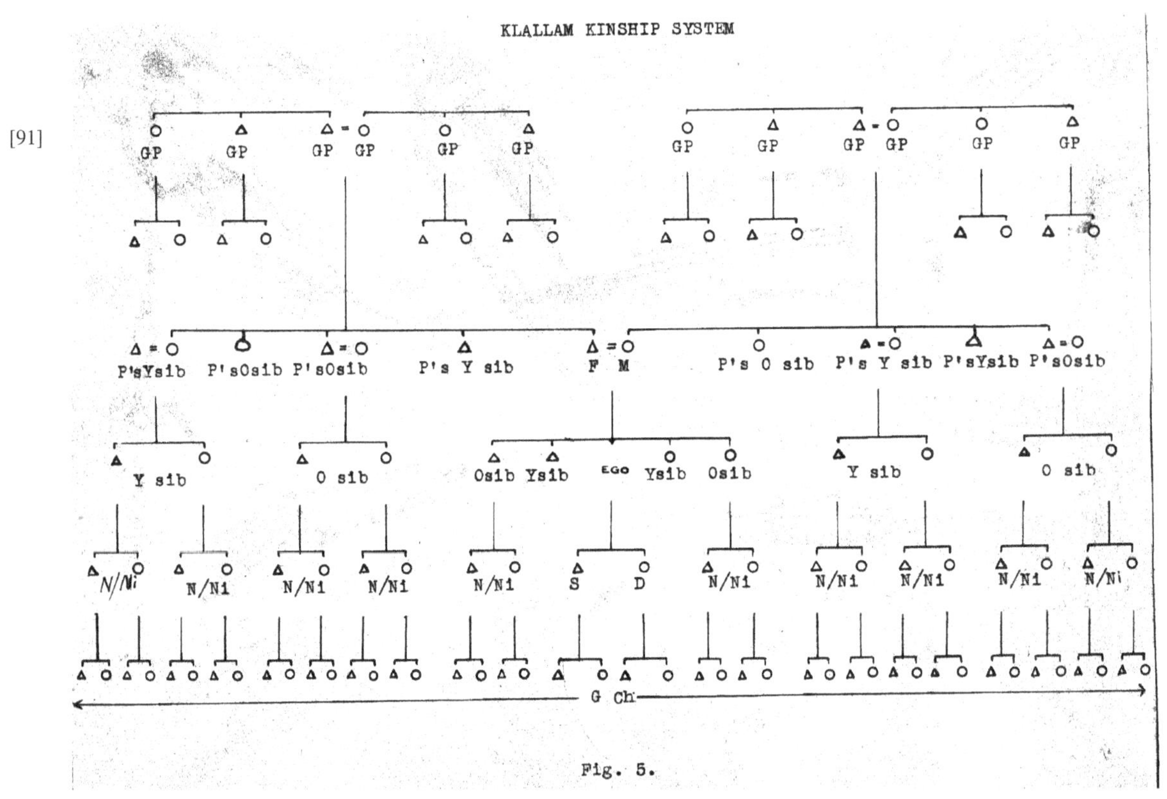

Fig. 5.

## Additional Terminology

As in the case of the Interior Salish, the terms for certain kin, including siblings' children, spouse's relatives, aunts and uncles, were changed after the death of the connecting relative. Also, the deceased himself was called by a different term following his death. Thus, the Klallam and Quinault had terms for "deceased wife," "deceased husband," and "deceased parent."

In some of the coastal tribes, as in the Lillooet of the interior, special terms of address (as distinct from terms of reference) were used for certain relatives, including husband, wife, mother, father, son, daughter.

All the tribes had different terms for children of different ages. Thus it was customary to speak of an eldest, youngest, or middle child.

Other terms used by the Coast Salish included those for step-parent, step-child, half-sister, half-brother, parent-in-law of one's child, brother's mother-in-law, etc. [92]

## Extension of Kinship Terminology

The terms extended to distant blood relatives were the terms for immediate lineal relatives or near collateral relatives. Thus, siblings and cousins of grandparents were equated with grandparents; parents' cousins were equated with parents' siblings; cousins, both far and near, were called by sibling terms; children of all "siblings" were called by the nepotic term; grandchildren of siblings were "grandchildren." Kinship consequently had a wide lateral spread, just as among the Interior peoples, and an individual's relatives were legion. The Coast Salish varied in the extent to which kinship was reckoned vertically; the Puyallup-Nisqually individual could carry his genealogy back only two or three generations, but in the Strait of Georgia tribes, kinship was reckoned to the fifth or sixth generation or even further. Some of the Coast Salish also applied consanguineal terms to step-relatives and relatives by adoption. Olson, commenting on kinship extension among the Quinault, says:

> The kinship bond was strong and effective no matter how remote the genealogical relationship. The result was that every person counted his kinsmen in hundreds. The duties of aid, of hospitality, of blood revenge, of not quite formal visits between relatives seem to have held between an exceptionally large number of persons. Close blood kinship, however, naturally counted for more than remote relationship.[190]

Affinal terminology was also extended to more distant relatives by marriage. For example, in the Puyallup-Nisqually tribes affinal terms were extended, as follows:

1. The term for sister-in-law was applied to "cousin [female] of living spouse; wife of living male sibling or cousin; females related by marriage to siblings or cousins."

2. The term for brother-in-law was used for "cousin [male] of living female sibling or cousin; males related by marriage to siblings or cousins." [93]

3. The term for parent-in-law was extended to "all blood relatives of living spouse in second,

---

[190] Olson, *op. cit*: p. 89.

third and fourth generations."[191]

## Differences in Coast Salish Kinship

Two variant systems also appear in Coast Salish kinship.  (See fig. 4 and 5.)  The first of these is found among the southern Puget Sound tribes, and among the Quinault and Bella Coola.  The second occurs among the Klallam and the Strait of Georgia tribes.  These two systems differ in two respects:

1.  The southern Puget Sound, Quinault, and Bella Coola tribes make a sex differentiation in the case of relatives of the first and second ascending generation; the other tribes do not.
2.  The former tribes extend sibling terms to cousins according to whether they are younger or older than *ego*; the latter make the extension according to whether they are the children of *ego*'s parents younger sibling or older sibling.

A further variation is found in the case of the Klallam system.  The Klallam emphasize age distinctions more than do the other tribes, differentiating between parents' older and younger siblings, between children of *ego*'s older and younger siblings, and between *ego*'s younger sibling's spouse and his older sibling's spouse.  The writer suspects that the tribes of the Strait of Georgia may also have made these age distinctions, the ethnographers failing to record them.

## Kinship Behavior

### The Life Cycle

<u>Birth</u>. – A woman at childbirth was secluded in a corner of the house or in some isolated spot.  Usually she was attended by one of the village midwives, although occasionally the husband might assist. [94]

According to Smith, there was no ceremony during or after childbirth among the southern Puget Sound groups.[192]  Gunther does not describe a ceremony so far as the Klallam are concerned, either, but does state that while the child was being born the husband, parents and parents-in-law of the woman prayed for a safe delivery.[193]  In the Tillamook tribe all of the relatives were called into the house at the birth of a child because it was believed that if they were present and each called the child by the correct term of relationship, it would not die.[194]

<u>Infancy</u>. – It seems to have been the custom in several of the tribes to have a child's ears pierced when it was very young by the mother or some other older female.  No special ceremony was involved, however.  Most of the Coast Salish tribes also practiced head deformation of the young.  In the more northern tribes, head flattening was a sign of good birth, and there seem to

---

[191]  Smith, *The Puyallup-Nisqually*: p. 175.

[192]  *Ibid*: p. 179.

[193]  Gunther, *op. cit*: p. 234.

[194]  Franz Boas, "Notes on the Tillamook" ("University of California Publications in Archaeology and Ethnology," XX [Berkeley, 1899]: 6.

have been different degrees of it corresponding to the different ranks, slaves being forbidden to deform their children's heads.  In the Puyallup-Nisqually tribe, however, "it was done to all children as a mark of parental care and solicitude .... for an undeformed head was not beautiful."[195]

A naming ceremony was held for children when they were about one year old or had reached walking age.  The name was bestowed by one of the grandparents from either the maternal or the eternal side.  Often the name given a person when he was very young was not an important one, and later he might assume a better [95] one.  According to Gunther, any time a person of the Klallam tribe had enough property "to do honor to a great name in his family" he might give a potlatch and take the name.[196]  Similarly, among the Strait of Georgia tribes, new family names could, be taken by individuals at puberty, marriage, or on other occasions; in con- action with each naming a potlatch was given by the maternal or paternal kin of the person taking the name.  In all of the coastal groups names were considered the property of families and the use of a certain name was exclusive to members of the family owning those names.

<u>Childhood</u>. – As among the interior peoples, this was a period of play and training.  The favorite childhood games were those imitative of adult occupations.  In the winter evening hours, children were told myths and led in indoor games by adults. Girls and boys played together until puberty.

Children were quite strictly disciplined by their elders.  In the Puyallup-Nisqually tribes they ate after the older people had eaten; they were not given the better portions of food and were not allowed to visit the family larder between meals, when they played indoors they were expected to keep very quiet.  Smith says:

> Rules on quiet in the house and against taking food were enforced by frightening the children with tales of tsiātko or wild Indians and of the cannibal woman who carried children off in the basket on her back and devoured them.[197]

Such methods of scaring children into behaving themselves, however, were not employed by the children's own parents but by other elders of the house or village.  Parents punished their disobedient offspring by whipping them. [96]

From the time they were about five or six years old until puberty, children of the Coast Salish tribes were required to go through a Spartan-like training designed to prepare them for the acquisition of guardian spirits, as well as to make them strong, healthy, and of good moral fiber.  The program included waking at dawn, bathing in the icy waters of the creeks, taking brisk rub- downs, and going on trips into the woods.  In the Puyallup-Nisqually tribes there were special "trainers" in charge of the program and the children's parents never interfered with them.

During the years preceding puberty, too, the children were instructed in the various duties connected with maintaining a living.  Boys learned how to fish and hunt by accompanying their fathers and uncles on fishing and hunting expeditions.  Girls practiced the various female tasks such as cooking and making mats and baskets.

---

[195]  Smith. *The Puyallup-Nisqually*: p. 185.
[196]  Gunther, *op. cit*: p. 239.
[197]  Smith, *The Puyallup-Nisqually*: p. 187.

<u>Puberty</u>.  Barnett's statement that this was the "time par excellence" for seeking guardian spirits seems to hold in all of the tribes.[198]  During the winter training period, pubescent or near-pubescent boys would go to secluded spots and stay there until they had acquired guardian spirits or had become so weak they had to return to camp.  While thus isolated, they fasted, bathed, rubbed themselves with boughs, swam, and dived; finally, they were visited by their spirits.  Barnett, in describing the spirit visit as it occurred in the Strait of Georgia tribes says that when the seeker had reached a point of exhaustion or unconsciousness, "he received a vision, a song, a spirit cry, and promise of help according to the nature of his wishes.  Otherwise his experience came in a dream .... Dreams .... gave luck in hunting, in acquiring wealth, in fighting, in doctoring."[199]  [97]

Smith states that though boys of the southern Puget Sound tribes were urged by their trainers, fathers, and grandfathers to undertake spirit quests, actually only a small percentage of such quests were successful.  However,

> .... power could be obtained in other ways and there was no particular power which could be obtained solely by quest, so it formed no necessary part of' the training of shamans, warriors and other important 'power men'.[200]

At the approach of the first menses, a girl was secluded behind a mat partition in the house or in a separate hut.  While in isolation, she bathed, rubbed herself with boughs, underwent a period of fasting, did not drink or talk, and slept vary little.  She also made mats or baskets and was trained in the behavior expected of an adult female in the society.  During her seclusion, she was attended and instructed by a close female relative – mother, aunt, or grandmother.

In the Klallam and Strait of Georgia tribes a very important public ceremony was held after the girl's seclusion, the purpose of which was to mark her entrance into the adult life of the society and to announce the fact that she was now of marriageable age.[201]  Gunther says that the girl for whom the ceremony was not given really had no social standing, and so if the parents were too poor, some other relative – uncle, aunt, grandparent on either side – might give the feast for her.  The first part of the ceremony consisted of a sing to which families only were invited, and this was followed by the presentation of gifts to the guests by the girl's father or relative; then on the last day men were invited to a feast.[202]

As among the Interior Salish, during the period between [98] puberty and marriage, a girl was closely guarded, and carefully chaperoned by her mother or some other female relative wherever she went.  She was supposed to act "shy," especially when boys were near, and was expected to speak very little.

<u>Marriage</u>. – Relatives perhaps figured more prominently in the ceremony and practices relating to rnarriage than in those attending any other life crisis.  The preferred type of marriage

---

[198]  Barnett, *op. cit*: p. 136.

[199]  *Ibid.*

[200]  Smith, *The Puyallup-Nisqually*: p. 194.

[201]  Gunther, *op. cit*: 239.

[202]  *Ibid*: p. 210.

as that involving an exchange of goods between the two kin groups. Such a marriage was costly and a boy needed the assistance of his relatives in gathering together the property required for the bride payment and for distribution among her relatives. Indeed, it was probably only among the wealthier people that this type of marriage was possible.

The marriage proposal was made by the young man, his father, or his uncle. If accepted, the boy, with his relatives and friends, would go to the girl's house and present her father and relatives with gifts. The two families would usually feast together and then the girl's father would distribute food or gifts among the boy's relatives. Exchange of visits and gifts between the two families generally continued for some time afterward, and the marriage placed them in a permanent reciprocal relationship, economically and socially.

Polygyny was permissible in the Coast Salish tribes and practiced by all who could afford supporting several wives. Sororal polygyny was the usual type. The sororate and levirate, though not compulsory, were usually observed. There seem to have been no rules governing marriage except that forbidding the wedding of relatives. In some tribes, such as the Quinault, the rule forbidding marriage between kin applied to all relatives, no matter how remote. Olson says this may explain the rarity of intratribal [99] marriages in the case of the Quinault for since most of the members of the village were related, a mate often had to be sought outside of the local, or even tribal group.[203] In other tribes, distant relatives could marry; among the Bella Coola and a number of the Strait of Georgia tribes, for instance, the union of third cousins was allowed.

Village exogamy was the mechanism through which the kinship group was spread over a large territory among the Coast Salish. Barnett says that members of the Strait of Georgia tribes married outside of the village "to insure help in trouble" and to have as many 'homes' as possible."[204] Intervillage marital unions were expensive, involving exchanges of large quantities of goods, and hence prohibitive so far as the poor people were concerned. {Dynastic} Marriages between distant villages or between tribes were especially important, almost "political" in nature, and usually concerned the families of village chiefs or other persons of high rank. Gunther says in regard to the desirability of this sort of marriage in the Klallam tribe:

> People of high rank want their sons and daughters to marry outside of the tribe on account of the political ties that are established in this way. If, however, such a marriage cannot be arranged, then it becomes necessary to marry a first cousin in order to avoid union with a person of lower rank.[205]

The emphasis on wealth and rank in marriage of the noble class reached a rather ridiculous peak in groups such as the Comox. According to Barnett,

> The Comox aristocrats performed a travesty {!} of marriages without a bride for the sole purpose or acquiring privileges in the exchange. This was their chief concern and consequently marriages were unstable.[206] [100]

---

[203] Olson, *op.cit*: p. 89.

[204] Barnett, *op. cit*: p. 135.

[205] Gunther, *op. cit*: p. 241.

[206] Barnett., *op. cit*: p. 153.

<u>Death</u>. – At the death of an individual much wailing and weeping was done by his relatives and friends, and close relatives further showed their grief by fasting, cutting their hair, and blackening their faces.  Among the Puyallup-Nisqually, the deceased's spouse had to go through a period of purification consisting of sweatbathing, plunges in icy water, and body rubbing.  Smith says:

> Because of every day and of sexual contacts between spouses a strong identification was felt to exist between them.  The purification was designed to complete the separation caused by death, to 'remove the smell' of the deceased, to 'make the one who was alive a whole person'.[207]

Frequently, in the case of the rich, a potlatch was given by a close relative of the deceased either at the time of the death or later at reburial of the remains.  The avowed purpose of the potlatch was "to honor the dead"[208] but it also served the living in helping to increase or maintain the donor's prestige just as did all potlatches.

## Patterns of Kinship Behavior

The behavior characterizing the various kinship relationships found among the Coast Salish resembled that existing among the Interior Salish.  An individual's relatives, in the coastal tribes, celebrated the different life crises with more elaborate ceremonies – feasts, gift distributions, and the like – than was the case among the interior tribes; however, the same <u>patterns</u> of kinship behavior existed among both branches of Salish.

Parents instructed, and disciplined their children and did all they could to see that their children were properly oriented in the society.  They encouraged their sons in their quests for [101] guardian spirits; if wealthy enough, they paid the required fee for their children's initiation into the secret societies; and, assisted by relatives, they attended to the gift giving and other social obligations involved in their children's marriage.

Uncles and aunts assisted the parents in their duties toward their children.  Gunther's description of the uncle-nephew relationship among the Klallam is typical:

> An uncle gives advice to his nephew just as a father would to his son.  He is always interested in his nephew's welfare.  If the parents should be too poor to have their son join the secret society his uncle might help him.  A nephew gives a larger share of fish or game to his uncle than he would give to any other older person.[209]

An aunt would aid a girl's mother in instructing her in the women's duties and helped attend her while she was in her puberty seclusion.

Likewise, the behavior connected with other relationships was similar to that associated with corresponding relationships among the Interior Salish.  There existed the same close

---

[207] Smith, *The Puyallup-Nisqually*: p. 304.

[208] *Ibid*: p. 205.

[209] Gunther, *op. cit*: 260.

relationship between siblings, the same friendly relationship between grandparents and grandchildren, the same economically reciprocal and jealous relationship between husbands and wives.  There were no parent-in-law tabus.  [102]

## CHAPTER V
## THE CLASSIFICATION OF SALISH KINSHIP AND
## THE RECONSTRUCTION OF THE EARLY KINSHIP TYPE

In Chapter II It was shown that Interior Salish kinship systems could be divided into two types: that found among the Northern Okanagon, Sinkaiatk, Kalispel, Spokan, and Flathead; and that occurring among the Thompson, Shuswap, and Lillooet. This separation could be made on the basis of the fact that while the former groups distinguish between, maternal and paternal relatives in the first and second ascending generations, the latter tribes do not. In Chapter IV it was pointed out that two kinship types also exist among the Coast Salish. The Puget Sound tribes, the Quinault, and the Bella Coola, on the one hand, share with the Thompson, Shuswap, and Lillooet in their type of kinship system. The peoples of Vancouver Island, the Lower Eraser area, and the Strait of Georgia region, on the other hand, possess a system which is distinct from all other Salish systems in that there is an absence of terminologic distinction of sex. This latter system is also characterized by an increased differentiation as to relative age.

Within the three main divisions of Salish kinship certain minor variations occur. Thus, the systems of the Kalispel, Spokan, and Flathead differ from those of the Northern Okanagon and Sinkaietk in that they are characterized by the use of self-reciprocal terms between members of the first ascending and first descending generations. The chief point of difference between the systems of the Thompson, Shuswap, and Lillooet and those of the [103] Puget Sound, Quinault, and Bella Coola tribes lies also in nepotic terminology. While the former call nephew and niece by terms equivalent or similar to the terms for son and daughter, the latter use a generalized nephew-niece term. In the third division the Klallam represent a variant in that they make an age distinction between the parental siblings and between children of *ego*'s older and younger siblings.

In short, the terminologies of the three divisions of Salish kinship can be summarized as in the following table:

## TABLE 2
## SALISH KINSHIP TERMINOLOGIES

| Generation | I<br>K., Ok., Sink., Kal., Sp., Flthd. | II<br>Thomp., Shus., Lit., P-N., Quin., B.C. | III<br>Vancouver Is., L Fraser, St. of Geo. |
|---|---|---|---|
| Second ascending | FF, FM, MF, MM | GP, GM | GP |
| First ascending | FS, FB, MS, MB<br><br>F-in-L, M-in-L | U, A<br><br>Sh., Th., F-in-L, M-in-L<br><br>Others: P-in-L. | Par. sib. (with age differentiation in Klallam)<br><br>P-in-L |
| *Ego*'s | OB, YB, OS, YS<br>B-in-L, Sis-in-L | O sib, Y sib<br>Th, Quin.: Sib-in-L<br>Others: B-in-L, Sis-in-L | 0 sib, Y sib<br>Sib-in-L |

| First descending | N., Ok., Sink.;<br>N/Ni<br>Flathd: self-reciprocal<br><br>S-in-L, D-in-L | Th,, Sh., Lil: S, D, or N, Ni<br>Others: N/Ni | N/Ni (with distinction between children of *ego*'s Osib and Ysib in Klallam) |
|---|---|---|---|
| Second descending | G Ch or self-reciprocal | G Ch | G Ch |

[104]

The setting up of these divisions raises the historical question of what the early Salish kinship system was like before differences developed.  To a certain extent, by comparing the various systems and their native terminologies, we can reconstruct the old system.  We know, to begin with, that those characteristics which are common to all of the Salish system probably belonged also to the parent type.  These characteristics may be listed as follows:

1. The differentiation of lineal and collateral relatives in the first ascending and first descending generations, but the merging of lineal and collateral relatives in the second ascending, *ego*'s and second descending generations.

2. The distinction of generation, each generation having its own set of terms.

3. The extension of terms to collateral relatives by equating either siblings or cousins, or both. Thus, in the second ascending generation, grandparents are equated with their siblings and cousins, and the terms for grandparents-in-law are extended to their siblings and cousins.  In the parental generation, uncles and aunts are equated with the parental cousins, and terms for parents-in-law are extended to their siblings and cousins.  Similarly, in *ego*'s generation and the generations below him, the terms for lineal relatives or immediate collateral relatives are extended to other relatives, and the terms for *ego*'s close affinal kin are applied to his more distant affinal relatives.


Knowing these more general characteristics of the early Salish kinship type, then, we are left with the problem of determining the more specific features of terminology.  There remain such questions as:  In the generations above *ego* were relatives on the two parental sides differentiated or lumped together?  To what extent were sex and age differences indicated?  How were nephews and nieces termed?

In order to answer these questions we must compare the native kinship vocabularies and determine cognate forms, knowing that if a cognate form is of wide distribution it probably represents a feature of the original system.[210]  The reconstruction [105] attempted here on the basis of such a comparison, however, is limited by two factors:  (1) the incompleteness of the individual kinship schedules, and  (2) the writer's lack of knowledge of sound shifts in the Salish languages (by which are determined the linguistic cognates).  Because of these limitations the reconstruction of the early Salish kinship type is but a tentative one, subject to later correction.


<u>Grandchildren</u>. – Although self-reciprocal terms are used in several of the interior tribes

---

[210] Alternatively, of course, it may have spread by diffusion at a later time, but this is less likely.

and in at least one of the coastal tribes, the term <u>grandchild</u> is found in practically all of the Salish groups and the native words are cognate.  Compare:  Okanagon, <u>snemats</u>; Lillooet, <u>ēmatc</u> Thompson, <u>ē'mitc</u>; Shuswap, <u>ēmts</u>; Puyallup-Nisqually, <u>ebats;</u> Quinault, <u>ane'mats;</u> Squamish, <u>ē'mats</u>; Bella Coola, <u>stlēmts</u>.  It appears certain, then, that a term grandchild was a feature of the early system.  There is a possibility too that self-reciprocal terminology was used, but whether this was an actuality cannot be stated; it seems more probable because of its limited distribution that this usage was a later development.

    <u>Nephews and nieces</u>. – Although a good deal of variance exists in nepotic terminology among the Interior Salish, the occurrence of a generalized nephew-niece term among the Northern Okanagon and Sinkaietk which is cognative {cognate} with corresponding terms in coastal systems would seem to suggest that such a term was characteristic of the early system. Compare:  Sinkaietk, <u>sɫEɫEwīlt</u>; Puyallup-Nisqually, <u>stálaɫ</u>; Squamish, <u>stai'atl</u>; Songlsh, <u>stēkwEn</u>. The use of self-reciprocal terminology found among the Flathead probably represents a more recent development due to influence from the Kootenay, whose kinship system closely resembles [106] that of the Flathead.[211]

    <u>Parents and Children</u>. – Coastal and interior terminologies have diverged so greatly in regard to terms for parents and children that we cannot draw any definite conclusions as to original terminology.  There must have been terms for mother and father and probably a term each for son and daughter, although the present Coast Salish do not differentiate between the two.

    <u>Uncles and Aunts</u>. – The Sinkaietk, northern Okanagon, Flathead, Kalispel, and Spokan have four terms:

TABLE 3

UNCLE AND AUNT TERMINOLOGY

| | Northern Okanagon | Sinkaietk | Flathead | Kalispel | Spokan |
|---|---|---|---|---|---|
| FB | sumī'ɫ$^x$ | smīɫ | səmiɛl | sm'ē1 | si-māhl |
| FS | sqō'kwē | sk!ō'qwe (♂ sp) <br> stata'kwa (♀ sp) | skukwi (♂ sp) <br> titi•kwɛ (♀ sp) | skokoi (♂ sp) <br> tikul (♀ sp) | sko'-qe-i |
| MB | sEsī' | sEsī' | si: or sī•ɛ | s' si'i | si-i |
| MS | suwa'wa'sa | swawa'sa | kágɛ | ka'ge | ká-ha-e |

    The Thompson, Shuswap, Lillooet, Puyallup-Nisqually, and Bella Coola have two terms:

---

[211]   See H.H. Turney-High, *Ethnography of the Kutenai* ("Memoirs of the American Anthropologist Association," #56 [Menasha, 1941]: pp. 140-143.

## TABLE 4

### UNCLE AND AUNT TERMINOLOGY

|  | Thompson | Shuswap | Lillooet | Puyallup-Nisqually | Bella Coola | Tcilqeuk |
|---|---|---|---|---|---|---|
| Uncle | cī'ckah | si'sa la'ua | cēck'ā'a | kasi | sī'si | squmElē'k•Q |
| Aunt | skōz' | to'ma k'ō'ya | stā'a | pos | siskHsō'm | t'scwumElek |

[107]

The other tribes have one term "parental sibling":  Kwantlen, cqEmnēkq; Squamish, sīaī; Siciatl, tcāp'ts; Songish, satc'a; Klallam, tsa'tcts, kłē'tłk; Bella Coola, sī'si.

Cognate forms of sEsī appear rather consistently throughout the terminologies and this suggests that they may represent a term of the old Salish system.  There is the question, however, of whether sEsī (or some form of it) originally meant "mother's brother," "uncle," or "parental sibling."  If the early system was characterized by the use of the term "parental sibling," we should expect to find in the tribes retaining that usage a reasonable number of cognates of sEsī.  Such is not the case, however, as an inspection of the above terms for "parental sibling" will show.

The next possibility is that sEsī, as originally used, meant "uncle."  We find in examining the terms for "uncle" in those tribes which do not differentiate between the two parental sides, that all with the exception of one are cognate.  If it were not for this one exception, it would be just as reasonable to assume that in the old Salish system sEsī meant "uncle" as it would be to assume that it meant "mother's brother."  However, the one exceptional term – the Tcilqeuk term squmElē'k•Q – appears to be a cognate of the Interior Salish terms for father's brother (e.g., compare with Okanagon sumī'ł$^x$).  This would make it seem somewhat more likely that formerly there were two terms, mother's brother and father's brother; most of the tribes retained the native term for mother's brother and applied it to both maternal and paternal uncles or all parental siblings, regardless of sex, but the Tcilqeuk kept the native term for father's brother and used it to designate both kinds of uncles.

Corresponding to two uncle terms would be two aunt terms, [108] father's sister and mother's sister.  To support belief as to the existence of the latter is the tacit of similarity in the native terms meaning "aunt" in the Thompson, Shuswap, Lillooet, Puyallup-Nisqually, and Bella Coola tribes.  If the more generalized term "aunt" characterized the old system, rather than the two terms mother's sister and father's sister, again we should expect in the tribes retaining such a usage a reasonable number of cognate forms.  But inspection of the terms shows that they are not at all similar.  The Thompson term skōz' seems related to the Okanagon, Flathead, Kalispel, and Spokan terms for father's sister (♂ speaking), whereas the Lillooet term stā'a is similar to the terms used by these same tribes for father's sister (♀ speaking).  This suggests that the Okanagon, Flathead, Kalispel, and Spokan system represent the original contributing system from which the Thompson, Shuswap, Lillooet, and coastal systems diverged.  Thus, the evidence, though not by any means conclusive, points more toward the existence of four terms for parental siblings rather than just two or one.

Grandparents. – The Sinkaietk and Flathead, have four terms:

TABLE 5
GRANDPARENTAL TERMINOLOGY

|  | Sinkaietk | Flathead |
|---|---|---|
| Father's father | sxa'xba | s̲gɛpɛ |
| Father's mother | ka'qEna' | k'e'nɛ |
| Mother's father | k!ēk!wa | si'•lɛ |
| Mother's mother | stEmtī'ma | tc•tc•γ'ɛ |

[109]

The Thompson, Shuswap, Lillooet, Puyallup-Nisqually, Quinault, and Bella Coola have two terms:

TABLE 6
GRANDPARENTAL TERMINOLOGY

|  | Thompson | Shuswap | Lillooet | Puyallup-Nisqually | Quinault | Bella Coola |
|---|---|---|---|---|---|---|
| Grandfather | capazā | slɑ'a | dz'itsp'ā'a | sápa | anstco'pa | ko'kpi |
| Grandmother | k•zā' | gyā'a | ku'koāa | káiya | anstci' | gigia' |

All the other tribes have one term "grandparent," and the native words are all cognate: Tcilqeuk, sē'la; Kwantlen, se'la; Squamish, se'la, Siciatl, se'la; etc.

The widespread distribution of forms of sí•lɛ indicates that a parent form of it must have been one of the early Salish terms. This means that sí•lɛ at one time meant either "grandparent" or "mother's father." If we were to conclude that it originally meant "grandparent," this would mean that the Thompson, Shuswap, Lillooet, Puyallup-Nisqually, and Bella Coola tribes all dropped sí•lɛ when their system changed to one with two grandparental terms, not one of them keeping it, and devised two new native terms, all of the same stem (a remarkable fact considering the geographical separateness of the Bella Coola from the other tribes). A much much <ok> more likely explanation would be that primitive Salish had four grandparental terms; that the Thompson, Lillooet, Shuawap, Bella Coola, and Puget Sound tribes took the terms for father's father and father's mother and applied them to grandfather and grandmother on both sides; and that the other coastal tribes kept the term for mother's father and used it for all grandparents.

Siblings and cousins. – Unfortunately, a comparison of native [110] terms tells us nothing here. There seem to be no Coast Salish sibling terms which are cognates of Interior Salish sibling terms. However, since the early Salish system as reconstructed so far appears to be like the modern Sinkaietk-Flathead system, it would seem that four terms are more likely.

On the basis of the above very sketchy comparison of Salish terminologies, the writer would hazard a tentative conclusion that the early Salish kinship system was much like the modern system found among the Sinkaietk peoples and probably other central Interior Salish (cf. chart on p. 106). Such a conclusion would be consistent with the conclusion reached by Verne Ray and others that the culture of the central Interior Salish groups appears to be most representative of the "pure" or "original" Plateau culture. It also supports the hypothesis that the Salish peoples moved from the Interior regions to the coast where their culture underwent a number of changes.

It would perhaps now be well to consider the question of how Salish kinship fits into a larger kinship classification. Examining Spier's classification of kinship systems we find that the

Salish systems fall under three of his types.  The systems of the Sinkaietk, Northern Okanagon, Kalispel, and Spokan (?) are of Spier's Mackenzie Basin Type, the characteristic feature of which is that "all cousins, parallel and cross, are siblings."[212]  The Flathead system would belong to Spier's Acoma Type, which is characterized by "verbal reciprocity between grandparents and grandchildren and between avuncular and nepotic relatives."[213]  In the Salish Type itself Spier includes the systems of the Siciatl, [111] Squamish, Songish, Bella Coola, Lillooet, Shuswap, Snuqualmi, Duwamish, Nisqually, Klallam, Quileute.  He describes this type as being marked by

> merging of father's and mother's siblings; that is, there is only one term for 'aunt' and one for 'uncle. '  Conversely, there is but one term for nephew and niece.  There are terms for 'grandparent', 'child', and grandchild'.  Brothers and sisters are usually distinguished as 'older sibling' and 'younger sibling'.  Sibling terms are applied to both parallel and cross-cousins.[214]

Strictly speaking, the systems of the Klallam and the Strait of Georgia tribes do not entirely fit this description.  It will be remembered that in these tribes parental siblings are not differentiated as to sex; there is not a term for "aunt" and a term for "uncle" but rather only one term PSb for both, "parental sibling."

It appears that Spier's designation "Salish Type" is rather misleading, for, as we have just seen, the Salish systems fall under other of Spier's types besides this one alone, and furthermore, included in it are non-Salish systems such as those of the Makah, Nootka, and Kwakiutl.  It would thus perhaps be well to do away with the designation "Salish Type" and employ some other name which does not connote a linguistic stock or geographical region, such as, for instance, Kroeber's term "Lineal."[215]  In this type then would be included the systems of the Thompson, Shuswap, Lillooet, and the Salish of Vancouver Island, Puget Sound, and the Strait of Georgia, as well as the systems of non-Salish tribes such as the above mentioned Makah, Nootka, and Kwakiutl, and certain Sahaptin groups of the Plateau.  The remaining Interior Salish systems and the other non-Salish systems which Spier puts in his Mackenzie Basin Type might be given some such designation [112] as Kroeber's "Bifurcate Collateral."[216]  The writer feels that the Flathead system is not sufficiently different to be placed in a separate type but that it should probably be considered a sub-category of the latter type.  All of these systems would come under the major heading; "Non-Classificatory Kinship Systems" (i.e., systems in which, in the first ascending generation at least, lineal relatives are distinguished from collateral relatives).

---

[212]  Leslie Spier, *The Distribution of Kinship Systems in North America* ("University of Washington Publications in Anthropology," I [Seattle, 1925]): 76.

[213]  *Ibid*: p. 74.

[214]  *Ibid*.

[215]  A.L. Kroeber, "Relationship Terms," *Encyclopedia Britannica*, XIX (14th ed. 1936): p. 86.

[216]  *Ibid*. Although, strictly speaking, these systems do not entirely ascribe to Kroeber's definition of "Bifurcate Collateral," as cousins are not separated from siblings but classed with them.

# CHAPTER VI
## CHANGE IN SALISH SOCIAL ORGANIZATION AND KINSHIP

In the earlier part of this thesis the type of social organization found, among the Interior Salish was described and the ways in which Coast Salish social organization differed from it were shown. Considered in the light of the hypothesis of a Salish migration from the interior to the coast and the theory that the culture of the central Interior Salish represents an old Plateau culture, the Interior Salish type of social organization becomes the early Salish type, and the differences from it found among the Coast Salish become _changes_. It is the purpose of this chapter to deal with the nature of these changes in social organization and to consider the question of how they are related to one another as well as to the changes which have taken place in kinship.

Before considering the question of change, however, it might be well to review the character of Interior Salish social organization and the role played by kinship in early Salish society. The Interior Salish social organization, it will be remembered, was an exceedingly simple one. The individual internal structures composing the larger social structure were few in number and chief among them was the kinship structure, which together with the related age and sex structures, controlled practically all of social life.

Kinship was, for instance, an important regulating force in the economic area of life. The various kinship relationships, characterized by certain duties, obligations, and privileges, were basic to the organization of economic activities. The mutual [114] dependence and co-operation of the husband-wife relationship were manifested in the economic division of labor between them; the obedience of children to parent was shown in the dutiful assistance which they gave in the various tasks connected with securing and maintaining a living; the close bond between siblings was demonstrated in their labor together in economic enterprises. Such cooperation between members of the family resulted in an economic self-sufficiency for the family. There was scarcely any economic organization outside of the family working units; there was no larger organization according to which an apportionment of economic tasks could be made among members of the community and an exchange of services or goods carried on.

Kinship also had its ramifications in the political structure. The political organization, consisting of rule by local chief, was itself patterned after a fundamental kinship relationship – that between parent and child. Many times in the literature the chief is described as a sort of "father" to the group, his duties being much the same as those of the family head and consisting of advising his "children" concerning their moral conduct, exhorting them to industrious living, seeking to keep order and peace among them. It was he, too, who, when the occasion demanded it, applied organized negative sanctions,[217] such as public whipping. It must be pointed out, however, that social control for the most part did not consist of organized sanctions but of unorganized expressions of disapproval as, for instance, ridicule – a really powerful means of social control in this society in which relationships were largely of a personal character.

Retaliation for an injury done to an individual or group was often considered to be a matter of kinship behavior rather [115] than the concern of the political authority. Thus, we find among the Interior Salish the institution of blood revenge, or the avenging of a person's death or injury by his kinsmen.

---

[217] See A.R. Radcliffe-Brown, "Sanctions," _Encyclopedia of the Social Sciences_.

The political and legal structures were thus not very highly organized.  Such political organization as did exist, to repeat, was patterned after a basic kinship relationship, and many of the functions assigned to political authority in more sophisticated societies were taken care of by the kinship group.  It should be pointed out here that political organization was one aspect of Salish organization which did not undergo any change.  On the coast, as in the interior, government lay in the hands of village chiefs whose authority was quite limited; and there was no comprehensive structure unifying the individual village groups in a larger political group.

Relationships of subordination and superordination also arose principally out of the kinship system and age structure.  There was no organization of the society into formal classes or castes; such relationships of superiority and inferiority as did exist were, for the most part, those between the old and the young.  An individual, we have seen, was subordinate to his parents and other members of the generations above him.  This generational character of kinship was reinforced by the age structure.  There was no rigid age-grading in Interior Salish society, but there was a structure of a semi-formal character based upon the divisions of the individual's life.  These age periods were:  (1) a period of infancy in which the individual was considered a social non-entity, terminated by the naming ceremony,  (2) a pre-puberty period, or childhood,  (3) a post-puberty period, or early adulthood, and  (4) a post-marital period, or mature and late adulthood.  All adults were considered superior to the younger individuals; they were [116] possessed of wisdom and their advice was sought on all matters of life.  It was the elders of the group who occupied the positions of house leaders and who lectured the young on morals and the traditions of the society.

Not all relationships of subordination and superordination arose out of the kinship and age structures; some were involved in the system of differentiating individuals according to their special "powers."  Certain persons, because of their outstanding abilities in certain spheres of life, were separated out and recognized as "leaders."  They possessed authority in their respective fields and the people granted themn their respect and followed their leadership.  They did not, however, constitute a formal class with an organized body of privileges.

We have seen, then, that in the Interior Salish society there were few organized structures, besides kinship, by which social behavior was regulated.  In the change from the original Salish social organization, the component structures of the larger social structure multiplied, making for a greater complexity in the system of social relationship and a diminished importance of kinship.

The change in Salish social organization was one not only of increased complexity, but also of greater formalization.  Especially was this true in the case of the more northern coastal tribes – the Bella Coola and Strait of Georgia tribes on both the island and mainland.  It is among these tribes, for example, that we find the most rigid and highly developed system of social stratification, society here being divided into four social classes:  chiefs, nobles, commoners, and slaves.  We have seen that membership in these classes was purely a matter of birth, that nobility was inherited, that marriage was strictly within class boundaries, and that mobility within the structure was at a [117] minimum.  It was shown, too, that associated with the nobility was a well-defined body of privileges – and also obligations – and that between the nobles and commoners there existed certain prescribed manners of behavior, especially exhibited on formal occasions such as potlatch affairs and public ceremonials.

The existence of several Salish societies whose systems of social stratification are intermediate in character between this rigid class structure of the Strait of Georgia tribes, on the one hand, and the democratic early Salish society, on the other, suggests a series of steps through which the change may have been wrought.  First, there is to be considered the situation found among the Puyallup-Nisqually.  Here, persons of high status were those who because of their special abilities, ultimately attributable to "powers" from the supernatural, held specialized postitions – such persons, for instance, as hunters, harpooners, canoe makera, gamblers, political chiefs, and warriors.  This differentiation of individuals on the basis of personal abilities recalls a similar sort of social specialization found among the interior tribes.  In the case of the Puget Sound peoples, however, there is the additional fact that the special abilities of individuals constituted a means of accumulating wealth, if the individuals so desired; for due to the greater development of economic organization on the coast, they could exchange their services or products for wealth.  We thus find entering here into the system of super-ordination and sub-ordination the concept of property or wealth.  According to Smith, it was the common possession of the capability of "producing, procuring, or manipulating property" that welded persons into a high class.

We also find in Puyallup-Nisqually society the beginning of the inheritance factor in social stratification.  This manifests itself in the tendency of chiefs and their families to [118] preserve their authority and status through passing them down to their descendants.

Among the Puyallup-Nisqually, actual possession of wealth was not so necessary or important in establishing status as was the ability to acquire it.  In the ease of the Klallam and Quinault tribes, however, we find that the possession of wealth is of much greater importance, social position being determined by it and/or the quality of birth.  The concept of good birth is rather "ill-defined" here but nevertheless, there is a growth of the inheritance factor as a determinant of status in these societies.  The chiefly lineage is definitely established, and we find among the Quinault the existence of a nobility composed of persons who are of good birth.  But in the Quinault system there are also persons of high status who are not noble but rich, or who are of good birth but poor; in fact, a series of gradations between nobles and those who are definitely commoners.  This fact makes it appear all the more likely that the Quinault system of social stratification is intermediary in character between the strictly hereditary rank structure of the Strait of Georgia tribes and the non-hereditary class structure of the Puyallup-Nisqually.

Thus, we find that the change from the classless early Salish society to the definitely stratified Coast Salish society is characterized by the development first of a wealth factor and secondly of an inheritance factor.  It is possible that the second is a growth from the first, that the inheritance of rank had developed as a result of the tendency to keep property, and hence rank, within families.

A second instance of formalization on the coast is found in the development of sept organisation among the more northern Coast Salish groups.  Here the extended kinship group has been given a formal character by the possession of an origin tradition, [119] certain crests, rights to secret society dances, names and property.  The development of sept organization is probably connected with the inheritance of rank, and the associated custom of keeping family genealogies.  If the sept organization were similar to the *numaym* system found among the Kwakiutl, septs were ranked according to the order of birth of their ancestors, as were also the families within septs; hence, the custom of keeping family genealogies, and hence the traditions as to sept origin.  Just as in the case of individuals, the comparative rank of septs was marked by the kinds of rights and privileges which they possessed.

The secret societies of the Coast Salish represent an organization of persons with regard to ceremonial life.  It will be remembered that the public ceremonies of the Interior Salish consisted largely of the winter guardian spirit dances.  A dance was given by a single individual but all other members of the community were free to participate in it. There was, however, no organization connected with the singing of the songs and the performing of the dances of a particular guardian spirit. Each person had his own song and dance given him by his spirit and he could exhibit these at any one of the dances; thus, the typical winter dance was something of a free-for-all. These guardian spirit dances were retained on the coast, but here, in addition, we find the formal grouping of persons around the songs, dances, and secrets connected with a single supernatural personage. Each society had traditions relating how the society's secrets had been given to the group's ancestor by the supernatural being and possessed formal rules concerning the entrance of individuals, the initiation of novices, and the behavior between members. In the more northern tribes, the associational organization may have been a reinforcement of the rank structure for it appears that in some of these groups heavy entrance fees had to be paid and at the potlatch given [120] in connection with the initiation ceremony{,} the initiate's relatives had to distribute large amounts of property.

With the increase in complexity of the social system, kinship lost its absolutely paramount importance as a regulator of social behavior. The kinship system itself, however, did not undergo a very great change but remained the same in the following basic characteristics:

1. The emphasis on generation.

2. The merging of lineal and collateral relatives in the second ascending and descending generations, and the separating of them in the first ascending and descending generations.

3. The extension of kinship through the equating of siblings or cousins.

On the coast, as in the Interior, the kinship system continued to be built primarily on two fundamental principles which have been termed by A.R. Radcliffe-Brown as the "generational principle" and the principle of the "equivalence of siblings." The first of these, the generational principle, has been defined by [Sol] Tax as: "Persons of one generation tend to respect those of the generation above." The fact has often been repeated in this thesis that among the Salish the relationship between parent and child was such that the parent was placed in a position of discipliner and teacher and the child was placed in a position requiring obedience and respect. The corollary to the generational principle, that "alternate generations (grandparents and grandchildren) tend to behave reciprocally" also holds throughout Salish society. Though a person also respected his grandparents, he was not strictly disciplined by them and the relationship between them tended to be one of friendly comradeship. The Salish extended these relationships to distant as well as close relatives and thus made generation one of the chief means of differentiating kinship behavior. [121]

The principle of the equivalence of siblings has been defined as "a group of siblings tends to be considered as a unit." In the Salish system it underlies the equating of grandparents with their siblings and of a sibling's grandchildren with one's own grandchildren, and indirectly, the extension of sibling terms to cousins. Behaviorally, the principle manifests itself in the close solidarity of siblings, especially those of the same sex. The principle does not seem to operate in the case of the first ascending and descending generations, in which lineal relatives are distinguished from collateral relatives. Whatever may lie behind this distinction, however, it must be pointed out that in actual behavior the distinction is not so great, for we do find the practices of sororate and levirate throughout Salish society and the corresponding tendency for a person to treat his mother's sister and father's brother as sort of potential parents. Furthermore, the behavior relationship with his uncles and aunts was very similar in character to that involved in his relationship with his parents.

Seemingly nothing in the basic characteristics of Salish kinship conflicted with the changes in social organization, at least to a great enough extent to produce any drastic changes in the kinship system. The fact is that the generational character of kinship was consistent rather than conflicting with the new developments in social organization; for age distinction, of which the differentiation of generations is a manifestation, becomes of increased importance in Coast Salish kinship. The classing and treatment of cousins as siblings must have been somewhat inconsistent with the rank structure of coastal society, which prescribed marriage within class bounds. We are told that if a person could not arrange a marriage outside of his local group, he was sometimes forced to marry a cousin or "sibling" in order to marry [122] within his class, and the Salish ordinarily frowned upon marital unions with cousins. Such conflicts, however, were evidently not frequent enough or serious enough to bring about alterations in the kinship system.

Changes in Salish kinship consisted of the loss of distinction between maternal and paternal relatives, a decreased differentiation as to sex, and, as mentioned above, an increased differentiation as to age. The first of these changes, the failure to distinguish between maternal and paternal relatives, was characteristic of all the coastal groups. In the Puget Sound tribes, decreased distinction of sex consisted of the use of the terms "older sibling" and "younger sibling" rather than "older brother," "older sister," etc., and the use of the terms "parent-in-law" and "sibling-in-law" instead of terms in which sex was indicated. In the Klallam and Strait of Georgia tribes there was practically a complete loss of sex differentiation. Age differentiation reached its greatest extent in the Klallam system, in which a distinction was made between older parental sibling and younger parental sibling and between one's older sibling's children and his younger sibling's children. All of the coast tribes possessed kinship terms denoting the relative ages of children.

Just how important a social change was represented by the shift from a differentiation to a non-differentiation of maternal and paternal relatives cannot be determined. On the coast, the non-distinction between relatives on the two parental sides had its behavioral correlates. But it seems that in the Interior Salish system also, so far as actual behavior was concerned, there was not much difference between maternal and paternal kin; however, this may be a false impression due to the fact that students failed to observe the difference though such existed.

The failure to distinguish between maternal and paternal [123] relatives on the coast was consonant with the rules governing sept membership. An individual could belong to either his mother's or his father's sept, the sex of the parent evidently not being as important in determining sept affiliation as the comparative rank and wealth of each. The fact that property considerations were more important than the sex factor was also illustrated in the practice mentioned as existing among the Comox (and found among the Kwakiutl, too) of performing "a travesty of marriage without a bride for the sole purpose of acquiring privileges in the exchange."[218] Unfortunately, because of the incompleteness of our information, we cannot cite other instances of the lessened importance of the sex factor among the Coast Salish but the writer believes that such instances did exist. It appears then that a decreased differentiation as to sex in kinship terminology was correlated with a diminished importance of sex in actual social behavior and the latter, in turn, seems to have been connected with an increased emphasis upon wealth and rank.

---

[218] Barnett, *op. cit*: p. 155.

The greater distinction of age, too, is related to the emphasis upon property. It was pointed out above that the larger part of a patrimony descended to the first son and the rest of it was portioned out to the other children according to their ages, with the youngest getting the smallest amount {a "ramage"}. Persons were also ranked according to their order of birth and this was basic to the ranking of septs. The sept of highest rank was supposedly descended from the eldest son of an original ancestor. Families within the sept were similarly ranked. Now the differentiation in the kinship system between children of different ages, between parent's older sibling and parent's younger sibling, and between older sibling's child and younger sibling's child appears to be correlated [124] with the inheritance of property and rank according to relative age.

An emphasis upon property or wealth thus appears to be fundamental to change in general among the Coast Salish. It was found to be related to the organization of class structure among the Puyallup-Nisqually, and it was suggested that through the continued efforts to keep property, and the status which it gave, in families, there developed the inheritance of wealth and rank with the consequent formation of the rigid rank structure of the Strait of Georgia tribes. In turn, correlated with the growth of inherited nobility was the formalization of the sept. Then, so far as kinship is concerned, we have just seen that property was emphasized at the expense of {gender} sex differentiation, but with an increase in age distinction.

It is of interest now to note that the environment of the coast was more favorable than that of the interior for the development of an emphasis upon wealth. Because of the greater amount of rainfall in the coastal region, food was more plentiful. Food, in fact, was present in great abundance. Consider, for instance, the following description of the Puyallup-Nisqually environment by Smith:

> It was a land which offered food for the taking, a land in which people were said to be starving if their winter diet of smoked and dried food was not varied daily by the addition of fresh fish or meat.[219]

And, according to Barnett, in the Strait of Georgia area, "every river and creek once literally seethed with salmon in the spawning season."[220]

The coast and interior environments were alike in that the [125] means of subsistence which, they offered was of a seasonal nature necessitating a seasonal dichotomy in their life. Thus, we found that the same type of local organization characterized both groups of Salish, that in the summer the people were divided into family groups following a nomadic life in the quest for food, and that in the winter they were organized in village communities, the component units of which were the households. In the case of the coastal peoples, however, on a basic substratum consisting of this type of local organization and fundamentally the same type of kinship structure as was found in the interior, there grew a much more complex social system; and we are pointing out here that the greater favorableness of the coastal environment may have been an important factor in this development.

Because of the larger amount of food to be had and the greater ease with which it could be secured, a surplus could be accumulated, and, also, an increased density of population was

---

[219]  Marian W. Smith, "The Puyallup of Washington," *Acculturation in Seven American Indian Tribes*, Ralph Linton, ed (New York 1940): p. 4.

[220]  Barnett, *op. cit*: p. 118.

made possible.   This produced a situation conducive to the development of economic specialization; persons especially adept at certain techniques or crafts could spend the greater part of their time in those occupations and exchange their products for the surplus food of others. This would result in a greater production of wealth, and from this to a cultural emphasis upon wealth and consequent development of class structure, it seems to the writer, would be but a short step.

The writer is not suggesting a necessary relationship between a favorable environment and the development of the wealth concept and social stratification on the basis of it, but is merely pointing out that in this particular case the environment offered certain possibilities which the inhabitants seized upon with the resultant growth of a complex social organization. Whether a scientific correlation exists between a favorable [126] environment and such a cultural development can be ascertained only by studying comparable instances {especially place-based names and TEKW knowledge} elsewhere.

## BIBLIOGRAPHY

Curtis, Edward S. *The North American Indian.* Vol. IX. Cambridge [Mass]: University Press, 1907-1922.

Eggan, Fred (ed.). *Social Anthropology of North American Tribes.* Chicago: University of Chicago Press, 1937.

Gunther, Erna. *Klallam Ethnography.* University of Washington Publications in Anthropology, Vol. I. Seattle: University of Washington Press, 1927.

Hill-Tout, Charles. *British North America.* Vol. I. London: Constable, 1907.

Hodge, F.W. *Handbook of American Indians.* Bulletin of the Bureau of American Ethnology, No. 30. Washington, 1907, 1910.

Kroeber, A.L. *Cultural and Natural Areas of Native North America.* University of California Publications in Archaeology and Ethnology. Berkeley: University of California Press, 1959.

Morgan, Lewis H. *Systems of Consanguinity and Affinity,* Smithsonian Contributions to Knowlcdgc, Vol. XVII. Washington: Smithsonian Institute, 1871.

Olson, Ronald L. *The Quinault Indians.* University of Washington Publications in Anthropology, Vol. VI. Seattle: University of Washington Press, 1936.

Ray, Verne. *Cultural Relations in the Plateau of Northwestern America.* Publications of the Frederick Webb Hodge Anniversary Publication Fund, Vol. III. Los Angeles: The Southwest Museum, 1959.

______ *The Sanpoil and Nespelem.* University of Washington Publications in Anthropology, Vol. V. Seattle: University of Washington Press, 1932.

Smith, J. Russell. *North America.* New York: Harcourt, Brace & Co., 1925.

Smith, Marian W. *The Puyallup-Nisqually.* Columbia University Contributions to Anthropology, Vol. XXXII. New York: Columbia University Press, 1940.

Spier, Leslie. *The Distribution of Kinship Systems in North America.* University of Washington Publicatlons in Anthropology. Vol. I. Seattle: University of Washington Press, 1925. [128]

Spier, Leslie (ed.). *The Sinkaietk or Southern Okanagon of Washington.* General series in Anthropology, No. 6. Menasha: George Banta Co., 1938.

______. *Tribal Distribution in Washington.* General Series in Anthropology, No. 3. Menasha: George Banta Co., 1936.

Teit, James. *The Middle Columbia Salish.* University of Washington Publications in Anthropology, Vol. II. Seattle: University of Washington Press, 1925.

Turney-High, H.H. *Ethnography of the Kutenai.* Memoirs of the American Anthropological Society, No. 56. Menasha: George Banta Co., 1941.

______. *The Flathead Indians of Montana.* Memoirs of the American Anthropological Society, No. 48. Menasha; George Banta Co, 1937.

Wissler, Clark. *The American Indian.* 2d ed. New York: Oxford University, 1922.

### Parts of Books

Smith, Marian W. The Puyallup of Washington," *Acculturation in Seven American Indian Tribes.* Ralph Linton, ed. New York: D. Appleton-Century Co., Inc., 1940.

Teit, James. "The Lillooet Indians," *The Jesup Expedition Publications*, Vol. II, New York: American Museum or Natural History, 1900.

______. "The Shuswap Indians, " *The Jesup Expedition Publications.* Vol. II. New York:

American Museum of Natural History, 1900.

______. "The Thompson Indians of British Columbia," *The Jesup Expedition Publications*, Vol. I. New York: American Museum of Natural History, 1900.


## Reports


Boas, Franz. "Preliminary Notes on the Indians of British Columbia," *Report, Fifty-eighth Meeting of the British Association for the Advancement of Science*, (1889).

______. "Second Report on the Indians of British Columbia," *Report, Sixtieth Meeting of the British Association for the Advancement of Science*, (1891).

______. "Third Report on the Indians of British Columbia," *Report, Sixty-first Meeting of the British Association for the Advancement of Science*, (1893).

Hill-Tout, Charles. "Ethnological Studies of the Mainland Halkomelem," *Report, Seventy-second Meeting of the British Association for the Advancement of Science*, (1903). [129]

Hill-Tout, Charles. "Notes on the N'tlaka'pamuQ of British Columbia," *Report, Sixty-ninth Meeting of the British Association for the Advancement of Science*, (1900).

______. "Notes on the Skqomic of British Columbia," *Report, Seventieth Meeting of the British Association for the Advancement of Science* (1901).

______. "The Salish Tribes of the Coast and Lower Fraser Delta," *Ontario Annual Archaeological Report,* 1905 (1906).

Smith, Harlan I. "Recent Archaeological Discoveries in Northwestern America," *Bulletin of the American Geographical Society*, No. 38 (1906).

Teit, James. "The Salishan Tribes of the Western Plateaus." Franz Boas, ed. *Forty-fifth Annual Report of the Bureau of American Ethnology* (1950).

Tolmie, W.F., and George Dawson. "Comparative Vocabularies of the Indian Tribes of British Columbia." *Geological and Natural Survey of Canada* (1884).


## Articles


Barnett, H.G. "The Coast Salish of Canada," *American Anthropologist*, XL (1958).

Boas, Franz. "Notes on the Tillamook," *University of California Publications in Archaeology and Ethnology*, XX (1899).

Dawson, George M. "Notes on the Shuswap People of British Columbia. *Royal Society of Canada Transactions*, (1891).

Hill-Tout, Charles. "Ethnological Report on the Stseelis and Skaulits Tribes," *Journal of the Royal Anthropological Institute*, XXXIV (1904).

______. "Report on the Ethnology of the Okanaken of British Columbia," Journal of the Royal Anthropological Institute, XLI (1911).

______. "Report on the Ethnology of the Siciatl of British Columbia," *Journal of the Royal Anthropological Institute*, XXXIV (1904).

______. "Report on the Ethnology of the Southeastern Tribes of Vancouver Island," *Journal of the Royal Anthropological Institute*, XXXVII (1907).

______. "Report on the Ethnology of the Stlatlumh," *Journal of the Royal Anthropological Institute*, XXXV (1905).

Kroeber, A.L. "Relationship Terms," *Encyclopedia Britannica,* 14th ed., Vol. XIX.

Radcliffe-Brown, A.R. "Sanction," *Encyclopedia of the Social Sciences*, Vol. XIII. [130]

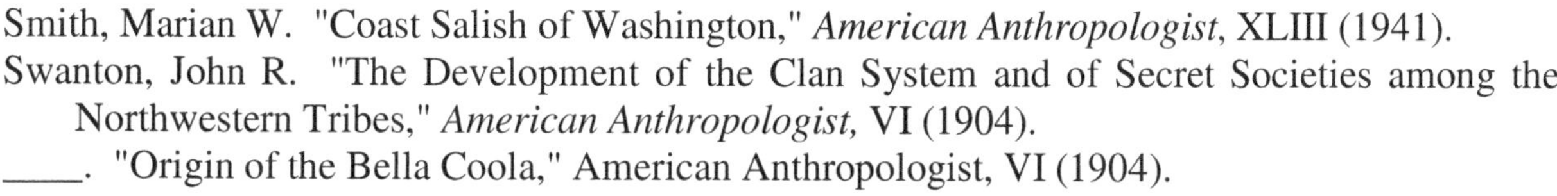

Smith, Marian W.  "Coast Salish of Washington," *American Anthropologist*, XLIII (1941).

Swanton, John R.  "The Development of the Clan System and of Secret Societies among the Northwestern Tribes," *American Anthropologist*, VI (1904).

_____. "Origin of the Bella Coola," American Anthropologist, VI (1904).

Iva Osani Schmitt Springstead died in September 1969 at Nagoya, Japan.  She was a social anthropologist, specializing in kinship, formerly on the faculty with her husband Karl Schmitt of the University of Oklahoma where a memorial funds the Springstead Award recognizing the best overall graduating senior in anthropology.  The recipient's name is engraved on a plaque located in the department lounge.  Contributions may be sent to: U of Oklahoma Library, Iva Springstead Memorial Fund, U of Oklahoma, Norman, OK 73069.

https://anthrosource.onlinelibrary.wiley.com/doi/epdf/10.1111/an.1970.11.3.3.5

# System Change in Salish Kinship Terminologies[221]
William W. Elmendorf

THIS PAPER is concerned with one specific diachronic problem suggested by a major system difference between the kinship terminologies of different Salish-speaking peoples in the Pacific Northwest. The problem may be defined generally as: given certain comparative evidence, can we infer anything definite as to the nature and direction of change in the several Salish terminologies?

The question seems open to approach from both ethnological and linguistic directions. Consequently, evidence bearing on this problem is sought through comparative analysis of Salish terminologies as *systems of term usage* and as *linguistically related morpheme sets*. I have restricted both types of comparison to grandparent-grandchild and uncle-aunt-nephew-niece term sets. The reason for this restriction is that term usage in these classes of relations seems to illustrate most clearly the basic system difference referred to above. Finally, results of the systemic and linguistic comparisons are applied as independent lines of evidence to suggest a most plausible hypothesis as to change processes in Salish kinship usage.

## Features of Salish Kinship

Some preliminary observations on Salish kinship systems will serve to define more exactly the scope of our problem. Two of these are assumptions in part derived from theoretical considerations as to the nature linguistic relationship of Salishan peoples implies an original Salishan kinship terminology. Lexically, this terminology would have been part of the proto-Salish language; ethnologically, part of the social culture of the proto-Salish language community.

A second assumption, derived in part from data presented below, is that whatever type of kinship terminology characterized the proto-Salish speech community, this original system has developed into two distinct types among modern Salish peoples, and these types correlate with a series of linguistic and cultural differences.

Despite considerable differences in term usage, modem Salish kin-term systems [366] share certain common features.[222] These may be summarized as: (1) All PSb are distinguished from P, and SbC from own C.[223] (2) PSb and PP terms are extended to same generation

---

[221]  1/ A preliminary draft of this paper was read at the Northwest Anthropological Conference, University of British Columbia, April, 1961. I am indebted to Wayne Suttles and Allan H. Smith for permission to use or refer to unpublished field notes.

[222]  3/ Spier, 1925, p. 74, for a somewhat different formulation of common Salish kinship traits.

[223]  4/ Symbols and abbreviations for kin relations are basically those of Murdock, 1949, with some additions and slight modifications: Hu, Wi, So, Da, Fa, Mo, Br, Si, El (elder), Yo (younger) are as in Murdock. I introduce 3-letter terms for sex-generalized relations: Spo (spouse), Chi (child), Par (parent), Sib (sibling); also Dec (deceased), Ma (male), Fe (female), Mn (man's), Wm woman's). Other symbols, representing relations between terms are:  - (hyphen), linking two or more terms defining a term set, e.g., PP-CC terms: ~ "reciprocal with"; = "same as"; ≠ "different from"; ≅ "same as reciprocal."

collaterals of those relatives, and similarly for SbC and CC (i.e. PSb = PPSbC, PP = PPSb, etc.). (3) Sibling terms are extended to cousins (Sb = PSbC), although one or two systems include a special supplementary reference term for "cousin" (e.g., Spokan). (4) Special status-change terms for PSb and SbC applied following death of a connecting relative (P or Sb) are very widespread. (5) Terminology for lineal relatives beyond the second ascending or descending generation (e.g., PPP, CCC) tends to be "generation" in type; often a single term applies reciprocally to members of both generations. It may be added that Salish reference terms are in general not distinct in morpheme form or pattern of usage from terms used in address. We may assume that these universally shared features characterized proto-Salish kinship terminology, and represent stable retentions from that original system of terms.

Apart from common features, Salish peoples of the present are divided as to kinship terminologies into two main sets: (1) Those with *lineal* systems of terms for PSb and PP.[224] (2) Those with *bifurcate collateral* systems in designating these relatives. Lineal terminology does not distinguish PSb or PP according to the {gender} sex of the connecting relative; thus, all FSb = MSb, all FP = MP. Bifurcate collateral terminology does so distinguish these sets of relatives; thus FSb ≠ MSb, FP ≠ MP.[225]

This twofold division of lineal and bifurcate collateral systems coincides in general with the linguistic division between Salish languages of the Bella Coola, Coast Salish, and Oregon divisions on the one hand and of the Interior division on the other.[226] It also coincides generally with the ethnographic division between [367] Salish tribes of Northwest Coast and Plateau culture types. In general, the Bella Coola, Coast Salish, and Oregon (Tillamook) linguistic divisions fall into the Northwest Coast culture area, and show kinship terminologies of lineal type, while the Interior Salish linguistic division falls into the Plateau culture area, and shows terminologies of bifurcate collateral type. The Thompson are an exception to this generalization. Culturally they are a Plateau people, and linguistically Interior Salish, but their PSb and PP terms are lineal. They are, of course, an interior group territorially adjacent to Coast Salish peoples.

Both Salish types of terminology, lineal and bifurcate collateral, occur among other, neighboring, non-Salish peoples. Lineal terminologies characterize Wakashan and Chemakuan as well as Salish peoples on the Pacific coast, and others to the south, including the Yurok in northwestern California.[227] Bifurcate collateral terminologies occur widely among non-Salish groups east of the coastal ranges, including Sahaptins and Upper Chinook (Wishram),[228] Thus, the lineal versus bifurcate collateral division seems to correlate primarily with a culture-type division of Northwest Coast and Plateau rather than simply with a linguistic division within the Salish stock. These facts suggest that diffusional factors, or cultural changes associated with the development of regional social-culture differences, may be among the ultimate causes of the

---

[224]  5/ Spier, 1925: p. 74, defines this system as "Salish type." Some Interior Salish systems, as we shall see, do not accord with the criteria of this type, but fit better his "Mackenzie Basin" or "Eskimo types *(idem,* pp. 76, 79).

[225]  6/ Lowie 1928, and Kirchhoff 1932, originally defined these types independently; see also Murdock, 1949: pp. 141-142, for usage of this system of classification.

[226]  7/ Classification of the Salish stock in these four main linguistic divisions, on comparative lexical evidence, is presented in Swadesh 1930.

[227]  8/ See Spier, 1925: p. 74 and Plate 1, and Kroeber, 1934.

[228]  9/ Jacobs 1932, Spier and Sapir 1930: pp. 262-266.

split in Salish terminologies.

## Hypotheses of Change

Three logical possibilities occur as to the direction of this Salish development.

(1)  The original proto-Salish terminology was of neither lineal nor bifurcate collateral type, but developed into these two types in coastal and interior regions, respectively, as a result of linguistic and cultural separation of the proto-Salish speech community.  Under this view, coastal and interior systems would represent independent innovations in these two areas.

(2)  Proto-Salish terminology was of lineal type, which has been preserved among coastal groups, while Interior Salish peoples have innovated in developing bifurcate collateral terminologies.  This view restricts major system innovation to the interior terminologies.

(3)  Proto-Salish terminology was bifurcate collateral in type.  This system has been preserved among Interior Salish tribes, while coastal groups have innovated in developing lineal terminologies.  In this view major innovation was restricted to coastal systems.

Considering the three possibilities above as mutually exclusive hypotheses, it [368] is the purpose of the ensuing discussion to show that a combination of comparative linguistic and systemic evidence demonstrates greatest plausibility for the third interpretation:  that coastal lineal terminologies have undergone major innovation, and that they have been derived from an original bifurcate collateral system.

We dismiss the first hypothesis mainly for lack of any clear supporting evidence.  It is, of course, not to be assumed that only one of the divergent systems, coastal or interior, has undergone developmental change.  This is in fact directly contradicted by significant variations among Interior Salish groups in their PSb-SbC usage.  The comparative results presented below do suggest, however, that coastal systems have changed most, and in a particular direction, while interior systems have remained relatively conservative and hence approximate more closely to an original hypothetical proto-Salish system.  The second hypothesis, the converse of the third, seems directly contradicted by the results which support the latter hypothesis.

## Grandparent-Grandchild Terms:
## Systemic Features

Let us first consider PP-CC terms, since these form somewhat simpler and more manageable systems and lead to clearer conclusions than do Salish PSb-SbC terms.  There are usable data for ten coastal and four interior systems: Bella Coola, Squamish, Musqueam, Nooksack, Lummi, Klallam, Twana, Puyallup, Qumault, and Tillamook (Siletz) on the coast; and Thompson, Southern Okanagon, Spokan, and Wenatchee-Columbia in the interior.[229]  Systemic

---

[229]   10/ Sources are:  McIlwraith 1948 vol. I: pp. 150-156 (Bella Coola); Wayne Suttles, unpublished field notes (Squamish, Nooksack, Lummi); Elmendorf and Suttles, 1960: pp. 20-21 (Musqueam); Gunther, 1927, pp. 258-260 (Klallam); Elmendorf, 1946: pp. 422-424 (Twana – two errata in this source should be noted:  p. 424, relations 3 and 4 should read

results of a comparison of these terminologies may be summarized as follows.

(1)  All coastal groups, and Thompson, agree in differentiating PP and CC.  All these, except Tillamook, use a single term for the CC relation.  All, except the South Georgia groups (Squamish, Musqueam, Lummi, Klallam, Nooksack), use two terms for PP (PF, PM).  The South Georgia [369] groups, forming a linguistically closely related branch of the Salish stock, have a single PP term.[230]

(2)  The three Interior Salish systems – Southern Okanagon, Spokan, Wenatchee-Columbia – show four PP terms, differentiated according to sex of the referent and sex of the connecting relative; thus, FF, FM, MF, MM.  Further, these terms are used reciprocally for descending-generation relatives; thus, FF $\cong$ ♂SC, FM $\cong$ ♀SC, MF $\cong$ ♂DC, MM $\cong$ ♀DC.  The system results in the descending generation relatives being distinguished not by own sex but by sex of the speaker and sex of the connecting relative.  Spokan has an additional self-reciprocal status-change term to designate PP $\cong$ CC after death of the connecting relative.

If the coastal system has been derived from one like that of the interior, then its major innovative changes must have been:  (1) Reduction of PP terms from four to two (or one), by disregarding sex of connecting relative as a differentiating factor;  (2) restriction of PP terms to the ascending generation only, by abolishing generation reciprocity;  (3) assigning a single new term (except in Tillamook) to the CC relation.[231]  Such a system would retain only part of the lexical stock of the original system.

If the coastal system were the result of a single innovative change, then we should expect the modem coastal terminologies to agree, in a lexical comparison, with *a particular part* of the interior term sets; the other original terms would have been lost to the coastal languages at one innovative stroke, so to speak.  On the other hand, if the coastal system has resulted from

---

tca'c-a•lı'c; p. 427, in first diagram or fig. 2 lines for maternal grandparents should be transposed); Smith 1940: pp. 173-178 (Puyallup); Olson 1936: pp. 90-92 (Quinault); Frachtenberg 1917: pp. 45-46 (Tillamook, Siletz dialect); Wayne Suttles, unpublished field notes (Thompson); Walters 1938: pp. 88-90 (Southern Okanagon); W.W. Elmendorf, unpublished field notes (Wenatchee-Columbia, Spokan).  Spokan terminology was compared with that of the Kalispel in field notes of Allan H. Smith; the two are virtually identical.  The same appears true of the Flathead terms given by Krueger, 1961.  I have modernized the orthography or native terms in the older sources in some instances, for consistency.  Transcription is in accord with modern Americanist usage and follows in general the prescriptions of George Herzog *et alia, Some Orthographic Recommendations* (American Anthropologist, vol. 36: pp. 629-631 1934).

[230]  11/ For the South Georgia branch as a special linguistic grouping within the Coast Salish division, see Swadesh 1950.

[231]  12/ The new coastal CC term was apparently innovative, at least in that usage, although it also appears in Thompson (and Shuswap).  Tillamook (Siletz) usage for their two CC terms is hard to make out from Frachtenberg's definitions, but this system lacked the morpheme used for CC in other coastal systems.

multiple parallel innovations undergone independently by earlier forms of different Coast Salish languages, then modern coastal terminologies could be expected to agree lexically with *various parts* of the interior term sets. This last condition would result from survival of different terms from the original set in different independently innovating coastal systems.

Grandparent-Grandchild Terms:
Linguistic Features

These two derivative hypotheses can be tested by linguistic comparison. We first note, for the three interior bifurcate collateral terminologies, that three (and possibly four) of the four Wenatchee-Columbia PP terms are apparent [370] cognates of corresponding Spokan terms, while Wenatchee-Columbia and Spokan share two cognates in this set with Southern Okanagon.

Turning to the coastal terms, we note the following cognate correspondences with terms for which at least two cognates can be found in interior languages.

(1)  Coastal (PF): BC kukpi, Puy sápa, Quin čopə, Til xɛha?s, Interior (FF): SOk sxáxba, Spok s<u>x</u>apɛ, WC s<u>x</u>ə<u>x</u>ápə.

(2)  Coastal (PF, PP): Twa si•la (PF); Squa sé?la, Mus si?la, Nook sil?ai, Lum síla, Klal síya (all PP).  Interior (MF): Spok sí•la, WC stəti•la (WC possibly a noncognate analogical loan from Sahaptin).

(3)  Coastal (PM): BC kik<sup>y</sup>a, Twa káya, Puy káiya, Quin či (and Thom kiɛ).  Interior (MM): Spok čɩčciyɛ, WC kəkiya.  (Initial k- in the Twana and Puyallup words involves a phonological difficulty).

(4)  Coastal (PM): Til qɛna?s.  Interior (FM): SOk káqəna, Spofe qan•a, WC qəqan•a.

(5)  Coastal (CC): BC slemc (apparently s-l-emc, cf. emc SbC), Squa íməþ, Mus ?iməþ, Nook ?iməþ, Lum ?iŋəs, Klal ?iŋəc, Twa íbac, Puy ébac, Quin émac (also, Thom iməč, Shuswap émc).  Interior: Nil, except possibly SOk snémat "inclusive term for all grandchildren," apparently supplementary to generation-reciprocal use of PP terms.  This seems, like the Bella Coola term, a derivative; the hypothetical stem *-emat* does not occur as a kinship term (in Walters' material), unlike BC slemc CC, emc SbC.

(6)  Coastal ("CC"); Til sila?s.  Interior (MF ≅ ♂DC): see 2, above.

(7)  Coastal ("CS/D"):  Til čiya?s.  Interior (MM ≅ ♀DC): see 3, above.

The correspondence may be tabulated as follows:

| *Interior* | *Coastal* | *Coastal Systems* |
|---|---|---|
| FF | → PF | BC, Puy, Quin, Til |
| FM | → PM | Til |
| MF | → PF | Twa; So. Georgia groups (→ PP) |
| MM | → PM | BC, Twa, Puy, Quin (also Thom) |
| MF | → "CC" | Til |
| MM | → "CS/D" | Til |
| (nil Ø) | → "CC" | All (except Til), and Thom |

These results are in striking agreement with the assumption of derivation of coastal

132

systems from an original system like that of interior groups, and of multiple independent innovations in coastal systems, all leading to lineal terminologies. [371]

If the assumed direction of derivation is reversed, an apparently impossible situation results. We note that all of the coastal-interior cognates appear in the Spokan PP-CC term set. Then, an interior system such as the Spokan would have resulted from the lexical amalgamation of several different term sets, which is hard to credit. This consideration leads to dismissal of the second hypothesis, referred to above (p. 367)

Three main patterns of derivation appear from these data:

(1)  FF → PF, MM → PM;
(2)  MF → PF (→ PP, SoGeorgia groups), MM → PM (→ zero Ø, SoGeorgia groups);
(3)  FF → PF, FM → PM, MF and MM (generation-reciprocal) → CC terms.

The first and second patterns involve restriction of original generation-reciprocal usage to older generation only, with a new CC term supplied. The third pattern also restricts original generation reciprocity, in male-side terms to older generation, in female-side ♀ terms to younger; and, of course, like the other patterns, it removes the male-side and female-side distinction.

The first pattern is shared by the Bella Coola with Puyallup and Quinault, but doubtless represents two independent innovations, in Bella Coola and southern Coast Salish division languages respectively. Intervening Coast Salish terminologies show the second pattern. The third pattern is restricted to the Tillamook.

Our analysis thus far indicates that Salish kinship system changes have taken place in accordance with the hypothesis that major innovation has been restricted to coastal systems. We conclude that coastal lineal grandparent terminologies were formed by reduction-selection from an original four-term bifurcate collateral system, such as that of the Wenatchee-Columbia, Spokan, and Southern Okanagon. Further, reductions of the original system seem to have been effected independently in different coastal groups, since linguistic cognates of the coastal PP terms appear among all four of the interior terms. The coastal system is basically the same throughout, except for further reduction to a single PP term in groups of the South Georgia linguistic branch; however, it has not been arrived at by any single innovative selection of terms. Instead, at least four separate innovations seem to have taken place – among the ancestors of the Bella Coola, the northern coastal division tribes (south to the Twana), the southern coastal division tribes (Puget Sound and Olympic branches), and the Tillamook.

It is noteworthy that, while the linguistic innovations have been multiple, the systemic results are consistently similar. All coastal systems have reduced the number of PP terms to two or one; all have restricted their usage to the ascending generation (where the original term set was apparently generation reciprocal, [372] applying also to CC); and all but the Tillamook have supplied a new term for CC (in Bella Coola a derivative of the term for SbC). Tillamook is unique in having restricted original female-side terms (MF ≅ ♂DC and MM ≅ ♀DC) to the younger generation.

The only consistent feature in these coastal system changes seems to be sex of the designated relative (in the ascending generation); that is, FF and MF terms are preserved as PF, FM and MM terms as PM. Even here the South Georgia groups are an exception in their special generalizing of an original MF term to usage as PP. We may assume, somewhat speculatively, that this special South Georgia development followed an earlier two-term innovation in which original MF and MM were generalized as PF and PM, and the latter term was then lost.

Uncles, Aunts, Nephews, Nieces:
Systemic Features

One's first impression on examining Salish kin terms for the PSb-SbC class of relatives is that these show the same clearcut distinction between coastal lineal and interior bifurcate collateral usages as do the PP-CC terms. Closer analysis discloses greater complication and more special problems than arise in a comparison of PP-CC terms. Salish PSb-SiC term sets are more variable, both systematically and linguistically, than are the term sets for PP-CC relations. It may be assumed that they resulted from more numerous and extensive innovative processes than in the case of the grandparent-grandchild terms. Yet the general results of a comparison of PSb-SbC terminologies are in agreement with the conclusions derived above from analysis of PP-CC terms.

We find the following five patterns of usage for PSb-SbC terms among the ten coastal systems examined and the Thompson, who here, as in PP-CC usage, agree in general with the coastal systems.

(1) PB, PZ, SbC  (Bella Coola, Squamish, Puyallup, Quinault).
(2) PSb, SbC  (Musqueam, Nooksack, Lummi, Klallam).
(3) PB, PZ, ♂SbC, ♀SbC (Twana).
(4) PB, PZ, SbS, SbD  (Thompson).
(5) FB, MB, PZ, BC, ZC  (Tillamook).

The most widely distributed coastal system has three terms as listed as #1 above, in which Bella Coola agrees with several other linguistically diverse groups. Four groups of the South Georgia linguistic branch (Musqueam, Nooksack, Lummi, Klallam) have reduced distinctions in this class to one of generation only, m accord with their general tendency to generation terminology, as in PP-CC terms. [373] Klallam has essentially the same system as the others, but introduces a distinction of PoSb and PySb, and designates their younger-generation reciprocals as ySbC and oSbC, respectively; the latter two terms are obvious derivatives of the same stem. It is not difficult to derive this South Georgia system from usage like #1 above, as we have already done in the case of the South Georgia PP-CC terms.

Twana agrees with the most general coastal system (#1), except in introducing a unique distinction according to sex of speaker in SbC terms. Thompson also has two SbC terms, but distinguishes these according to own sex.

Only Tillamook distinguish PSb by means of bifurcation, and then only with reference to males; nieces and nephews are not distinguished by own sex, but by sex of the connecting relative, a kind of bifurcation. The system is not like that of other coastal tribes, but, like these, can apparently be derived from an original system similar to those of the Southern Okanagon, Spokan, and Wenatchee-Columbia.[232]

---

[232]  13/ A not dissimilar system for PSb-SbC relations appears in Siuslaw (Lower Umpqua dialect); see Leo J. Frachtenberg, "Siuslawan (Lower Umpqua)," in Franz Boas, ed., *Handbook of American Indian Languages, Part 2* (Bureau of American Ethnology, Bulletin 40, 1922): pp. 461-462.

In addition to the term usages listed, most coastal systems have also two status-change terms (DecPSb, DecSbC); Tillamook has one ("relative after death of connecting relative").

In the three Interior Salish systems – Southern Okanagon, Wenatchee-Columbia, and Spokan – PSb terms are consistently bifurcate collateral. All three distinguish PSb from P, and in addition distinguish these relatives by sex of the P and by own sex, resulting in a four-term system (FB, FZ, MB, MZ). Spokan in addition distinguishes ♂FZ and ♀FZ. Thus, in comparison with interior usage the systems of coastal groups show the same pattern of reduction of number of terms in the PSb category as in that of PP. In both categories Thompson, as noted, goes with coastal usage.

Descending-generation usage is very different, not only between coastal and interior systems, but among the latter. Southern Okanagon has a single SbC term, and generation-reciprocity does not, apparently, apply to the PSb terms. Wenatchee-Columbia shows four terms for SbC relations, ♂BC, ♀BC, ♂ZC, ♀ZC, all apparently distinct from P-Sb terms. Spokan has a complex system in which the principal term distinctions are:

♂FB = ♂BS, FB = ♂BC (partially overlapping the first term in meaning), ♂FS = ♀BS, ♀FZ = ♀BD, MB, MZ, ♂ZC, ♀ZS, ♀ZD. [374]

Spokan has in addition two status-change terms, DecPSb and DecSbC. Southern Okanagon shows one such term, DecPSb; the material used has no item for DecSbC, though one suspects some special term usage in this case. My Wenatchee-Columbia data likewise show no status-change terms in the PSb-SbC class, though this may be due to failure to record such designations.

It may be observed of the Spokan system that no terms refer to both paternal and maternal relatives, that all paternal terms are generation-reciprocal, and that maternal and female-side terms form a different system in which there is no generation-reciprocity and sex of speaker distinguishes terms only in younger-generation referents.

The diversity in descending-generation usage, within the PSb-SbC class of terms, among these three Interior Salish systems is striking. The three tribes concerned speak fairly closely related languages, especially close in the case of Southern Okanagon and Spokan (whose SbC usages differ most markedly), and are probably very similar in their social systems. Obviously innovative change has strongly affected these interior systems in their PSb-SbC usages, so that no one of them can be taken as representative of original proto-Salish usage in this class of relations. Yet they do all show a common feature, bifurcate collateral usage in PSb designations, which contrasts systemically with coastal usage.

Uncles, Aunts, Nephews, Nieces:<br>
Linguistic Features

In determining directions and patterns of change between interior and coastal systems, it would be helpful if we could arrive at some conclusions regarding the relative conservatism of the three interior term sets designating PSb-SbC relations. If, for example, we could arrive at evidence suggesting that one of the interior systems was closer to or more typically representative of proto-Salish usage than the other two, this would assist in placing interior-coastal comparisons on a sounder foundation and would enable us to draw surer diachronic conclusions from such comparison.

Linguistic comparison of Southern Okanagon, Spokan, and Wenatchee-Columbia terms for PSb-SbC relations does seem to provide such evidence. In the data tabulation on page 375 {p136} terms cognate among the three systems are arranged horizontally on the same lines.

In cognate relationships, Spokan is obviously the most interconnected of the three systems, while Southern Okanagon and Wenatchee-Columbia are less connected with each other than is either with Spokan. Further, the Southern Okanagon and Wenatchee-Columbia connections include no cognate relationships not also shared by both these systems with Spokan. Spokan also shows a meaningful [375]

| *Southern Okanagon* | *Spokan* | *Wentachee-Columbia* |
|---|---|---|
| | Łp'úsəmən | |
| | ♂FB ≅ ♂BS | |
| *smił* | səmɛʔł | səmʔɛl |
| FB | FB ≅ ♂BS | FB |
| sk'oq$^{w}$e[2334] | sk'úk'$^{w}$i | |
| FZ | ♂FZ ≅ ♀BS | |
| statak$^{w}$a | tä•tik$^{w}$ə | tik$^{w}$a |
| FZ | ♀FZ = ♀BD | FZ |
| səsi | sɩsi | |
| MB | MB | |
| | | qása |
| | | MB |
| swawása | | |
| MZ | | |
| | qáx̱a | qáx̱a |
| | MZ | MZ |
| | tú•nš | tú•nx |
| | ♂ZC | ♂ZC |
| | sk$^{w}$səʔ'ɛlt[234] | sq$^{w}$ə'sə[235] |
| | ♀ZS | ♀ZC |
| | st'mʔčɛlt | |
| | ♀ZD | |
| łuístən | łuwɛstɩn | |
| DecPSb | DecPSb | |
| słəłwílt | słuwɛlt | słuwɛlt |
| SbC | DecSbC | ♂BC |

---

[233] 14/ Apparently the Northern Okanagon term, used as an alternative to staták$^{w}$a at Tonasket. The cognate Spokan term looks like a reduplicative diminutive of *sk'ui* (♂M).

[234] 15/ This and the term below contain the derivative suffix -ɛlt, "child, young one." Cf. Spokan *sk$^{w}$sɛʔ* (S), st'mčɛʔɛlt (D); the term for ♂ZD is apparently formed from that for D by a glottal-stop infix, of possibly diminutive import. The forms were carefully checked phonetically.

[235] 16/ WC ♀BC was attested by informants as a separate term, but the form is uncertain.

distinction of terms for ♂FZ and ♀FZ which are apparently lumped as synonyms for FZ in Southern Okanagon.[236]

We can derive several immediate conclusions from these observations. The system differences in SbC usage, in particular, indicate that innovations have occurred in all three systems, but probably most extensively in Southern Okanagon and Wenatchee-Columbia. Linguistic considerations make it apparent that the innovations are not shared by any two of the three systems, and that the Spokan PSb-SbC terminology is the most likely to have been least affected by innovation; it is therefore relatively conservative within this group of three Interior Salish systems. We can further conclude that the Southern Okanagon and Wenatchee-Columbia terminologies have been independently affected by innovations which can be roughly characterized as (a) term reduction, and (b) restriction of reciprocal generation usage.

If coastal PSb-SbC terminologies have been derived from an original system perhaps best represented by recent Spokan PSb-SbC usage, then these same innovative processes must have played a major role in the formation of the coastal systems. However, linguistic evidence indicates again that the innovations were adopted separately in different coastal groups.

Linguistically, the terms for PSb-SbC relations in coastal Salish groups are extremely diverse, much more so than the reasonable uniformity of system usage for these terms would lead one to suppose. Cognate terms for this class among coastal languages, with interior cognates noted where apparent, seem to be limited to the following cases.

(1) Coastal (PB): BC sisi, Squa sése. Interior (MB): SOk səsí, Spok sısí?

(2) Coastal (PB): Twa kási?, Puy kasé, Til qɛ'sa?s (MB). Interior (MB): WC qása. (The *k-q* correspondence makes this comparison doubtful for Twana and Puyaliup, unless *k-* is misrecorded for *q-*).

(3) Coastal (FB): Til swaáls. Interior (FB): SOk, smił, Spok səmɛ?l, WC səm?ɛl.

(4) Coastal (PSb): Lum *sɛčs*, Klal cáčc (PoSb), Til čac (PZ). Interior (oSb): Spok łčíčɛ (♀oZ), WC čáka (♂oZ). (The Spokan cognate is doubtful; it may represent a reduplicated stem *či-čɛ plus ł- prefix, and thus cognate with Wenatchee-Columbia kə'x (♀oZ) and Twana čə'š (oZ).

(5) Coastal (SbC): Squa stáeł, Twa sta•yıł (DecSbC). Puy stálał [377] (SbC) and Twa staláł (♀SbC) are possibly connected. No interior cognates are apparent.

(6) Coastal (SbC): Mus stíwən, Nook, stíwən, Lum stík$^w$ən, Klal stíq$^w$in (oSbC). Interior (FZ): SOk staták$^w$a, WC tik$^w$a, Spok tä•tik$^w$ə (♀FZ ≅ ♀BD). The Spokan generation-reciprocal usage suggests that the other interior systems and coastal usage have here developed in different directions by different restrictions of generation reciprocity.

(7) Coastal (SbC): Twa słua•laš (♂SbC), Til sıgálš (BC). Interior (SbC): SOk słəłwílt, WC słəłwílt (♂BC), Spok słəłwílt (DecSbC). (As noted previously, the element -ɛlt (etc.) in the interior terms is a suffix denoting "child, young one").

---

[236] 17/ Or perhaps represent Northern and Southern Okanagon terms, used as synonyms by some Southern Okanagon.

(8)    Coastal (DecSbC):   Squa swɪnəmáɫ, Mus swənmɛyɫ, Nook swɛnimaiƛ̓, Lum skʷənŋíčƛ̓. All are languages of the South Georgia branch.  No interior cognates appear.

(9)    Coastal (DecPrSb): Lum k'sɪčäɫ, Klal skésačaiɫ (DecSbC).    Note reversal of generation-reciprocity.  No interior cognates.

(10)  Coastal (DecPSb): Squa saʔɪxʷɫ, Quin sixʷɫ (SbC; cf. síxʷən, DecPrSb).  Interior: Spok scixʷəlt (C, CC, lineal descendant; səxʷsixʷlt, "children and grandchildren").

(11)  Coastal (SbC): BC emc; cf. BC slemc CC, and other coastal (and Thompson, Shuswap) CC terms cited above, p. 370.

We should also note that while the Thompson terms for PB and PZ are difficult to find cognates for, their terms for SbC have clear interior but no coastal cognates:  Thom skʷəsɛ (SbS), Spok skʷəsɛʔ (S), skʷəʔɛlt (♀ZS), WC sqʷəsə (♀ZC); Thorn sƛ̓əmqéit (SbD), Spok st'mʔčɛʔɛlt (D), st'mʔčɛʔɛlt (♀ZD).  Thus, Thompson is terminologically more like other interior languages, despite its agreement in system of usage with the coast.  This suggests that the accordance of Thompson usage with the coastal lineal system, both in PP-CC and in PSb-SbC terms, is the result of contact influence from coastal cultures, and thus represents a special Thompson innovation due to this factor.

Patterns of cognate correspondence in the above material are not as clear as in the case of PP-CC terms, yet in so far as we can define them they do not seem to be at variance with the conclusions regarding derivation of coastal systems arrived at from analysis of the PP-CC terminologies.  The following patterns are apparent in PSb-SbC terms; in each case the interior application is cited first, followed by the meaning or meanings in coastal systems.

(1) MB → PB.  (2) MB (another term) → PB.  (3) FB → FB.  [378]  (4) oZ → PrSb (Z).  (5) FZ → SbC.  (6) SbC → SbC.  (7) C (etc) → DecPSb, SbC.[237]

There are indications in the list of a change in generation, reference among coastal terminologies.  Pattern #5, for example, shows a cognate correspondence of Southern Okanagon and Wenatchee-Columbia terms for FZ (and a cognate term of broader meaning) with coastal (South Georgia branch) terms for SbC.  This can be explained by assuming, as we have done on other grounds, that Spokan generation-reciprocal usage is here original (♀FZ ≅ ♀BD).  Usage in the other two interior systems, on the one hand, and in the South Georgia coastal systems, on the other, would then represent secondary restrictions of generation reciprocity to ascending and descending relatives, respectively.  Indications of an old generation-reciprocal usage may also appear in pattern #7.

Three of the four Interior Salish PSb terms show cognate correspondences in coastal terminologies – patterns # 1, 2, 3, and 5 above.  Meanings or range of application are usually different, but only the interior terms for MZ seem to lack cognates in coastal terms.  We thus have a situation comparable to the coast-interior relations in PP terms, which can be interpreted plausibly only by assuming derivation of coastal systems from something more like the interior

---

[237]   18/ The symbols used express both cognate correspondences, for terms of designated meaning, and hypothetical direction or derivation.

systems.

The linguistic data on PSb-SbC terms shows a high degree of noncomparability of terms in this set between the various coastal terminologies. Most of such cognates as appear are shared by adjacent groups or those closely related linguistically. On the other hand, the number of distinct terms in this class is generally less in any coastal system than in the three interior systems with bifurcate collateral arrangement.

We infer that if present coastal PSb-SbC systems were all (or most of them) reflexes of a single original Coast Salish innovation which reduced an original proto-Salish system from bifurcate collateral to lineal terminology, then these systems would show higher cognate ratios in their term sets than is actually the case. But, since the coastal systems are lexically quite heterogeneous, it appears more reasonable to conclude that their reduction from an original bifurcate collateral terminology was the result of a number of independent innovative changes. All of these independent changes brought about the same systemic results: reduction of the number of terms in the PSb-SbC set, and (except in Tillamook) consistently lineal term usage. However, since these changes went on independently in different earlier coastal systems, the linguistic results were lexical diversity and a considerable number of noncognates among the different terminologies. [379]

Innovative change has in this case operated more extensively on the coast than in PP-CC term sets, yet the same pattern of diverse correspondence in cognates with different parts of the interior term sets appears as in the case of the PP-CC terms. Thus, consideration of PSb-SbC terminologies does not contradict but rather strengthens the conclusions derived from analysis of PP-CC terms.

## General Conclusions

The principal findings and conclusions of this study may be indicated in general summary.

(1) Major innovative change in Salish kinship terminologies has affected coastal systems, including such linguistically diverse {branches} divisions of the Salish stock as Bella Coola, Coast Salish, and Tillamook. These peoples have developed varieties of lineal terminology in the PP-CC and PSb-SbC classes of relations.

(2) Coastal lineal terminologies have been derived from an original bifurcate collateral terminology similar to systems found among some Interior Salish, and perhaps best exemplified by the Spokan, through two main processes: reduction of number of distinctive terms through generalizing meanings; and, restriction of generation-reciprocity by distinguishing ascending from descending generation usage. Certain common features of Salish kinship usage have been retained in both systems, coastal and interior.

(3) Linguistic comparison indicates derivation of coastal terminologies not only in the direction indicated above – bifurcate collateral to lineal – but through multiple independent but parallel innovations.

## Further Problems Suggested

Granting the applicability of these conclusions, a number of problems respecting kinship usage may be settled or illuminated in new ways.

First, we may enquire if both the systems examined for Salish peoples – coastal lineal and interior bifurcate collateral – show common features of Spier's "Salish system."[238]  Or, put another way, are all Salish peoples properly to be lumped as having a single type of kinship terminology?  The common features of all or most Salish systems cited above are impressive, but equally striking are the divergences in methods of classifying ascending-generation relatives shown by coastal and [380] interior groups.  In his Salish type Spier included as defining criteria certain common Salish kinship features and others referring only to lineal terminologies.  This Salish type was held to include Coast Salish, a number of other coastal non-Salish groups, and the Interior Salish Lillooet, Shuswap, and "possibly" Spokan.  The Lillooet and Shuswap may turn out to go with coastal peoples – their interior British Columbia neighbors the Thompson certainly do – but we must remove from this category not only the Spokan, but probably all southerly Interior Salish, of the Wenatchee-Columbia, Okanagon, Spokan-Kalispel-Flathead, and Coeur d'Alene groups.  It is not implied that Spier intended to restrict his Salish type to Salish peoples (as he obviously did not), nor has he categorically included in it all Salish groups.

Secondly, coastal and interior systems of Salish kin terms appear to present an example of two "bilateral" systems with a different number of term distinctions, the interior systems having more for the classes of relations examined (PP-CC and PSb-SbC). Murdock has presented an hypothesis according to which "distinctions in kinship terminology should appear in association with relatively insignificant functional differences between kinsmen more often in bilateral than in unilinear societies."[239]  Coast Salish and Interior Salish societies are both bilateral, yet the latter make more distinctions in term usage than do the former. It is not impossible that a greater number of "insignificant functional differences" between kinsmen appear in Interior Salish societies than in those of coastal tribes, yet I know of no clear-cut ethnographic data which would lead us to this conclusion. This is a perhaps profitable direction of future research.

A third problem involves the question of whether the lineal terminology of coastal Salish groups is an ancient and conservative system, retained perhaps from some remote proto-Mosan-Algonkian past, and therefore shared by such linguistically and geographically discrete peoples as Wakashans, Salish, and Yurok. Kroeber seemed to think that such was the case.[240]  If the results of the present study have been interpreted correctly, then we must abandon this view, at least so far as Salish lineal systems are concerned, since these can be explained as innovative within the framework of Salish data alone, and do not require reference to historically wider (or deeper) linguistic units.

A much more general and perhaps more significant problem has to do with whether there are any

---

[238]  19/ Spier 1925: p. 74 and Plate 1.  Among the defining features of the "Salish type" are: merging of father's and mother's siblings; one term for "uncle" and one for "aunt"; one term for nephew or niece; terms for "grandparent," "child," "grandchild."  These criteria fit most coastal systems, but not those of the interior (other than Thompson).

[239]  20/ Murdock 1949: p. 110.

[240]  21/ Kroeber 1960: pp. 347-348 (fn.); also, 1934.

causal or influencing factors which can be shown to correlate with the particular line of change in Salish kinship terminologies defined in this study. It is not proposed to explore this problem here, but there do seem to be [381] several promising lines of investigation which might shed light on the wider question of kinship systems as indicators of organizational level or degree of social development.

One striking difference in social culture between coastal and interior Salish tribes is the prevalence of ranked status distinctions in the former groups. This is, of course, a general distinction between Northwest Coast and Plateau societies, and applies to peoples on the coast other than Salish. We have already noted, however, that Coast Salish lineal terminology is shared with other coastal peoples; there is therefore a correlation with some aspect or aspects of coastal culture.

It is not perhaps easy at first glance to see how this distinction between Northwest Coast and Plateau types of social structure could reflect itself in the coastal reduction of kin term distinctions. Yet something along this line could probably be worked out in terms of a general theory of evolution in kinship systems recently proposed by Service.[241] I was struck by the fact that his formulation seems to fit well such a specific case as we have here: the smaller number of terminological distinctions for immediate kin and the presumably more complex structure of general status relationships in coastal cultures, vis-a-vis those of the Plateau area. Service's notion of "devolution" or progressive simplification of "egocentric-familistic" systems of nomenclature in more complex societies is suggestive and worth pursuing in this connection.

BIBLIOGRAPHY


Elmendorf, William W.
  1946 *Twana Kinship Terminology* (Southwestern Journal of Anthropology, Vol. 2: pp. 420-432).
Elmendorf, William W., and Wayne Suttles
  1960 *Pattern and Change in Halkomelem Salish Dialects* (Anthropological Linguistics, Vol. 2, No. 7: pp. 1-32).
Frachtenberg, Leo J.
  1917 *A Siletz Vocabulary* (International Journal of American Linguistics, Vol.1: pp. 45-46).
Gunther, Erna
  1927 *Klallam Ethnography* (University of Washington Publications in Anthropology, Vol. 1, No.5).
Jacobs, Melville
  1932 *Northern Sahaptin Kinship Terms* (American Anthropologist, Vol. 34: pp. 688-693).
Kirchoff, Paul
  1932 *Verwandtschaftsbeuichnungen Und Verwandtenheirat* (Zeitschrift für Ethnologie, Vol. 64: pp. 46-49). [382]
Kroeber, A.L.
  1934 *Yurok and Neighboring Kin Term Systems* (University of California Publications in American Archaeology and Ethnology, Vol. 35, No. 2).
  1960 *Comparative Notes on the Structure of Yurok Culture* (Research Studies, Washington State University, Monographic Supplement No. 2; Published With W.W. Elmendorf, *The*


---

[241] 22/ Service, 1960.

*Structure o Twana Culture*).
Krueger, John R.
 1961  *Miscellanea Selica II: Some Kinship Terms Of The Flathead Salish* (Anthropological Linguistics, Vol. 3: pp. 11-18).
Lowie, Robert H.
 1928  *A Note on Relationship Terminologies* (American Anthropologist, Vol. 30: pp. 265-266).
Mcilwraith, T.F.
 1948  *The Bella Coola Indians* (2 Vols., Toronto).
Murdock, George Peter
 1949  *Social Structure* (New York).
Olson, Ronald W.
 1936  *The Quinault Indians* (University Of Washington Publications in Anthropology, Vol. 6, No. 1).
Service, Elman R.
 1960  *Kinship Terminology and Evolution* (American Anthropologist, Vol. 62: pp. 747-763).
Smith, Marian W.
 1940  *The Puyallup-Nisqually* (New York).
Spier, Leslie
 1925  *The Distribution of Kinship Systems in North America* (University of Washington Publications in Anthropology, Vol. 1, No. 2).
Spier, Leslie, and Edward Sapir
 1930  *Wishram Ethnography* (University of Washington Publications in Anthropology, Vol. 3, No. 3).
Swadesh, Morris
 1950  *Salish Internal Relationships* (International Journal of American Linguistics, Vol. 16: pp. 157-167) ,
Walters, L.V.W.
 1938  "Social Structure" (In Leslie Spier, ed., *The Sinkaietk or Southern Okanagon of Washington*: pp. 73-99, General Series In Anthropology, No. 6).

WASHINGTON STATE UNIVERSITY
PULLMAN, WASHINGTON

William Welcome Elmendorf  System Change in Salish Kinship Terminologies  *Southwestern Journal of Anthropology* VOL. 17 (4): 365-382, 1961 Winter

# Kinship Terminology in Upper Chehalis in a Historical Framework
M. Dale Kinkade

*University of British Columbia*

Abstract.
The Upper Chehalis kinship system has an unusual pattern of terminology for siblings, distinguishing elder from younger, male from female, and inclusive from exclusive. The last applies only to elder siblings, and sex is not distinguished for inclusive siblings; the result is a five-term system. Other parts of the system are less unusual (aside from one or two decedence terms). Some of the meanings of these terms are not well identified; comparative data from other Salishan languages help provide a fuller understanding of the use of this terminology and suggest a source for the complex sibling terms.

1. **Introduction**. Kinship systems in the Tsamosan (earlier Olympic) branch of Salish appear to be almost totally unstudied, Olson (1936) reports Quinault terminology, although he does little more than offer a list of most of the terms. Elmendorf (1961) includes data from this source in his comparative study of grandparent-grandchild and uncle-aunt-nephew-niece terminology in Salish, but apparently had no access to other Tsamosan data. This neglect is unfortunate, since it turns out that Upper Chehalis has an extremely unusual set of terms for elder siblings and uncle. An attempt will be made in this paper to explain how this system developed, although no suggestions will be made as to why it did so. This explanation requires comparative evidence from Cowlitz and Lower Chehalis, the languages spoken to the east and west, respectively, of Upper Chehalis. These comparisons will then be expanded into speculations on relevant parts of the Proto-Tsamosan kinship system. The remainder of the Upper Chehalis kinship system is less problematic, and is not unlike other kinship systems of the area. However, it does have features that are of interest for comparative Salish and for kinship studies in general.

2. **Siblings**. Upper Chehalis has separate terms for siblings distinguished according to age relative to *ego* and according to sex of the sibling. However, there are five terms, rather than the four that would be expected from this statement, because the external reference of the relationship is also a factor for elder siblings. Specifically, there is a single term for elder siblings (regardless of sex) of the speaker or addressee (that is, first or second person), while there are two terms for elder siblings of a third person. This opposition will be labeled *inclusive* and *exclusive* (adapting pronominal terminology).[242] [85]

---

[242]  1/  In this paper the parallel to pronominal terminology is only approximate, since in pronomial reference exclusive unites first and third person against second, while here exclusive merely represents the reverse of inclusive: third person against first and second, versus first and second against third. My adaptation is based simply on the need for labels to refer to the Upper Chehalis categories.

(1)  EXCLUSIVE                 INCLUSIVE                PLURAL
     oB  *čit'-n's*[243]                                *nsčit'utn*
                               *x̲ʷáł*
     oZ  *yáy'-n's*                                     *nšyáy'a'tn*
     yB          *ne'sči, nəsči*                        *nšne'sčitn*
     yZ          *pesn', pəsn*                          *nšpase•n'tn*

In the singular, *čit'-* and *yáy'-* can occur *only* with third person possessive suffixes; *x̲ʷáł* can never occur with them. Usage in the plural is not entirely clear; I was only able to elicit the plural terms given in (1), which are used with *any* possessive affix, although Boas (1927) reports plural forms *of x̲ʷáł* as well *(nšx̲ʷáłtn)*. Furthermore, when no possessive affix is used at all, only *x̲ʷáł* can occur; hence *čit'u-* and *yáy'a-* are bound forms.

It is important to add about *x̲ʷáł* that it is only the *term* which can be ambiguous in reference to sex. Since the language requires definite or indefinite articles with all lexical arguments (subjects, objects, and objects of prepositions), and these articles distinguish gender, the actual usage of the term would specify whether the referent is male or female. In fact, the use of articles provides the only means of distinguishing the sex of the referents of several Upper Chehalis kin terms: offspring, one of the four terms for sibling's offspring, grandchild, great-grandparent, and parent-in-law. What is interesting here, then, is the fact that there are separate *terms* for older brother and older sister in the exclusive system, and for younger brother and younger sister; these pairs could, after all, also have been distinguished solely by preceding articles, as they are in some other nearby Salishan languages.

There is no information on whether or not there are cultural reasons or implications for these data, and such information is no longer recoverable. It is certainly an oddly skewed system, however, and an explanation of some kind seems desirable. It is typologically quite aberrant, partly because inclusive-exclusive oppositions using totally different lexical items are not usual in kinship systems (although vocative forms are often different). The Upper Chehalis exclusive system (with a third person possessor) fits into Murdock's (1968: 3) Type D: Dravidian or Age-Sex Type (which would have four terms divided by sex and relative age). However, with a first or second possessor (the Upper Chehalis inclusive type), it fits none of his categories except by turning on its head his Type C: Algonkian or Skewed Age Type (which distinguishes sex for elder siblings, but not for younger siblings). Nerlove and Romney (1967: 182), on the other hand, allow for twelve types of sibling systems, as contrasted with Murdock's six, and recognize as a rare exception to their type 5 just such a system as occurs in Upper Chehalis inclusive terminology (the exclusive system is again no problem, and is their type 6).

Although the Upper Chehalis system as a whole is highly unusual and not found elsewhere in the area, there are neighboring parallels for both the inclusive [86] and the exclusive systems. Cowlitz (also Salish), spoken to the southeast of Upper Chehalis, had a system identical to the Upper Chehalis inclusive system (and there is no evidence that it ever had contrasting inclusive and exclusive systems). This system is illustrated in (2) below.

---

[243]  2/ This *-n's or -ns* suffix is a variant of third person possessive *-s;* it occurs commonly with kin terms, but is not limited to them.

(2) Cowlitz

| | |
|---|---|
| $\underline{x}^{w}\acute{a}\mathord{?}\ell$ ($\underline{x}^{w}\acute{a}\mathord{?}\ell$-I 'his...) | 'oB/oZ' |
| *ne?sk (nske-w'i* 'his ...'; root nəski'-) | 'yB' |
| *pe•sn (psn-á•w'i* 'his...', *nx-paisen'-tn* 'PL yZ') | 'yZ' |

Note that the three terms above are similar in form to the Upper Chehalis inclusive terms,[244] Furthermore, the same system was also apparently found in Tenino Chehalis, the upriver dialect of Upper Chehalis and the one contiguous to Cowlitz; neither *čit'-ns* nor *yáy'-n's* is attested for that dialect, although the entire set of sibling terms is attested for the Oakville Chehalis and Satsop dialects.  This three-term pattern occurs even further afield, however, in both Kathlamet Chinook and Lower Chinook.  Both these languages were spoken on the Columbia River downriver from the Cowlitz (who were along the Cowlitz River nearly down to its confluence with the Columbia).  These Chinookan groups were thus south and southwest of the Upper Chehalis, although not immediate neighbors of them.  The two systems were as follows:

(3)  Kathlamet (Hymes 1955: 129-30)

| | |
|---|---|
| -*lxt* | 'oB/oZ' |
| -*mxix* | 'yB' |
| -*mtx* | 'yZ' |

(4)  Lower Chinook (Boas 1911: 611-12)

| | |
|---|---|
| *ká-pxo• (voc)*, -*xk'un* | 'oB/oZ' |
| *ao• (voc)*, -*wux* | 'yB' |
| *a-ts (voc)* | 'yZ' |

Neither of these systems bears any phonological resemblance to the Salishan systems (or apparently to each other), so if there is influence in one direction or the other, it is strictly on a systemic basis, and not a matter of borrowing of terminology.

The Upper Chehalis exclusive system, a more usual kind of sibling system, is the same as that found in its western neighbor.  Lower Chehalis, shown in (5) (again all terms are phonologically similar to the Upper Chehalis equivalents).[245]

(5)  Lower Chehalis

| | | |
|---|---|---|
| *čit'* | 'oB' | [87] |
| *yáy'* | 'oZ' | |

---

[244] 3/ I avoid calling these cognates because of the possibility of borrowing, as discussed below.

[245] 4/ Upper Chehalis, Cowlitz, and Lower Chehalis forms are from my own field notes except where otherwise noted.  Some Lower Chehalis forms cited are from the 1967-68 field notes of Charles T. Snow (indicated by CTS).  Quinault forms are primarily from the 1968 field notes of James A. Gibson (indicated by JAG), although forms given by Olson (1936) were also consulted; Gibson's materials are in a narrow phonetic transcription from which I have extrapolated the possible phonemic rendition used here.  Forms cited from the *Comparative Vocabularies* of Boas (1925) are marked CV.

*nəsc*　　'yB'
*pəs*　　'yZ'

As an aside, it should be pointed out that Quinault, the fourth Tsamosan language, seems to have a completely different system of sibling terminology, with at most one term *(yə* 'oZ', given by Olson 1936: 92) that is similar to anything in the other languages.[246]

The source of the complicated Upper Chehalis system, then, does seem explainable as being at least in part a result of diffusion, although it cannot be explained why it was maintained or what cultural implications it may have had. Either a Cowlitz-type system was overlaid as the inclusive system on a Lower Chehalis-type system, or a Lower Chehalis-type system was overlaid as the exclusive system on a Cowlitz-type system. The first of these seems the more likely possibility for two reasons: (1) the three-term system is typologically unusual, and (2) Proto-Salish appears to have had at least a four-term system, which would presumably have been retained in daughter languages until altered by outside influences or internal social changes.

To date no one has attempted a complete reconstruction of the entire Salishan kinship system; Laurence Thompson and I have reconstructed a number of terms, including five terms for siblings in Proto-Salish. We reconstruct a term for Proto-Salish only if reflexes occur in at least two of the five branches of the family (Bella Coola, Interior Salish, Tsamosan, Central Salish, and Tillamook); if only two languages are involved in a reconstruction, they must not be contiguous. The five sibling terms, with tentative glosses (tentative because of meaning differences in individual languages), are given in (6), along with an indication of which branches have reflexes of the terms.

(6) Proto-Salish

      **ʔalix*　　　　'cross-sex Sib' (Central Salish, Tillamook)

      **qá-*　　　　　'oB' (Interior Salish, Central Salish)

      **kət*　　　　　'oB' (Tsamosan, Central Salish)

      **kəx ~ *kix*　　'oZ' (Interior Salish, Central Salish)

      **s-ʔuqʷay*　　'ySb' (Interior Salish, Central Salish, Tillamook)

The evidence from Proto-Salish for solving the question of the development of the Upper Chehalis system is not as clear-cut as one might like. Only one Upper Chehalis term goes back to one of the Proto-Salishan terms in (6), namely, the second oB term (cf. Upper Chehalis *čit'u-*). However, note that Proto-Salish did apparently distinguish elder siblings according to sex. Furthermore, even if it did not distinguish younger siblings according to sex, as do at least three of the Tsamosan languages, the oB-oZ-ySb pattern is typologically not unusual (and is the pattern found in Tillamook). It may be assumed, [88] then, that the exclusive Upper Chehalis and Lower Chehalis elder sibling terms derived from Proto-Tsamosan, but not the inclusive Upper Chehalis and Cowlitz term *x̲ʷáɫ*. I would suggest the following terms for Proto-Tsamosan:

---

[246] 5/ Other Salishan languages in the area have the following sibling patterns: Tillamook oB, oZ, ySb; Twana oB, oZ, myB, myZ-mySb; Lushootseed and Clallam oSb, ySb.

(7)  Proto-Tsamosan
>     *kit'u-          'oB'
>     *yáy'a-          'oZ'
>     *nəski-          'yB'
>     *pəsən-          'yZ'

The reconstruction *kit'u- is supported by Upper Chehalis and Lower Chehalis, as well as Central Salish cognates. The form *yáy'a- is also supported by Upper Chehalis and Lower Chehalis, and Olson's (1936: 92) Quinault yə 'oZ' is probably related as well.[247] The two younger sibling terms can be reconstructed on the basis of Upper Chehalis, Lower Chehalis, and Cowlitz (the vowel and stress reconstructions are based on various oblique forms),[248] even though both terms and the division of a single younger sibling term from Proto-Salish into two terms in Tsamosan are innovations.

3. **Uncle**. An inclusive-exclusive opposition is found in one other part of the Upper Chehalis kinship system, in terms for uncle.

(8)      qási² (PL: ns-qási²-tn)                    'FB/MB' (inclusive)
         t'át'-ns 'his ...' (PL: nš-t'at'a-tn)      'FB/MB' (exclusive)

Again the exclusive term is similar to Lower Chehalis and Quinault (although not attested for either the Satsop or Tenino Chehalis dialects of Upper Chehalis).

(9)      Lower Chehalis
         t'á²t' (CTS)

         *Quinault*
         t'át²                    'U'

There is nothing else in Tsamosan similar to qási²; cognates for it do occur in Interior Salish, Central Salish, and Tillamook, and a Proto-Salishan term for uncle can be reconstructed:

(10)     Proto-Salish
         *qasáy²        'U' (Interior Salish, Tsamosan, Central Salish, Tillamook) [89]

---

[247] 6/ This form may also go back to Proto-Salish. It is possible to reconstruct a Proto-Salishan form *yá'ya', meaning something like 'friend, relative' (based on Central Salishan forms). The meaning difference is not bothersome, but the fact that Upper Chehalis has a root yáy'a- 'to like, love', and Cowlitz yáy~ 'to like, respect', adds a further complication. This latter seems a more likely cognate for the Central Salishan forms, although a semantic split of the root in Tsamosan is not impossible.

[248] 7/ Plurals, possessed forms, and other oblique forms will be given wherever they are necessary to show the underlying form of a morpheme.

This form must, therefore, have occurred in Proto-Tsamosan.  However, because the other word for uncle occurs in three of the four Tsamosan languages, it should also be reconstructed for Proto-Tsamosan:

(11)  Proto-Tsamosan
      *tát'a- 'PB'

An alternative hypothesis is that (11) is an innovation in Lower Chehalis-Quinault, and borrowed by Upper Chehalis as part of its exclusive kinship terminology (note that it was the exclusive sibling terms that were similar between Upper Chehalis and Lower Chehalis).  Nevertheless, two uncle terms seem likely for Proto-Tsamosan.  Three terms can be reconstructed to Proto-Salish as possible terms for uncle; besides *qasáyʔ, given in (10) above, there are the following:

(12)  Proto-Salish
      *(si)sádyʔ          'U' (Bella Coola, Interior Salish, Central Salish)
      *s-məʔál            'U' (Interior Salish, Tillamook)

In addition, Lower Chehalis and Quinault have two terms each, those in (9) above and those in (13).

(13)  Lower Chehalis
      si•x^w               'U'

      Quinault
      si'•x^wən (MDK)          'U; U, A when P is deceased'

These forms may properly be decedence terms (see section 4.4 below for possible other meanings).
        Cowlitz is of no help on uncle terms.  It has a single term for both FaBr and MoBr:

(14)  Cowlitz
      k^wáłamn (k^wáłamn-awi "his ...')    'U'

This term is a compound of k^wáła(w) - 'aunt' and mán- 'father'.  The *Comparative Vocabularies* (Boas 1925) do give *ke'.se,* although this form was not known to my informants.  All the Tsamosan languages have a single word for 'aunt', reconstructible as:

(15)  Proto-Tsamosan
      k^wáłáw-                 'PZ'  [90]

This reconstruction is based on the Cowlitz form and other Tsamosan cognates.

(16)  Upper Chehalis
      k^wáł  (PL: nš-k^wəłá•w'-tn, nš-k^wáł-tn) 'MZ/FZ'

Cowlitz

$k^w \partial tu\mathit{?}$  ($k^w \partial t\acute{a} \bullet w'$-$i$ 'his ...')          'A'

Lower Chehalis

$k^w \acute{a} \mathit{ł}$                              'A'

Quinault

$k^w \partial t\acute{a} w\mathit{?}$                          'A'

This term does not go back to Proto-Salish, however, where three terms can be reconstructed for 'aunt':

(17)  Proto-Salish

*$xk\acute{a}k^w c$                    'A'  (Central Salish, Tillamook)
*$\mathit{?}\partial p\acute{u}s\partial\mathit{?}$                    'A'  (Interior Salish, Central Salish)
*$sat\acute{a}$-                      'A'  (Interior Salish, Central Salish)

4.  **Other terms**.  The inclusive-exclusive opposition is not used anywhere else in the Upper Chehalis kinship system, and reconstruction of the rest of the Proto-Tsamosan kinship system presents fewer difficulties, although there are many terms in these languages that do not appear to have cognates in other branches of the family.  However, the kinship *system* that can be reconstructed for Tsamosan is compatible with what we have been able to reconstruct for Proto-Salish.  The remaining kin terms are discussed below in four sections:

> terms for ascending generations (parents, grandparents, and step-parents);
> equal and descending generations (cousins, children, step-children, nieces, nephews, and grandchildren);
> relatives by marriage (spouses and in-laws);
> and decedence terms (terms for relatives after the linking relative has died).

4.1.  **Ascending generation terms**.  Ascending generation kin terms in Upper Chehalis are general in the way they are in English, that is, no distinction is made between one's mother's and one's father's siblings or parents:  FB = MB, FZ = MZ, FM = MM, and FF = MF.  In addition, all great-grandparents are designated with a single term, which was, furthermore, reciprocal with descending generations.  (Uncles and aunts were discussed in section 3 above.)

Upper Chehalis terms for parents are simple.

(18)  $k^w \acute{u}y$              'M'
      $k^w um\acute{a} \bullet \mathit{?}$          'F' [91]

Both terms have good Salishan histories, although the word for 'father' is disguised with a prefix and loss of a final consonant.  That the $k^w u$- on 'father' is a prefix can be seen from terms for step-parents in (19), where a different prefix is used.  In addition, the final consonant of the root is present (as well as a suffix -$m$).

(19) *sčəłtán'm*          'step-M'
     *sčəłmán'm*          'step-F'


Note further that the word for 'step-mother' uses an entirely different root for 'mother', and it, too, can be reconstructed in Proto-Salish. Having two terms each for 'mother' and 'father' is typical of several Interior Salishan languages and Tillamook, although not otherwise usual on the coast; the distinction is between the parents of a male referent and those of a female referent. Coast languages have retained reflexes of one or the other term; recognition that two forms for each kin type must be reconstructed accounts for the inconsistent distribution of their reflexes on the coast. The Proto-Salishan forms are given in (20).


(20) Proto-Salish
       *mán*           'F'  (Bella Coola, Tsamosan, Central Salish, Tillamook)
       *l(a)ʔáw*       'F'  (Interior Salish, Tsamosan, ?Central Salish, Tillamook)
       *k'uy*          'M'  (Interior Salish, Tsamosan, Central Salish, Tillamook)
       *tán*           'M'  (Tsamosan, Central Salish)


The function of the $k^wu$- prefix on $k^wumá•ʔ$ is unclear, and is apparently lexicalized in Upper Chehalis. It does occur on Cowlitz parent terms, too, and it may be the same prefix found on Lower Chehalis and Quinault words for 'grandchild'; it is possibly also the beginning of the Quinault words for 'son' and 'daughter'. These forms are:


(21) Cowlitz
       $k^wu$-*máʔ*, *kə-máʔ* (*mán-awi* 'his ...')          'F'
       $k^wu$-*máʔ*, *kə-máʔ* (*mán-awi* 'his ...')          'M'


Lower Chehalis
       $k^wəʔim$                 'GC'


Quinault
       $k^wiʔím$ (JAG)           'GC'
       $k^witún$ (JAG)           'S'
       $k^wəmíł$ (JAG)           'D'
       $k^witán$ (JAG)           'yB, yZ'  [92]


Additional forms in Cowlitz with a *k*- prefix were also recorded: *kəkáyʔ* 'grandmother' and *kak^wúpaʔ* 'grandfather' (see (24) below). At first glance they might appear to be reduplications; however, it is not a usual reduplication pattern in Cowlitz, and they are more likely additional instances of this prefix. The latter may be a vocative marker, although none of these forms were recorded as specifically or exclusively vocative.[249]

---

[249]   8/  Besides the prefix *kə-/ka-/$k^wu$-*, there are two other inflections peculiar to kin terms in Upper Chehalis and Cowlitz. (1) Cowlitz, for several terms, and Upper Chehalis, for a very few terms, adds an augment *-aw-* before a third person possessive suffix (see examples in

None of the other Tsamosan languages has retained a reflex of Proto-Salishan *k'uy* for 'mother'; Cowlitz has the other 'mother' term (which Upper Chehalis uses in 'step-mother'), and three of the four languages have retained reflexes of *man* 'father'. Quinault also has a reflex of the second 'father' term. These other Tsamosan terms are:

(22)  Cowlitz
      *kʷu-má?, kə-má?* (*mán-awi*  'his ... ')      'F'
      *kʷu-tá?, ka-tá?* (*s-tán-awi*  'his ... ')      'M'
      *tcułma'nEm* (CV)      'step-F'
      *tcułta'nEm* (CV)      'step-M'

Lower Chehalis
      *qəx̲t*      'F'
      *kəh*      'M'
      *qá?ya* (CTS)      'step-M'

Quinault
      *mán* (JAG)      'F'
      *?ál'* (JAG)      'F'
      *kə* (MDK)      'M'
      *sxʷƛ̓íčməł* (JAG)      'M'
      *čəčimá?an* (JAG)      'step-F'
      *súp'əl* (JAG)      'step-M'

While the examples above support a reconstruction of Proto-Tsamosan *man* for 'father', the reconstruction of additional Proto-Tsamosan terms for 'father' and 'mother' can only be supported by knowing that terms found in only one or two neighboring languages go back to Proto-Salish. If the Quinault term for younger sibling (*kʷitán*) can be related to Upper Chehalis *sčəłtán'm* (and Proto-Salish *tán*), then *tán* also can be reconstructed for Proto-Tsamosan.  These terms indicate, however, that Proto-Tsamosan must have had all four parent terms, with shapes similar or identical to those for Proto-Salish in (20) above.

     Upper Chehalis grandparent terms are quite simple; only one term each for 'grandmother' (both FaMo and MoMo) and 'grandfather' (both FaFa and MoFa) occurs, and only one term has been recorded for a generation beyond.  This last term is reciprocal for 'great-parent' and 'great-grandchild'.  The three [93] Upper Chehalis terms are:

(23)    *kəy*      'FM, MM'      *camé•c'a*      'PPP, CCC'
        *čúp'a*      'FF, MF'

---

(2), (32), (33), and elsewhere); the function of this augment is unknown.  (2) Nearly all kin terms in these two languages (plus a very few other words) have distinct plural inflection: in Cowlitz they require a prefixed *nx-~*, and in Upper Chehalis *nš-* or *ns-*, and in both languages a suffixed *-tn* (or *-tan-* if an open syllable follows).

The first two terms have cognates in all three of the other Tsamosan languages, and the third term has cognates in Cowlitz and Lower Chehalis.  Thus all three terms can be reconstructed to Proto-Tsamosan. The various terms for grandparents and their reconstructions are:

(24)  Cowlitz
     *káy⁷* (*káyi⁷-i* 'his...')               'FM, MM'
     *kʷúpa⁷* (*kʷúpa-w'i* 'his ...')      'FF, MF'
     *camé•c'a*                         'PPP, CCC'

     Lower Chehalis
     *číca* (CTS *čəca*)          'FM, MM'
     *mí⁷a*                    'FF, MF'
     *čúlpa⁷* (CTS)            'FF, MF'
     *čəšəlm'əš* (CTS)       'FF, MF'
     *camíc'* (CTS *čamíč'*)    'FF, MF ?PPP'

     Quinault
     *čí⁷* (JAG)               'FM, MM'
     *čúpa⁷* (MDK)          'FF, MF'
     *c'amlə⁷čúpə⁷* (JAG)     'PPF'
     *c'amlə⁷əčí⁷* (JAG)      'PPM'

     Proto-Tsamosan
     **kəyí⁷*                 'PM'
     **ku(l)pa⁷*           'PF'
     **cam=ic'a*         'PPP, CCC'

The significance of extra grandparent terms in Lower Chehalis is unclear. They are apparently local additions to the kinship system, since no other Tsamosan language has more than one term for 'grandmother' or 'grandfather', and only single terms can be reconstructed to Proto-Salish, as shown in (25).

(25)  Proto-Salish
     **kəyá⁷*          'PM, MM'  (Bella Coola, Interior Salish, Tsamosan, Central Salish,
                          Tillamook)
     **kúpay'*         'PF'  (Bella Coola, Interior Salish, Tsamosan, Central Salish) [94]

Given the elaborateness of what is known of other parts of the Proto-Salishan kinship system (with two terms each for 'mother' and 'father', and uncles and aunts apparently distinguished by which parent they relate to), separate terms for FM, MM, FF, and MF might be expected, although such a system, cannot be reconstructed at this time.

**4.2.  Cousins and descending generation terms**.  Salishan languages usually do not distinguish cousins from siblings.  Upper Chehalis, however, has two terms that have been translated as 'cousin':

(26)  *suc's* (súc'is-s 'his ...')          'Cz'
      *(s)tax̱ʷálx̱*                          'Cz'

Neither term seems to have been unambiguously 'cousin'. Boas (1927) gives the additional gloss 'friend' for the first term, and "brothers, sisters' for the second. The first of these terms is known only from the Oakville Chehalis and Tenino Chehalis dialects, and the second only from Oakville Chehalis. Thus *suc's* may have been less specifically a kin term, and *(s)tax̱ʷálx̱* may have been a cover term for both siblings and cousins. Boas further suggests that *suc's* is derived from *ʔuc's* 'one' (the usual word for 'one' is the diminutive of this: *ʔoᵊc's*). Elsewhere in Tsamosan, a term for 'cousin' has been recorded only for Cowlitz:

(27) Cowlitz
       *súc's* (súc'us-i "his ... )          'Cz'

This is clearly cognate with the Upper Chehalis term. A cousin term has also been recorded for Quinault, but it is a derivative of something else.

All four Tsamosan languages have cognate forms for 'son, daughter'. In general in these languages, the sex of the offspring is determined by a preceding feminine or non-feminine definite or indefinite article. The forms and the Proto-Tsamosan reconstruction are:

(28) Upper Chehalis
       *mán'* (PL: *nš-mǝn'-tn*)          'S, D'

       *Cowlitz*
       *mánʔ* (*maníʔ-i* 'his..., his...')  'S, D'

       Lower Chehalis
       *mǝnʔ*                                'S, D'

       Quinault
       *mǝʔn* (JAG)                          'S' [95]

Proto-Tsamosan
       **mǝníʔ-*                            'S, D'

Quinault has additional distinct forms for 'son' and 'daughter'; these can be found above in (21). Both appear to include a prefix *kʷǝ-*; there are no obvious cognates for the root of either Quinault term. It is likely that the Proto-Tsamosan word for 'offspring' is derived from the term for 'father' (given above as **mán*); however, no word for 'son' or 'daughter' can be reconstructed for Proto-Salish.

It should further be noted that the Upper Chehalis word for 'step-child' is derived from the word for 'son, daughter':

(29) *sčǝlmáᵊn'am*      'step-child'

The derivation of this term is like that for 'step-mother' and 'step-father'.
    Terms for nieces and nephews are problematic in that there is insufficient information on them and their specific meanings to sort them out properly.  Upper Chehalis has four such terms:

(30)    *snúk^wł*        'Nw/Nc'
        *x̱^wún*         'Nw'
        *sšawácł*    'Nc'
        *swánačł*   'Nc'

Except for *snúk^wł* (which is attested from Oakville Chehalis and Satsop), these terms are documented only for Oakville Chehalis.  The last of them may be a decedence term (see section 4.4 below); it appears to be derived from the root *wánača-* 'be lost, get lost' with a lexical suffix *=ił* 'offspring, child'.  The meanings of the Cowlitz cognates for *snúk^wł* and *sšawácł* suggest a different alignment of meanings of the Upper Chehalis terms, although this would still leave one extra term, that for 'niece'.  Quinault, too, has a cognate for *snúk^wł*, making a reconstruction to Proto-Tsamosan possible, although it is not possible to provide a meaning for the term, other than a general 'nephew or niece'; rounding of the *k* is apparently secondary in Upper Chehalis and Cowlitz, but must have been early to prevent palatalization.  These additional forms are:

(31)  Cowlitz
      *s-núk^w-ił*        '♂BC, ♂ZC'
      *s-xawádc=ił*   '♀BC, ♀ZC'

      Quinault
      *snučáł* (JAG)     'Nw'
      *six^wəł* (JAG)    'Nc' [96]

      Proto-Tsamosan
      **s-núk-ił*        'Nw/Nc'

Terms for 'niece' and 'nephew' are not available from Lower Chehalis.
Upper Chehalis has a single word for 'grandchild', sex being made explicit by the appropriate feminine or non-feminine article (as with 'child*'), as seen in (32).

(32)  *ʔimc* (*ʔimac-aws*, *ʔimc-s* 'his ...')         'CC'

This form has cognates in all three other Tsamosan languages (see (21) above for the prefix in the second Lower Chehalis and Quinault forms):

(33)  Cowlitz
      *ʔém'c* (*ʔimac-awi* 'his ...')   'CC'

      Lower Chehalis
      *ʔim'əc, k^wəʔím*         'CC'

Quinault
*ʔímǝc, kʷiʔím* (JAG)          'CC'

The term 'grandchild' can easily be reconstructed for Proto-Tsamosan, and is further derivable from a Proto-Salishan term, both given in (34).

(34) Proto-Tsamosan
*ʔímac-*          'CC'

Proto-Salish
*ʔímac*          'CC' (Bella Coola, Interior Salish, Tsamosan, Central Salish)

Although several of the Interior Salishan languages use reciprocal terms for grandparents and grandchildren, reflexes of the form in (34) also occur there as a cover term for grandchildren.

4.3. **Affinal terms**. Affinal terms have been relatively more stable than other categories of kin terms, both within the Tsamosan branch and within the Salish family as a whole. Seven can be reconstructed for Tsamosan, and at least four of these can be traced back to Proto-Salish.

The Upper Chehalis terms for 'wife' and 'husband' are:

(35)  *čǝwł (čawáł-ns* 'his ...')          'W'
       sšǝn (s-šanís-s  'her ...')          'H' [97]

The underlying stem of the word for 'wife' is *cawali-*; this shape can be seen in *s-cawdli-t-n* 'he is marrying her'. The term for 'wife' has a cognate in Cowlitz, and that for 'husband' has cognates in Cowlitz and Lower Chehalis, as shown in (36).

(36) Cowlitz
       *kúwł (s-kawáł-ani* 'his ...)          'W'
       *(s)-xǝn (xǝn-i* 'her ...')          'H'

Lower Chehalis
*šǝn*                              'H'

On the basis of the three cognate terms for 'husband', a Proto-Tsamosan form can be reconstructed. Upper Chehalis and Cowlitz by themselves are not sufficient to reconstruct a word for 'wife'. However, cognates for *čǝwł* do occur in other branches of Salish, permitting a reconstruction to Proto-Salish; the form must therefore have existed in Proto-Tsamosan. Other spouse terms were replaced in Tsamosan; these replacements are given in (37), and the reconstructed forms in (38).

(37) Lower Chehalis
       *nǝkʷlákʷ*                          'W'

       Quinault
       *txʷíʔnu* (MDK)          'W'     *txʷí-n'up* (MDK), *tǝxʷíy'nup* (JAG)          'H'

(Gibson's field notes [1968] give *xʷəqʷtəm'ixʷ* for 'wife'; this looks like some sort of derived form, Gibson also has *ʔəʔənim* for 'husband/wife'.)

(38)  Proto-Tsamosan
      *kəwál-        'W'
      *s-xən         'H'


      Proto-Salish
      *kəwáx         'W'  (Interior Salish, Tsamosan, Central Salish, Tillamook)

Listed in (39) are the Upper Chehalis terms for other relatives by marriage.  There is some confusion in the translations available for these terms.

(39)  *smátaxʷn'*                      'P/l, S/l  parent-in-law, son-in-law'
      *sápn* (*sápan-s* 'his ...')     'D/l  D-in-law'
      *syáxʷtč*                        'B/l  B-in-law'
      *scáw*                           'Z-in-law' [98]
      *tsai'.a* (CV)                   'Sb-in-law'
      *skwokwe'nEp* (CV)               'Sb-in-law'
      *qʷílx̱ʷ*                        'in-laws'

In order to sort these out as much as possible, attention must be given to glosses found in the various sources on Upper Chehalis.  The first term, *smátaxʷn'*, probably referred to either parent-in-law or to son-in-law; it probably did not include daughter-in-law, since there is a separate term for this relative, at least in the Oakville Chehalis dialect.  It may have included 'daughter-in-law' in the Tenino Chehalis and Satsop dialects of the language; the *Comparative Vocabularies* of Boas (1925) give this form for all four kin types in those two dialects, and do not include *sápn* for 'daughter-in-law'.  The latter term (in Oakville Chehalis) was glossed 'daughter-in-law, sister-in-law' by one of my informants.  Boas (1927) gives 'man's sister-in-law', and Eells (1885) gives 'daughter-in-law, son-in-law'.  This term can be reconstructed to Proto-Salish as 'daughter-in-law', which is probably its primary meaning in Upper Chehalis; it may have been extended to other relatives as well.  The only glosses available for *syáxʷtč* and *scáw* are 'brother-in-law' and 'sister-in-law', respectively; Boas (1925) adds 'of a man' to his gloss of *scáw* and both terms are given with the same meanings for all three dialects of the language.  The terms *tsai'.a* and *skwokwe'nEp* are known only from the *Comparative Vocabularies* (Boas 1925; also there for Cowlitz).  Both are glossed there as "brother-in-law, sister-in-law, wife's sister, etc."; the first of these two terms is given only for the Oakville Chehalis dialect, and the second for both the Oakville and Tenino Chehalis dialects.  It is not clear what the exact designations were, or how they differed from *syáxʷtč* and *scáw*.  Finally, *qʷílx̱ʷ* is apparently a cover term for a child-in-law and all relatives.  Glosses include 'son-in-law, daughter-in-law, parents and other relatives of one's son- or daughter-in-law'; 'member of affine family except in-laws' (Boas 1927); "brother-in-law, sister-in-law, wife's sister, etc,' (for Satsop; Boas 1925); 'and in-laws to each other' (for Tenino Chehalis; Boas 1925).

All the in-law terms documented for the other Tsamosan languages are cognate with the Upper Chehalis terms.  They are given in (40) below.

(40)  Cowlitz

| | |
|---|---|
| *s-mátx$^w$tn (s-mátx$^w$tan-i* "his ...') | F/l  S/l  Fa-in-law, So-in-law" |
| sápn *(sápan-awi* 'his ...') | 'D-in-law' |
| *s-yálx$^w$tk (yálx$^w$tač-i* 'his ... ') | 'B-in-law' |
| *s-káw (s-káw-i* 'his ...') | 'Z-in-law' |

Lower Chehalis

| | |
|---|---|
| *smá•təx$^w$* | 'in-law' |
| *sq$^w$íl'əx$^w$* (CTS) | 'in-law'  [99] |

Quinault

| | |
|---|---|
| *(s)mátax$^w$n'* (JAG) | 'in-laws' |
| *ĵáltač* (JAG) | 'B-in-law' |
| *sčáʔn* (JAG) | 'Z-in-law' |
| *q$^w$íyləx$^w$* (JAG) | 'parents of child-in-law' |

The Quinault term for in-laws is specific as including mother-in-law, father-in-law, son-in-law, and daughter-in-law.

The correspondences in (40) above allow the reconstruction of five in-law terms to Proto-Tsamosan, One of these, daughter-in-law, is not evident on the basis of Tsamosan alone, but is reconstructible to Proto-Salish, and must therefore also have been in Proto-Tsamosan. This and two other in-law terms can be reconstructed to Proto-Salish. The reconstructions in both Proto-Tsamosan and Proto-Salish are given in (42) below.

(41)  Proto-Tsamosan

| | |
|---|---|
| **s-mátax$^w$-n* | 'P/S-in-law' |
| **sápan-* | 'D-in-law' |
| **s-yálx'tak-* | 'B-in-law' |
| **s-káw* | 'Z-in-law' |
| **q$^w$íl<u>x</u>$^w$-* | 'in-law' |

Proto-Salish

| | |
|---|---|
| **s-mátax$^w$-* | 'Sb-in-law' (Tsamosan, Central Salish) |
| **sápan* | 'D-in-law' (Interior Salish, Tsamosan, Central Salish, Tillamook) |
| **s-káw* | 'Z-in-law' (Interior Salish, Tsamosan) |

Note that Proto-Salishan **s-mátax$^w$-* requires a different gloss from the Tsamosan forms.

4.4.  **Decedence terms**. An unusual feature of kinship systems in the Northwest is the use of a special set of terms applying to relatives such as 'aunt', 'uncle', 'nephew', 'niece', etc., after the death of the connecting parent or sibling (see Miller 1985 for a discussion of decedence terms in the Northwest). A very limited set of these terms is documented for Tsamosan, and a single term seems to have been used for a deceased parent's sibling and deceased sibling's child (although the fourth term for 'nephew' in (30) above may belong here). The Upper Chehalis term is:

(42)  (s)ƛ̓ix̣ʷinut

This is attested in Oakville Chehalis and Tenino Chehalis only (and from the CV *Comparative Vocabularies* [Boas 1925] for Cowlitz with the meaning 'mother's sister').  The form is clearly derived from an otherwise unattested root and the [100] lexical suffix =*ínut* 'mind, feelings', suggesting a special mental attitude toward these kinds of relatives.  A similar form, with the gloss 'aunt', is listed in the *Comparative Vocabularies* (Boas 1925) for Cowlitz: *tiax̣wai'nut*.  The only other Tsamosan language for which this sort of term is recorded is Quinault, where the word in (13) for 'uncle' given above *(si-x̣ʷəsn)* is also glossed as 'uncle or aunt when the parent is deceased'.

     Words for 'widow' and 'widower' should be considered as part of this same category of surviving relatives. A distinction is made generally for these two only by means of a preceding gender-specific article. The Upper Chehalis term and a derivative for 'widower' are:

(43)  *čé•č*                    'widow, widower'
     *čič-wálm*              'widower'

An additional term is given for the Satsop dialect in the *Comparative Vocabularies* (Boas 1925); it is *.skwāla'ux* <ok>.  The cognate version of the latter term in Tenino Chehalis, however, is glossed "bachelor": *.sqwa'lux̣*. This variation may be well within the semantic range of this term, since the Quinault form in (44) below is glossed 'widow, widower, bachelor, spinster'.  The other three Tsamosan languages have cognates of (43) for 'widow, widower':

(44)  Cowlitz
     *číl'k*               'widow'
     *číl'k-awilm*     'widower'

     Lower Chehalis
     *čílč*                 'widow'

     Quinault
     *čílč* (JAG)       'widow(er)'

The four terms in (43) and (44) are easily reconstructible to Proto-Tsamosan as in (45) (assuming that the shift of velars to palatoalveolars had not yet occurred).  The loss of *l* before another consonant is regular in Upper Chehalis; the length of the preceding vowel may be either from compensatory lengthening resulting from this loss or it may indicate that the form is diminutive.

(45)  Proto-Tsamosan
     **k'ílk*  'widow'

No decedence terms can be reconstructed to Proto-Salish.

     One final Upper Chehalis term should be considered in this category, known from the Oakville Chehalis and Tenino Chehalis dialects:  [101]

(46)  *smák̓ʷtuɬn*

This is most likely a term referring to the practice of levirate marriage (and possibly sororate marriage as well). It may also have applied to other relatives-in-law after the death of a spouse. It is glossed variously by Boas (1927) and Adamson (1926-27) as 'reciprocal term for a widow and her husband's relations, woman to whom levirate rights may be applied, mother-in-law after the death of one's husband (?), in-laws after the death of one's wife, woman's relatives-in-law'. A similar form from Cowlitz occurs in the *Comparative Vocabularies* (Boas 1925) with the gloss 'sister-in-law': *.sma'kotułEn;* also given there is a Lower Chehalis form *.smā'kEtułEn* <ok> under a general in-law heading. This term must certainly refer to a relative for whom the linking relative has died, since the form is derived from the root *mák<sup>w</sup>t* 'dead'.

5. **Summary**. This completes the catalog of available kinship terms in Upper Chehalis (no attempt has been made to include all Cowlitz, Lower Chehalis, or Quinault terms, although a large number have been presented here). It is possible that some terms are missing from the record, but most are certainly here. The major gap in our knowledge of this system is specific meanings for many of the terms. When the best materials were collected from the most knowledgeable speakers (by Boas and Adamson in 1926 and 1927), interest in kinship systems was not as great as it later became, and the terminology seems not to have been collected systematically. We are thus left with only partial information on the system. By comparing the information available with the terminology from neighboring Salishan languages (which is also fragmentary and inadequately glossed), it is possible to learn more about the Upper Chehalis kinship system.

Notes

*Acknowledgments.* Material for this article was collected from 1960 onward under the auspices of the American Philosophical Society Library, Indiana University, and the National Science Foundation. Upper Chehalis data were collected from Silas Heck and Mrs. Lillian Young; Cowlitz data from Mrs. Emma Mesplie and Mrs. Lucy James; and Lower Chehalis data from Mrs. Irene Shale and Mrs. Nina Bumgarner. I am deeply grateful to these people for their assistance. I also wish to thank Laurence C. Thompson for helpful comments on early drafts of the first part of this paper. All Upper Chehalis kin terms discussed here, as well as variant spellings and variant forms from various early sources, can be found in Kinkade (1991).

*Abbreviations.* Standard kinship abbreviations (and their analogues) are used here:

Au = aunt, Br = brother, Ch == child, Co = cousin, Da = daughter, Fa = father, GrCh = grandchild, Hu = husband, Mo = mother, Ne = nephew, Ni = niece, Pa = parent, Si = sister, Sib = sibling, So = son, Un = uncle, Wi = wife. Older and younger sibling terms have o and *y*, respectively, prefixed to the appropriate sibling abbreviation. A prefixed *m* or *f* indicates that the term applies to the relative of a male or female, respectively. [102] These abbreviations are not used where a source does not, or a reconstruction cannot, specify a relationship with sufficient exactitude.

The following grammatical abbreviations are used: PL = plural; VOC = vocative.

References


Adamson, Thelma
  1926-27    Unarranged Sources of Chehalis Ethnology. Ms., Melville Jacobs Collection, University of Washington Archives, Seattle.
Boas, Franz
  1911    *Chinook.*    Handbook of American Indian Languages, Franz Boas, ed. Smithsonian Institution, Bureau of American Ethnology Bulletin 40, vol. 1: 559-677.  Washington, D.C. [103]
  1925    *Comparative Salishan Vocabularies.*    Ms., American Philosophical Society Library, Philadelphia. [CV]
  1927 *Chehalis Field Notes.*  Ms., American Philosophical Society Library, Philadelphia.
Eells, Myron
  1885 *Kwaiailk Vocabulary.* Ms., National Anthropological Archives, Smithsonian Institution, Washington, D.C.
Elmendorf, William W.
  1961 *System Change in Salish Kinship Terminologies.*  Southwestern Journal of Anthropology 17: 365-82.
Gibson, James A.
  1968  *Quinault Field Notes.* Ms.
Hymes, Dell H.
  1955  The Language of the Kathlamet Chinook. Ph.D. diss., Indiana University.
Kinkade, M. Dale, comp.
        1991    *Upper Chehalis Dictionary.* University of Montana Occasional Papers in Linguistics 7.  Missoula.
Miller, Jay
        1985 *Salish Kinship: Why Decedence?*  Paper presented at the Twentieth International Conference on Salish and Neighboring Languages, Vancouver, 15-17 August.
Murdock, George Peter
        1968 *Patterns of Sibling Terminology.*  Ethnology 7: 1-24.
Nerlove, Sara, and A. Kimball Romney
  1967 *Sibling Terminology and Cross-Sex Behavior.*  American Anthropologist 69: 179-87.
Olson, Ronald L.
  1936 *The Quinault Indians.* University of Washington Publications in Anthropology, vol. 6, no. 1.  Seattle.
Snow, Charles T.
  1967-68 *Lower Chehalis Field Notes.*  ms.


M. Dale Kinkade    Kinship Terminology in Upper Chehalis in a Historical Framework. *Anthropological Linguistics*  34 (1-4): 84-103

# Decedence
Jay Miller

## Abstract
Though recognized as a universal feature of kinship systems, decedence has received scant attention.  Among the Lushootseed, with over-20 Salishan speaking communities along the river drainages of the Puget Sound Basin, it is significant in past kinship terms and present behavior.  How and why this enables collaterals to assume parental responsibilities at the death of their siblings is explored, particularly in terms of family-held prestigious 'knowledge.'

A key feature of Lushootseed survivance has been tightening and firming up kin bonds since the distinctive features of Salish kinship were that it was descriptive, bilateral, and relied on factors of generation, gender, age, and decadence = whether a linking relative was dead or alive (Collins 1974: 86).  While the other criteria were common, decedence, a change of kin terms precipitated at the death of a linking relative, is rare.  The term (as a substitute for "condition of life," the last of 8 principles listed by Kroeber in 1909) was introduced by Murdock (1949: 101) as a possible feature of classificatory kinship systems featuring = generation, sex, affinity, collaterality, bifurcation, polarity, relative age, speaker's sex, and decedence: "the last and least important of the nine, based on the biological fact of death" (1949: 106).

Because biology provides the basis for so much of kinship, in terms of gender and age, the recognition of a kinsperson's death adds yet another dimension.

In most societies, death calls for circumlocutions and polite forms, rather than the use of separate kin terms.  Often, these consist of adding lexicals meaning "the late" , such as  the Lushootseed *tu-* prefix, to circumvent references to the deceased or the introduction of actual necronyms for defining classes of people who are mourning specific types of relatives (Cf. Buchler and Selby 1968: 170).  In most cases where decedence occurs, it is a reflex of the marital alliances between families, moving a former affine into the category of "potential spouse" in anticipation of the levirate or sororate.

Among the Salish, however, decedence was a prominent and wide-ranging feature, applied to both affinals and collaterals.  Yet it was the application of the terms to collaterals that appears problematic because it involves surviving siblings (aunts and uncles) and their niblings (nieces and nephews), the children of the deceased.

Few explanations have been proposed for decadence, such as concern with entitlements, with responsibilities, or with custodianship of family resources.

In general, Goodenough (1970: 90-93), who found decedence "of considerable interest," suggests that it represented how the "entitlements" of kin relationship are transferred at death.

More specifically, Galloway (1977: 530), who worked among the Fraser River Stō:lo (Upriver Halkomelem Salish), suggested that their decedence terms indicate a shifting of "responsibilities" to the survivors.  Among his examples are two terms which mean deceased person (other than a parent) responsible for *Ego*.  Among those kin specifically identified are uncle, aunt, and grandmother.  He concludes, "The Stō:lo way of viewing ... these terms is that you are related to a person who dies or you are related to a person through another person who dies. These terms are looked at as a process."

Thus, for much of your life you are supposed to be the responsibility of your parents, and, secondarily, of other adult members of your family. With the death of your parents, however, you become the responsibility of other surviving adults, especially aunts and uncles.

Modern Lushootseed elders explain that decedence terms are adopted "for the sake of the children," but not necessarily orphans. Among the Stō:lo, for example, the term for orphan (*weləm*) is indeed included within a term for "the orphan child of a deceased sibling."

The full explanation, however, involved more general considerations. Indeed, decedence is invoked for the sake of the "family," the broad bilateral kindred holding corporate rights to traditions, locales, and resources, but most particularly, the inherited ancestral wisdom sometimes called "advice." Moreover, since the children were the epitome of the family; its hope and pride for the future, special care had to be taken to give them continued access to family traditions and lore, which were put at risk by the death of a either parent, who belonged to separate kindreds.

Throughout the world, while the welfare of children is a central concern of kin term usages, corporate "ancestral house" characteristic of the Northwest is lacking. In other regions of North America where decedence also occurs, such as native California, it relies on other factors (Drucker 1937).

In aboriginal California, decedence is so common in the northern and southern regions (Gifford 1922: 257) that the Huchinom felt put upon to explain why they do not use it. Everywhere else, "The continued use of the terms {for parent and collaterals} is said to be 'on account of the ch{ildren}'" (1922: 119). After a mother died, her children are "fed" by her parents and brothers, in addition to their father. The implication, then, was that families stayed in contact for the benefit of the children.

Yet, of the fifteen Californian "tribes" listed (1922: 17, 33, 36, 56, 60, 68, 70, 71, 77, 115), almost all of the decedence terms involve only affines. For example, among the Karuk, "For all terms of affinity following the death of the connecting relative the term *gardim* is used" (1922: 33). Only the Tolowa (1922: 17) specify terms for parental siblings: *trixne* for deceased parent's sister and *trine* for deceased parent's brother, both of which were related to *trixne* meaning 'ghost, spirit'. In addition, they applied *tamage* to all affines after the death of the linking relative. Such data confirm the link between decedence and on-going marital alliances through the sororate and levirate.

Unlike other areas of Native North America where "The terminologies for American Indian cultures are rarely complete with respect to the relationships brought about by death of a relative or by death and remarriage" (Edmonson 1958: 13), Salish and within it Lushootseed terminology is well reported, although given little if any cultural context.

Among Lushootseeds, four terms reflect decedence. These are /yəlab/, /sqəla(y)jut/, /sbalutsid/, and /*cəłbaskayu/. These terms were first discussed by Ballard (1935: 111), who learned to speak Lushootseed as a child.

> Noteworthy is the change in nomenclature employed in certain cases upon the death of the intervening relative. Thus upon the death of one's spouse the term *sbalucid* is substituted for *kʷəliw*, in so far as any relationship is presumed to continue. Incidentally, it seems to

have been obligatory for brother, or sister as the case may be, to marry the surviving spouse of the deceased.  Upon the death of one's parent the surviving brother, sister or cousin of the deceased is called *yəlab*.  Upon the death of *yəlab* he or she is again called *'qəsi* or *əpus*.  Reciprocal to *yəlab* is *sqəla(y)jut{ał}*, substituted for the term *stalał*.  Accordingly the expressions *yəlab* and *sqəla(y)jut{ał}* are used between elderly persons and young persons distantly related.

According to the first Lushootseed dictionary (Hess 1976: 631.2), *yəlab* is "either parent's sibling of either sex when the parent is deceased."  The term *yəl-* means 'both, pair' (1976: 631.1) and *-ab* is a suffix that extends a meaning.  Thus, the designation seems to translate 'embracing both sides'.  Of related interest is the use of the term /*yəlyəlab*/ to mean 'ancestors' (1976: 631.3).  Skagit speakers explicitly recognized such collateral ties when speaking English, remarking that their genealogies traced the "fathers of our uncles."

The term *sqəla(y)jut* has been translated as "nephew/neice when sibling link is deceased, reciprocal of *yəlab*" (1976: 375.2).  It is based on the term *qəl* meaning 'bad' and may mean 'badly off, unfortunate.'  Also, there is some dialectical variation in the suffixes applied to it.  Ballard (above) used {-*əł*}, while the term in Suquamish as spoken by Lawrence Webster has {-*ut*}.

The third term (*sbalucid*) has been translated in nominal form as "in-law when link is deceased" (1976: 18.3), while the verbal form means "court a girl, be going after someone" (1976: 18.3).  Related words include *balbal* 'confused, mistaken' (1976: 17.3) and *-ucid* "lexical suffix for 'gap, opening' and 'mouth, language, door, river'" (1976: 541.5).  It seems to mean 'to cover a mistake (or embarrassment),' giving added credence to the observation by Ruth Underhill (1965: 69) that in the Northwest "Death was an insult that had to wiped out, not by avoidance of the dead but by glorifying them."  As applied to actual situations, the term connotes 'intended spouse', much as English refers to betrothed individuals as 'intended' for each other.

As diagramed by Hess (1976: 383), during the lifetime of a parent, a *yəlab* was known as either aunt (*'əpus*) or uncle (*'qəsi*), and the nibling was called *stalał*.  In the southern dialects, *pus* was the term for aunt, as recorded by Ballard.  Their vital link with living traditions is shown by the fact that, after their own deaths, parents' siblings are again called 'aunt' and 'uncle,' fitting back into their former genealogical role within the family.  The terms *yəlab* and *sqəlayjut* remain in effect while the uncle, aunt, nephew, or neice remain alive.  When they die, they are again called *qəsi*, *'əpus*, or *stalał*.

The last term – *tciłəbskayu'* "related through the dead," previously related by marriage (1935: 116) – includes actual reference to the dead: /*skayu*/ 'corpse, ghost' (1976: 232.1), and uses the productive prefix of *cəł* 'make, build' (1976: 95), which indicated step-relationships when applied to kin terms.  Thus, the term for a step-father meant 'made a father'.  The term under consideration seems to mean 'created by death'.  Other dialects used other prefixes.  At least some of the southern dialects used {*cił*} (cf. Ballard (1935) and Hess (1976: 52.2)).

Different from some Salish languages such as Squamish, Puget expresses step-kin by compound words rather than with prefixes.  In Snohomish the expression for a step-relative is compounded of {-*əł*} 'order, law' plus the regular consanguine term.  In Skagit it is {*cəł*} 'make' and the consanguine term" (Hess 1971: 69, note 12; Cf Hess 1976: 458.3

where *-əł* is corrected to 'make').

The medial *-b-* may refer to repetition and thus mean 'made again by death', but it may also derive from *-ab-* 'belonging to'. It applies to in-laws, especially parents-in-law who are called /sk*ʷ*əlwas/ during life (1976: 254.6). The term *kʷətiw* (1976: 261.1, cf. Ballard above) now means to 'change residence at marriage, to go to the home of in-laws'.

While the other three terms are known and used by present speakers, this fourth term is not, although its meaning makes transparent reference to the dead. Present confusion about this term may be due to the fact that it severed a relationship rather than created a new one. As Ballard (1935: 112-113) wrote

> Any relationship formerly existing between them {the blood relatives of the surviving spouse} and the blood kindred group of the deceased is regarded as severed. They are called *tsiłəbskayu*, 'related through the dead.'

This suggests that it might actually be more in the nature of an anti-kinship term, as with the English prefix *ex-* for relationships which have been denied or legally severed.

According to native speaker responses, modern Lushootseed are particularly insightful with regard to the collateral terms, but less clear on the affinal ones. For *yəlab*, people say that it signifies that "someone became like a mother or a father;" while a *sqəla(y)jut* "became like a son or daughter." The implication is that the shift to these terms moves the kinspeople closer together. Similarly, *sbalucid* is said to indicate "the person you're going to marry," or "the person you're next in line to marry." Of course, given the levirate and sororate, when a sibling died, their surviving spouse become "intended" for a surviving sibling.

In her rigorous UChicgo-style study of Skagit (Northern Lushootseed) terminology, June Collins (1974) gives careful attention to important features of this system. What she says about this specific instance has direct bearing on more general conclusions.

Collins confirms the fundamental importance of siblingship for understanding the system, regarding it as "the most tightly knit, firmest bond in the society" (1974: 91). When siblings die, their children become the concern of surviving brothers and sisters (1974: 94), who argue for levirate or sororate marriages out of "fear of unkind treatment by unrelated stepparents" (1974: 102).

Among the Skagit and other Lushootseed, divorce is infrequent among good families, particularly because "both parents had to give up the children because of the fear already discussed of allowing the children to live with stepparents. Parents could not dispose of a child as they wished ... Both families had to agree to the child's residence" (1974: 105).

Other reasons against divorce include an unwillingness to return any of the gifts and property exchanged, and the dangers that might befall a lone woman making the journey back to her parents (1974: 105). The only acceptable grounds for divorce are a barren wife, adultery, or excessive cruelty. Even after marriages are end by the death of a spouse, where children were involved, everyone in the immediate blood line has a say in the care of any underage children.

In all, then, the feature of decedence among the Skagit and other Lushootseed revolves around a concern for children, not for general family alliances, as is the case when decedence applied to affinal terms. The effect of the terminological changes is "a closing of ranks" to look after the welfare of younger heirs. This tightening is also consistent with the manner in which kinship is traced by Salish.

By a process of overlapping, people will adopt a kin claim to someone on the basis of a relationship that has already been acknowledged by a linking relative. Thus, people will often say, "I call that person as 'nephew' because he calls my close-cousin 'aunt'." Obversely, someone who lays claim to a relationship might find their statement rejected or acted upon coolly because that person and family is not highly regarded. Such a rebuff often takes the form, "s/he's the only one I ever heard about that connection from."

Other societies acknowledge such kin realignments in other ways, so the explanation for the Lushootseed system must be found internally. The tight bond among siblings and kindreds among the Salish rests firmly upon a belief in what Wayne Suttles (see above) has called "advice." Among the Lushootseed this might better be called "wisdom, teachings, knowledge" since these words were closer to the meaning of the native terms, which include /x$^w$dik$^w$/, /x$^w$dig$^w$id/, /g$^w$əƛ́ada/, and /'ug$^w$usaɬ/, the last specifically meaning 'teachings' (cf. Hess 1976: 681). People who consistently transmit and practice these teachings become appropriate members of the upper class. People who did not are either low class or considered descendants of former slaves.

These teachings include the full range of the traditional heritage and family treasures, including stories, dances, songs, and artistic traditions, all linked to a stock of immortal names.

These teachings encode proper, elite etiquette through hereditary names, moralistic narratives, and information about the effective use of prime resource areas. It is the importance of these inherited teachings that gives the Northwest much of its distinctiveness, providing the basis for distinguishing a variety of corporate groups localized within households.

In the north, these corporations were characterized by matrilineal sentiments, establishing clear channels of responsibility within matrilines (Durlach 1928), which are regarded as impervious to death because the immortal names are inherited across and through the generations.

Among the Salish and others of the central coast, these kindreds were ambilateral and localized in households. While the system itself recognized open bilateral components, actual choices were limited to the households of acknowledged great-grand-parents. In practice, households include three generations of actual residents, along with, at least, a fourth generation recalled through hereditary names (Amoss 1981: 237).

Among the Lushootseed, every individual represents the conjunction of several of these "families" (kindreds). In addition to the term for ancestors based on the collateral term, Lushootseed speakers also use /st'əx̣$^w$šəd/ meaning "root (especially cedar root), ancestors (figurative)" (Hess 1976: 531.3).

Cedar roots are widely used for basketry and (pre-string) all-purpose bindings, so they were much in evidence. Also, they grow in every direction away from the tree, sending tendrils through the landscape. Like a network of roots, Lushootseeds recognize that an individual represents both a 'coming together and stretching out' of links from many different places. As a tree feeds from diverse roots, so the person comes from many sources.

Of these, those of the father (*bad*) and the mother (*k$^{'w}$uya*) are most important. They are each terminologically distinguished (contra Spier 1925: 74) by terms translating as 'on the entire side of the father' (*badalig$^w$əd*) and 'on the entire side of the mother' (*k$^{'w}$uyalig$^w$əd*), likely also related to the word for 'born' ($g^w\partial c$).  Even the word for the House ($g^w\partial \acute{c}altx^w$ ~ ancestral House) derives from the same lexical.)

For ranking families, an argument can be made that the transmission process involves replacement rather than succession.  Names and possessions are defined in terms of the timeless age of epics.  Since the universal change that coincided with the arrival of human beings, people have been trying to recreate these immortal conditions by giving "people to the ancestral names."

Reviewing the four Lushootseed terms in the light of wider distributions, two emerge as having the greatest significance for understanding decedence.  The term referring to the dead can be removed from consideration because it has gone out of use.  Of the three remaining, that for intended spouse has a broad distribution, presumably reflecting the importance, noted above, of continuing marital alliances to safeguard children.  As Sapir (1916: 329) already observed "the levirate itself is known to have been in force among most or all of the tribes of Washington and Oregon."

Most distinctive of the system, therefore, are the two terms for parental siblings and for niblings, which occur only among the Salish and neighboring Southern Nootkans.  The neighboring Sahaptians do not have such terms probably because of the different strategies used by the Salishan and the Sahaptians to encourage intertribal contacts.

The Salishans use intertribal gatherings (to dance, visit, gamble, and trade) over many days, which also foster intermarriages, while the Sahaptians sponsor day-long feasts.  Because the Salishans, especially of important families, expect to marry among diverse groups, the death of a parent is more disruptive to the transmission of teachings because of the greater distances and differences involved.  As a hedge against this, collaterals change terms to assume greater closeness, at least when speaking Lushootseed.

Among the Salish, this close/remote relationship pervades the entire cultural system.  In Lushootseed, the term for close(ness) is $\acute{q}^w u$ 'gather, collect' (Hess 1976: 432.2), with a range that includes "assembly, council, and gathering."  Ballard (1935: 112) reports it signifies "join, unite, assemble," and features in the contrast between $\acute{q}^w u\textipa{P}\check{s}\partial d$ and $\textipa{P}ii\check{s}\partial d$, based on $\check{s}ad$- 'feet, leg' and literally meaning 'together feet' and 'apart feet'.

Appropriately, at large gatherings, individuals still donate money to someone through a speaker, who announces that the offering is intended to show that the donor is "claiming X (that specific someone) as a relative."  Given the extensive network of kindreds in such a bilateral system, such periodic reclaiming of some weakening links serves to strengthen the relational ties among elite families, functioning in the present as a reflection of its greater importance in the past.

Similarly, the Thompson Salish have two terms for affines after the death of the linking relative:  one for a decendence affine of a close relationship and one for that of a distant relationship (cf Miller 1985).

*nk'eł(ə)we?íy(e)x* = decadence affine of distant relationship (cousin or more),
    literally 'weep together'
*n(e)qíc't(e)n* = decadence affine of close relationship (sibling in law)

It was, therefore, logically appropriate and internally consistent for Salishans to invoke this symbolic distinction to 'close ranks' and bring kinspeople nearer together after the death of a linking relative.

While this solution was distinctly Salishan, it was based on practice which was much more widespread. Fred Eggan (1955: 94) noted the importance given to "brotherhood" in Plains and other Native American kinship systems. Among the Numic-speaking Comanche and H3kandika,

The institution of formal friendship among men also entails the use of the brother terminology. The friend ... takes the status of his brother in the relationship system of his comrade's family, thereby taking over all the privileges and restrictions which go with the new status (Hoebel 1939: 448).

By invoking kin terms and behaviors, friends become kin, intent becomes kinship. The next step in this process was shown by Nez Perce usage.

*yelept* = friend. One fights in war side by side with his *yelept*. When he dies, his son becomes the survivors's nephew, the survivor becomes the orphan's paternal uncle (Aoki 1966: 360).

The Nez Perce also had a term for friend (*lawtiwa*) that did not invoke quasi-siblingship. What was notable about *yelept*, of course, was that it moved a quasi-siblinghood into a stronger kinship relationship after the death of the linking person. In motivation and intent it was a weaker form of decendence, closing ranks and strengthening voluntary bonds between participants. Among the Salish, however, the vital store of teachings, class rankings, and family pedigrees were not left to emotional chance. Hence, the significant role given to decedence in their terminology reflects the greater corporate kin structuring of their society.

While the Salish are fairly well known ethnographically and very well known linguistically, there has been scant analysis of their cultural ramification although they are pivotal for understanding Native North America. Spier (1925: 74) first considered Salish terminology in its own right, and Elmendorf (1961) studied it in greater detail, tracing its diversification into lineal Coastal Salish and bifurcate collateral Interior Salish forms. While Murdock derived Salishan structures from the Hawaiian type (1949: 350), he later characterized the Salish system, because it combined bilaterality with alternative residence options (1965: 31), as the fundamental kinship system of North America.

Abbreviations Used:

A)unt, B)rother, C)hild(ren), Cz~cousin, D)aughter, d)eceased, F)ather, f)emale('s), H)usband, I)ntended, l)affine (in-law), M)other, m)ale('s), N)ibling, Nc~neice, Np~nephew, P)arent, R)elative, S)on, s)tep-relative, Sb~sibling, Sp~spouse, U)ncle, W)ife, X~term attested, Z~sister, = term overlap.

Decedence

Cells

| | dPSb | dSbC | dSbSp | dSpSb | dCSp | dSpP | other |
|---|---|---|---|---|---|---|---|
| Lushootseed | X | X | I | =I | | X | |
| Twana | X | X | X | =X | | | |
| Chehalis | X | dSbS | | | | dHM=I | |
| Klallam | X | X | dSbR | | | Rdl | |
| Samish | X | X | X | | | | |
| Nitinat | X | X | I | | | | |
| Saanich | X | X | | | X | | PSbdC=PdCl |
| Sechelt | | X | dZH | | | | dSbl |
| Squamish | X | X | | X(I?) | X = | X | |
| Chilliwack | X | X | | dSpR | dR | | dC(S, D) |
| Thompson | XdMZ | | | | | | dRl |
| Columbian | X,sS | X,sD | X = | X | X = | X | |
| | | | Non-Salish | Salish | | | |
| Ahousat | | | I=dBW | | | | |
| Hesquiat | | | I=mZl | | | | |
| Kootenay | | | X = | X | X = | X | |
| Klickitat | dMF | | | dSpSb | | | |
| Nez Perce | | | | | | | |
| Proto-Sahaptian | | | | dSpSb | | | |

Tribal Terms

Twana:  12 dusta.əł     dPSb                              (Elmendorf 1946)
        13  stai²əł      dSbC
        28  sk'wets      dSbSp,dSpSb

Chehalis:  (s)λ̓axinut   dPSh, dSbC (cf -inut "mind")
           swanačł       dSbS (?)
           smak'ʷtułn    dHM, I (cf mak'ʷt "dead")

Klallam:  sxʷsqəsa²čay'ł    dPSb
          sqəsa²čayəł       dSpC
          k'ʷłx̱ʷu²uŋ        Rdl, co-mourner
          smayəcən         dSpR

Samish:  qseče.ł     dPSb                              (Galloway 1984: 28, 55)
         skʷənəŋəč   dSbC

c'ae.yʔə         dSbSp

Nitinat  8 bitxtaʔk       dPSh (cf 13 hadʔe.qa  PSb)
      22 qaqay'ʔk     dSbC
      30 ƛu.ʔbiʔƛ̓     dSbSp, I

Saanich:  21 s.qsəčeeł       dPSh
      9 skʷənŋəčəł       dSbC
      5 čeeyə         dCSp
      33 t'•əłx̲ʷəʔaŋ       PdCl, PSpdC (literally "(those who) cry together")

Sechelt:
      wanwanem     dSbC
      c'ayaya       dZB
      čəmašoł       dSbl

Suquamish:  wałsayʔxʷał     dPSh
      swanimaay ł       dSbC
      c'ayayʔ         dSpSb, I(?)
      słigʷaył         dSpP, dCSp

Chilliwack: sməstiyeł  dPSb            (Galloway 1977: 524, 531)
      swəlme.y ł       dSbC
      c'łxe.m       dS, dD  (literally "(those who) cry along with")
      θe.ye         dSpR
      sxʷəmθiye.ł     dR
      qeye.ł         dR

Thompson:  sʔiʔtm'     dPSb, dPCz
      skíxze         dMZ
      sk'ełwewíyx     dRl

Columbian:  łwasn       dPSb, sS
      słwalt         dSbC, ₃D
      naq'ʷíc'tn       dSbSp, dSpSb, I
      k'aʔálp         dSpP, dCSp


Except for Elmendorf and Galloway, these terms were provided by Dale Kinkade and Thom Hess, whose list numbers are repeated herein.

Decedence

Ahousat:                                                      (Hess from Webster)
    8 čiin'psiqsu             SbSp
    15 huuʔaawitšiƛ       dBW, levirata
    33 qʷiiʔiqsu           Pl, C, NfW, NcH

Hesquiat: či.nucckʷi        mZl, levirate        (Fleisher: 245)

Kootenay:                         (Sapir 1919: 98, cf Boas 1919: 100
    38 gax̱atgax̱əniyatuʔmał     dSpP, dCSp  Turney-High: 142 #41, #45)
    39 gatłumatə            dSpSb, dSbSp

Klickitat:                       (Jacobs, Schuster: 62-64)
    11 aDwa'iʔətil         dMP
    28 (p)nuk             SbSp
    35 awiD               dSpSb

Nez Perce:                      (Aoki)
    37 čik'i.wn     WB, mZH
    42 qeqe.ʔyet   SW, DH, WP, WM, HF, HM

Proto-Sahaptian:
    34 pəmuk       SbSp (Aoki. 365)
    37 awit         SpdSb (cf ʔa.wit  'widow')


TABLE

|  | dPSb | dSbC | dSbSp | dSpSb | dCSp | dSpP | other |
|---|---|---|---|---|---|---|---|
| Lushootseed | X | X | I = I |  |  | X |  |
| Twana | X | X | X = X |  |  |  |  |
| Chehalis | X | dSbS |  |  |  | dHM=I |  |
| Klallam |  | X | X |  | dSbR | Rdl |  |
| Samish | X | X | X |  |  |  |  |
| Nitinat | X | X | I |  |  |  |  |
| Saanich |  | X | X |  | X |  | PSbdC=PdCl |
| Sechelt |  | X | dZH |  |  |  | dSbl |
| Squamish | X | X |  |  | X(I?) | X = X |  |
| Chilliwack | X | X |  | dSpR | dR |  | dC(S,D) |
| Thompson |  | X |  |  |  |  | dRl    dMZ |
| Columbian | X,sS | X,sD | X = X |  | X = X |  |  |

Decedence

Non-Salish:

| | | | |
|---|---|---|---|
| Ahousat | | I=dBW | |
| Hesquiat | | I=mZl | |
| Kootenay | | | X = X   X = X |
| Klickitat | dMF | dSpSb | |
| Nez Perce | | | |
| Proto-Sahaptian | | SpdSb | |

Decedence Bibliography


Amoss, Pamela  1981  Coast Salish Elders. *Other Ways of Growing Old*: 227-261.  Pamela Amoss and Steven Harrell, eds.  Stanford University Press.

Aoki, Haruo   1966   Nez Perce and Proto-Sahaptian Kinship Terms.  *International Journal of American Linguistics* 32 (4): 357-368.

Ballard, Arthur  1935  Southern Puget Sound Salish Kinship Terms.  *American Anthropologist* 37 (1): 111-116.

Bates, Ann M  1987  Affiliation and Differentiation:  Intertribal Interactions among the Makah and Ditidaht Indians.  Indiana University: PhD Dissertation, 310pp.

Boas, Franz  1919  Kinship Terms of the Kutenai Indians.  *American Anthropologist* 21 (1): 98-101.

Buchler, Ira and Henry Selby  1968  *Kinship and Social Organization ~ An Introduction to Theory and Method.*  New York: The MacMillan Co.

Collins, June  1966  Naming, Continuity, and Social Inheritance among the Coast Salish of Western Washington. *Papers of the Michigan Academy of Science, Arts, and Letters* 51: 425-436.

1950  Growth of Class Distinctions and Political Authority Among the Skagit Indians during the Contact Period. *American Anthropologist* 52 (3): 331-342.

1974  *Valley of the Spirits ~ The Upper Skagit Indians of Western Washington.*  Seattle: University of Washington Press.

Drucker, Philip  1937  Diffusion in Northwest Coast Culture in the Light of Some Distributions. University of California at Berkeley:  PhD Dissertation.

1951  The Northern and Central Nootkan Tribes.  Bureau of American Ethnology, Bulletin 141.

Duff, Wilson  1964  The Indian History of British Columbia.  Volume 1: The Impact of the White Man. Provincial Museum of British Columbia:  Anthropology in British Columbia, Memoir 5.

Durlach, Teresa  1928  The Relationship Systems of the Tlingit, Haida, and Tsimshian.  *American Ethnological Society*, Volume 11.

Edmonson, Munro  1958  Status Terminology and the Social Structure of North American Indians. American Ethnological Society, Monograph 30.

Eggan, Fred  1955  The Cheyenne and Arapaho Kinship System: 33-95.  *Social Anthropology of North American Tribes.*  Fred Eggan, ed.  Chicago: University of Chicago Press.

Elmendorf, William  1946  Twana Kinship Terminology. *Southwestern Journal of Anthropology* 2: 420-432.

1961   System  Change  in  Salish  Kinship  Terminologies.   *Southwestern  Journal  of*

*Anthropology* 17 (4): 365-382.

    1971   Coast Salish Status Ranking and Intergroup Ties.  *Southwestern Journal of Anthropology* 27: 353-380.

Fleisher, Mark  1984  Hesquiat Kinship Terminology:  Social Structure and Symbolic World View Categories.  *Anthropos* 79 (1/3): 243-248.

Galloway, Brent  1977  A Grammar of Chilliwack Halkomelem.  University of California at Berkeley: PhD Dissertation.

    1980.  Upper Halqemeylem Grammatical Sketch and Classified Word List.  Sardis, British Columbia:  Coqualeetza Education Training Centre.

    1984  Samish Fieldnotes from Victor Underwood and Lena Daniels.

Gifford, Edward  1922  Californian Kinship Terminologies.  *University of California Publications in American Archaeology and Ethnology* 18: 1-285.

Goodenough, Ward  1970  *Description and Comparison in Cultural Anthropology.*  Chicago: Aldine Publishing Co.  173pp.

Graburn, Nelson  1971  *Readings in Kinship and Social Structure.*  New York: Harper and Row. 450pp.

Hess, Thom  1971  Prefix Constituent With /x$^w$/: 43-69.  *Studies in Northwest Indian Languages.* James Hoard and Thom Hess, eds.  Sacramento Anthropological Society, Paper 11.

    1976 *Dictionary of Puget Salish.*  Seattle: University of Washington Press.  771pp.

    p.c  Kinship terms: Saanich from Ernie Olsen, Ahousaht from Peter Webster, and Nitinat from John Thomas.

Hoebel, Adamson  1939  Comanche and H3kandika Shoshone Relationship Systems.  *American Anthropologist* 41 (3): 440-457.

Jacobs, Melville  1932  Northern Sahaptin Kinship Terms.  *American Anthropologist* 34 (4): 688-693.

Kinkade, Dale  1981  Dictionary of the Moses-Columbia Language.  Nespelem: Colville Confederated Tribes.

    p.c  Kinship Terms: Upper Chehalis and Moses-Columbian from his own fieldnotes, Klallam and Thompson from the notes of Laurence Thompson, and Sechelt from Ronald Beaumont elicited from Jennie Erickson.

Miller, Jay  1985  Salish Kinship: Why Decedence?  20th International Conference on Salish and Neighboring Languages: 213-222.  August 15-17.  University of British Columbia.

Murdock, George Peter  1949  *Social Structure.*  New York: Macmillan Co.  387pp.

    1965.  Algonkian Social Organization.  *Context and Meaning in Cultural Anthropology*: 24-35.  Melford Spiro, ed.  New York: Free Press.

Sapir, Edward  1916  Terms of Relationship and the Levirate.  *American Anthropologist* 18 (3): 327-337.

    1918  Kinship Terms of the Kootenay Indians.  *American Anthropologist* 20 (4): 141-418.

    1919  Corrigenda to 'Kinship Terms of the Kootenay Indians'.  *American Anthropologist* 21 (1): 98.

Schuster, Helen  1975  Yakima Indian Traditionalism:  A Study in Continuity and Change.  University of Washington: PhD Dissertation.

Spier, Leslie  1925  *The Distribution of Kinship Systems in North America.*  University of

Washington Publications in Anthropology 1 (2): 69-88.

Suttles, Wayne  1958  Private Knowledge, Morality, and Social Classes among the Coast Salish. *American Anthropologist* 60: 497-507.

   1965  Linguistic Means for Anthropological Ends on the North West Coast. *Canadian Journal of Linguistics* 10: 156-166.

Suttles, Wayne and William Elmendorf  1963  Linguistic Evidence for Salish Prehistory. *Symposium on Language and Culture*: 41-52.  Proceedings of the 1962 Annual Spring Meeting of the American Ethnological Society.  Viola Garfield and Wallace Chafe, eds.  Seattle: University of Washington Press.

Turney-High, H.H.  1941  *Ethnography of the Kutenai*.  American Anthropological Association, Memoir 56.

Underhill, Ruth  1965  *Red Man's Religion*.  University of Chicago Press.

White, Ellen, and Peter Wilson  1975  The History of Where You Come From – What You Call One Another.  10th International Conference on Salishan Languages: 155-171.  Robert St. Clair, ed.  LEKTOS, Interdisciplinary Working Papers in Language Sciences, University of Louisville, Kentucky.  Special Issue.

Acknowledgements

Many people have helped me with this foray into Salishan kinship.  My stimulus was the Lushootseed Elders in a language class at Swinomish, Washington, during the winter of 1983-4.  The inspiration to do something with their insight came from Fred and Joan Eggan.  Laura Wilbur, Lawrence Webster, and Vi Hilbert went over coastal terms with me, and Isabel Arcasa went over interior ones.  Linguists who rallied to my aid include Dale Kinkade, Thom Hess, Brent Galloway, Pam Cahn, and, indirectly, Ann Bates, Larry and Terry Thompson, Ron Beaumont, Jay Powell, and others.

# Conclusions

The breakthrough into cognatic kinship systems, which long baffled researchers from Lewis Henry Morgan to Franz Boas (1920), who never grasped the nature of the Kwakwakwawak Kwakiutl *numaym* kindred, came from the Pacifc. Ward Goodenough (1955), working on what was then Truk, now Chuk, began to grasp its bilateral kinship units, and William Davenport (1959) brought these insights to North American data, especially those of Boas. As a side note, Jorgensen's statistical study of Salish, a unit defined by language, society, and culture provides glimpses of clusterings otherwise not obvious.

British style kinship flourished at the founding of the University of Chicago and its anthroplogy department, where Iva Osanai first applied it techniques to publications about Salish tribes and communities as a library based MA, later June Collins (1974) continued this tradition with fieldwork among the Skagit and a proposal to regard Salish kinship as 'multilineal' (1979).

Wayne Suttles provides the now standard model of the aboriginal society as an inverted pear, with the bulbous body comprised of those of 'good blood' and nobility, with the thin top consisted of slaves and low lifes.

## Kin and Kith Ship

Salish kinship was and is remarkably flexible and versatile. Traced through both mother and father (bilaterally), it followed "bloodlines" that were free flowing from past to present. Its full compliment of components have never been fully studied, but an attempt is made here to delineate them. They include at least six features.

DESCENT from both parents, with recognition of close kinship bonds that embrace the eight great grandparents, though more distant generations might be traced through the inheritance of ancestral names. Kin ties follow from blood and sharing, while kith ties follow from marriage and include inlaws.

RESIDENCE at familiar locales associated with family members and resources. Wealthy families had more than one house, shifting with seasons and events among them, as well making long visits to kin and friends.

INGESTION of resources associated with particular locales and events, providing commensal (co-eating) groupings composed of the same local nutrients fortifying their bodies.

LABOR contributed to food hunting, fishing, and harvesting, construction of houses and weirs, and the hosting of ceremonial events sponsored by the household, family, kindred, or deme.

CLASS defined by "good blood" and unblemished pedigree distinguished noble ranks from generic commoners, with slaves a stigmatized group not fully human.

TOTEM as emblem, logo, and ancestor tied kindreds to species and habitats, as well as providing vague behavioral characteristics, such a bird-like swiftness or bear-like grumbling. A story about spirit animals at a set location – such as Bears at Ellensberg's rodeo grounds, eagles at Grand Coulee, Otter's House at Orondo and one of Coyote's houses near Bridgeport – links these spirits to its human residents.

In all cases, kinship is socially defined, not limited to tracing either a definite shared substance or special affinity.


## Bibliography


Franz Boas  1920  The Social Organization of the Kwakiutl.  *American Anthropologist* 22: 111-126.

June Collins  1979  Multilineal Descent:  A Coast Salish Strategy.  *Currents in Anthropology*: Essays in Honor of Sol Tax.  Robert Henshaw, ed.  Hague: Mouton.

William Davenport  1959  Nonunilinear Descent and Descent Groups.  *American Anthropologist* 61: 557-572.

Ward Goodenough  1955 A problem in Malayo-Polynesian social organization.  *American Anthropologist* 57: 71-83.

Joseph Jorgensen  1969  *Salish Language and Culture*.  Indiana University, Language Science Monographs #3.

Jay Miller  1999  *Lushootseed Culture and the Shamanic Odyssey*:  *An Anchored Radiance*.  Lincoln: University of Nebraska Press.

Wayne Suttles  1987  *Coast Salish Essays*.  Seattle:  U of Washington Press.

Please Help Zap Away Typo Gnomes!

Sold @ Amazon.com

ACCULTURATING AMELIA ~ Round Valley 1937  California
ALASKA EDGE ISLAND ~ Siberian Yupiks of St Lawrence Island
ALL SOULS ~ Conjuring, Divining, Redeeming, Reviving Native Vitalities
ALLIED MOUNDS ~ Touching the Earth, Modeling the World, Reaching the Sky
ANIMAL PEOPLE ADVENTURES ~ Native North American Tribal Stories
AT BAY ~ Cultures Converging through Southwest Washington
BALLARD BULWARK ~
CHACO ECHOES ~ Pervasive Keresan Priesthoods
CHACOKIA ~ Chaco, Cahokia, Cities & Ceremonies ~ Bundles & Blood Lines Centuries Ago
CREEK MVSKOKI TALWA TOWNS ~ Speck, Swanton, Hewitt, Opler, Howard            > 10
CHEHALIS CHANGER ~
CHINOOK CONCERNS ~ Emma Millett Luscier, Isabella Bertrand, Verne Ray
CIRCLING FOUR CORNERS ~ Re-Viewing Native American Indiens
CROSSING ~ LINES:  An Educational Memoir of Native North America
DEL-AWARE ~ Lenape Legacies
DELAWARE INTEGRITY ~ Rituals, Removals, Reforms by Lenape Indiens
DISCLAIMING TREATIES I ~ Puget Tribes 1927 Testimonies
DISCLAIMING TREATIES II ~ Puget Tribes 1927 Testimonies
ELDERS' DIALOG ~ Ed Davis & Vi Hilbert Discuss Native Puget Sound Language, Culture, & Heritage
EVERGREEN ETHNOGRAPHIES ~ Hoh, Chehalis, Suquamish, and Snoqualmi of Western Washington     >20
FEDERAL FISH FILES ~ Swindell 1942 Treaty Rights Report
GEORGE GIBBS NORTHWEST ARRAY ~ Full Reports, Place Names, Word List, Artifact Names, and Guide
GRASSROOTS JANET ~ Advancing Salish and Traditional Cultures
HERMAN HAEBERLIN REGAINED ~ Anthropology and Artifacts of Puget Sound 1916-17
HERSTORY NW ~ Women Upholding Native Traditions
INDIEN ~ ETHNOGRAPHY:  Cultural Traditions of Native North America
INDIEN ~ ETHNOLOGY:  Grounded, Gendered, Meaningful Cultural Traditions
LESCHI IN LOVE ~ A Novel of Native Puget Sound  > x2
MARCO MUCK MASKS ~ Frank Cushing on Marshes and Mounds
MINTER BAY ~ Land, Lore, Loss, and Lucre in the South Salish Sea            > 30
NATIVE MET HOW ~ Improving Posterity
NATIVE PROPHECY NW ~ Dancing Hope
OLD LUKH ~ Native Puget Sound in Daily Life, Places, and Stories
OVER THE FALLS ~ Sdoqwalbixw Survivance Surrounding Seattle
PACIFIC PLATEAU PORTRAYALS ~ People Places Ponderings
RAY'S ARRAY ~ Raymond D Fogelson's Works
RIGHTING NATIVE PLACES ~ Adventures in Northwest Geography
SAHAPTINS STUDIES ~ Columbia River Plateau, Cora Du Bois, Homer Garner Barnett, Gerald Raymond Desmond
SALISH SYSTEMS ~ Kinship Networks of the Northwest
SDOQWALBIXW                                                       > 40
SDOQWALBIXW SURVIVANCE
SM TSM'SYEEN ~ Real Tsimshians; Coast, Sgüüks, Gitxsan, Nisga'a
SOUND SALISH STRAITS ~ Central Salish Sea Cultures
UNSETTLING SEATTLE ~ Arresting Local Talent and Academic Illiteracy
WICHITA KINSHIP & CULTURE
WRITING WORDS IN WARY WORLDS ~ World Wide Improved Spellings of Native America Languages > 46

JONA Memoirs ($ varies)
RESCUES, RANTS, & RESEARCHES ~ A Re-View of Jay Miller's Writings on Northwest Indien Cultures ~ #9
TRIBAL TRIO of the Northwest Coast by Kenneth D Tollefson ~ #10
INTERWEAVING COAST SALISH CULTURAL SYSTEMS ~ Collected Works of Pamela Thorsen Amoss ~ #14
ANCESTRAL MOUNDS ~ Vitality and Volatility Crossing Native North America
            University of Nebraska Press  2015                           > 50
Chehalis Bee